Beyoncé

Beyoncé

AT WORK, ON SCREEN, AND ONLINE

Edited by
Martin Iddon and Melanie L. Marshall

INDIANA UNIVERSITY PRESS

This book is a publication of

Indiana University Press
Office of Scholarly Publishing
Herman B Wells Library 350
1320 East 10th Street
Bloomington, Indiana 47405 USA

iupress.org

© 2020 by Martin Iddon and Melanie L. Marshall

All rights reserved
No part of this book may be reproduced or utilized in any form or by any means, electronic or mechanical, including photocopying and recording, or by any information storage and retrieval system, without permission in writing from the publisher. The paper used in this publication meets the minimum requirements of the American National Standard for Information Sciences—Permanence of Paper for Printed Library Materials, ANSI Z39.48-1992.

Manufactured in the United States of America

Library of Congress Cataloging-in-Publication Data

Names: Iddon, Martin, [date] editor. | Marshall, Melanie L., editor.
Title: Beyoncé : at work, on screen, and online / edited by Martin Iddon, Melanie L. Marshall.
Description: Bloomington : Indiana University Press, 2021. | Includes bibliographical references and index.
Identifiers: LCCN 2020005993 (print) | LCCN 2020005994 (ebook) | ISBN 9780253052827 (hardback) | ISBN 9780253052841 (paperback) | ISBN 9780253052834 (ebook)
Subjects: LCSH: Beyoncé, 1981—Criticism and interpretation. | Popular music—2001-2010—History and criticism. | Popular music—2011-2020—History and criticism. | Popular music—Social aspects.
Classification: LCC ML420.K675 B37 2021 (print) | LCC ML420.K675 (ebook) | DDC 782.42164092—dc23
LC record available at https://lccn.loc.gov/2020005993
LC ebook record available at https://lccn.loc.gov/2020005994

1 2 3 4 5 25 24 23 22 21 20

CONTENTS

Introduction / *Melanie L. Marshall and Martin Iddon* 1

I. *Beyoncé at Work, Making Beyoncé*

1. ***Emily J. Lordi*** / Surviving the Hustle: Beyoncé's Performance of Work 23
2. ***Will Fulton*** / "A Scientist of Songs": Beyoncé, the Recording Studio, and Popular Music Authorship 40
3. ***Lisa Colton*** / "Singing All the Time": Constructions of Cultural Identity in Beyoncé's *I Am . . . Sasha Fierce* 68

II. *Beyoncé on Screen, Reading Beyoncé*

4. ***Julia Cox*** / Beyoncé's Mixed-Media Feminism: Sounding, Staging, and Sampling Gender Politics in "***Flawless" 93
5. ***Jaap Kooijman*** / "At Last a Dream That I Can Call My Own": Beyoncé and the Performance of Stardom in *Dreamgirls* and *Cadillac Records* 114
6. ***Omise'eke Natasha Tinsley*** / For the Texas Bama Femme: A Black Queer Femme-inist Reading of Beyoncé's "Sorry" 136
7. ***Eduardo Viñuela*** / Gypsying Beyoncé: The Latin Crossover through Hispanic Stereotypes 157

III. *Beyoncé Online, Re-presenting Beyoncé*

8. ***Mary Fogarty Woehrel*** / Unlikely Resemblances: Beyoncé, "Single Ladies," and Comparative Judgment of Popular Dance 179
9. ***Áine Mangaoang*** / "I See Music": Beyoncé, YouTube, and the Question of Signed Songs 198
10. ***Melissa Avdeeff*** / "Girl I'm Tryna Kick It with Ya": Tracing the Reception of the Embodiment of Girl/Bedroom Culture in "7/11" 226

Index 251

Beyoncé

Introduction

MELANIE L. MARSHALL
MARTIN IDDON

Beyoncé Knowles-Carter, hereafter simply Beyoncé, has arguably been *the* central figure in popular music for the past decade, and, as a member of Destiny's Child, for a decade before that. Beyoncé is significant both as a musician and as a cultural figure shaping debates about race, sexuality, and female empowerment, both as a touchstone for a generation and through direct political interventions in the United States and further afield. Her activities within the worlds of music and the broader societies that music touches are inextricably linked, ineluctably intertwined: what she does as a musician directly impinges on the lived experiences of fans and haters alike, and many others besides. Beyoncé's public face is embedded in both popular political movements—including her support (perhaps most obvious since *Lemonade* [2016]) for Black civil and human rights, her earlier endorsement of same-sex marriage, and her particular version of third-wave feminism—and in a particular history of popular music in which she negotiates her role within a constellation of stars, including Michael Jackson, Prince, Whitney Houston, Etta James, Diana Ross, and Madonna. Her visual imagery, too, intertwines these narratives, including variously direct stylistic references to Josephine Baker and to the Black Panthers. Such issues seem to have crystallized around her 2016 Super Bowl performance, which, by turns, attracted praise for its direct embrace of the Black Lives Matter movement and criticism for its exploitation, as some saw it, of post-Katrina New Orleans. For all those reasons, what follows, by way of introduction to the issues framed by this volume, through and with Beyoncé, is just one *point de capiton*, one of the ways in which Beyoncé is anchored to, sutured to such debates, and the way in which they are ineluctably shot through *with her*.

Fireworks and drum rolls presaged Beyoncé's performance at the 2016 Super Bowl halftime show—headlined by Coldplay—and fireworks of a different variety followed it. Coldplay's flowery, faintly psychedelic performance of their main hits began with Chris Martin crouching and singing from the grass while fans streamed in, then bouncing onto the stage where youth musicians directed by Gustavo Dudamel, dressed in primary colors, joined the band. At five and a half minutes in, the colorful tie-dye vibe gave way to a funkier sound and a lot of black leather: first, Bruno Mars and his dancers moved onto the stage, dressed all in black leather costumes by Donatella Versace that alluded to 1980s Run-DMC, and then, after more fireworks, the action moved back to the field.[1] Beyoncé, in her second appearance at the Super Bowl, got in formation with her dancers to observe US Black History Month (February), perform Black pride, remember longstanding Black political activism, and celebrate Black feminine/femme womanhood. Beyoncé and her dancers evoked the Black Panthers with black-leather costumes and black berets—Beyoncé's costume suggesting, too, Michael Jackson's 1993 Super Bowl halftime show—and danced into an X formation in reference to Malcolm X, who delineated and opposed the operation of white supremacy in the north of the United States, and whose voice is sampled on *Lemonade*.[2]

The joyously choreographed cross kindled a particularly loud cheer from the stadium.[3] X marks sites of political unhappiness and dissent even while Beyoncé's voice asserts itself powerfully: "I slay." The music video, released the night before and, presumably, not digested by every National Football League (NFL) viewer before the show, made the wider political context even clearer. Yet here, before that context was quite so apparent, the sonic surface of Beyoncé's performance was celebratory, mashed up with faux-1980s Minneapolis electro-funk, if already a blank reproduction of that funk. The spectacle was all commodification and carnival—of Bruno Mars's performance of his and Mark Ronson's "Uptown Funk"; the strangeness of the musical surface of "Formation" undercut by the binding together of groove and a marching band's drumline; the brief sample of a sample from the Chi-Lites'

"Are You My Woman (Tell Me So)," now wholly indistinguishable from Beyoncé's own "Crazy in Love"—enabling the elision of "Formation" with "Uptown Funk."[4]

Beyoncé's dancers accentuated the political message of the performance by lending their support to the campaign for justice for Mario Woods, a young Black man killed by police in 2015. Two Black Lives Matter activists, Rheema Emy Calloway and Ronnisha Johnson, managed to buttonhole the dancers as they left the field, and their short film of the dancers with fists aloft, and holding a sign reading "Justice 4 Mario Woods" went viral. Beyoncé's support for Black Lives Matter extends beyond performance and *Lemonade* to practice: she also attends protests and provides financial support.[5] Protest movements need to be bankrolled: arrested protestors need bail and organizations need financial support to start up and keep running. This is one possible reading of the "Formation" line, the "best revenge is your paper."[6]

Beyoncé's performance took place during Black History Month and in the final year of the second term of the first Black president of the United States—a very different climate from what was in place in the United States as we wrote this introduction—but Alicia Garza argues it still required courage. "I was really proud of her," Garza said of Beyoncé's performance, one of the most overtly political statements a recording artist of that stature has made in some time. "That was a big risk that she took. Many artists are scared to take those kinds of positions. They're actively discouraged against it."[7] Garza acknowledges that there is room for criticism of Beyoncé's performance— for example, she mentions justifiable anger about the exploitative use of New Orleans, and the problematic systems of celebrity and capitalism—but suggests that criticism of such systemic issues should be dealt with separately. Her point makes sense: Beyoncé is as embedded in neoliberal capitalism as any other successful mainstream artist, and the issues are much bigger than any individual, even (or especially?) if that individual is a global superstar. Tamara Winfrey Harris recognizes that Beyoncé's wealth, stardom, and glamour is "the very thing that makes *Lemonade*'s social justice bent possible ... [and] is the thing that makes people doubt the sincerity of the message and messenger." Harris concludes, "Getting rich may not be radical, but richness can be leveraged for radical things."[8]

Writers have nonetheless combined evaluations of the impact of Beyoncé's performance with an assessment of the limitations of her statement, with particular emphasis on Beyoncé as an accomplished capitalist—famous for her work ethic, as Emily Lordi discusses in this volume—who is aware of her market. Sarah Olutola warns against "mythologizing Beyoncé as a radical black political figure": she "cannot be extricated from—and should not be decontextualized from—the larger white patriarchal heteronormative capitalist context within which she, her work, and her success exists."[9] Dianca London, bell hooks, and Alicia Wallace suggest that Beyoncé was able to take this chance only because it did not in fact pose much risk to her bottom line. London calls into question, too, the propriety of the cultural references noting the disjunction between Beyoncé's use of Black Panthers-inspired images for capitalist ends and the Black Panthers' critique of Black capitalism.[10] Wallace articulates how Beyoncé's is a "capitalist brand of social justice" and argues that in "Formation," Beyoncé uses colorism, respectability politics, and the trauma of Hurricane Katrina for her own financial gain, though simultaneously recognizing that Beyoncé's song "has made black people feel powerful and called to act."[11] hooks welcomed *Lemonade*'s "construction of a powerfully symbolic black female sisterhood that resists invisibility, that refuses to be silent. This in and of itself is no small feat—it shifts the gaze of white mainstream culture."[12] hooks also noted, however, that the commodification and display of Black women for capital gain is not new and dates back to the auction blocks of slavery, albeit Beyoncé has a different "purpose ... to seduce, celebrate, and delight—to challenge the ongoing present-day devaluation and dehumanization of the black female body."[13] Olutola draws out the complexities of the politics around the skin colors of Beyoncé and her Super Bowl backing dancers, in a subtle consideration of Beyoncé's "strategies of negotiation around her blackness," keeping in mind the neoliberal context.[14] (Omise'eke Natasha Tinsley's contribution to this volume goes further than London and hooks in exploring the woman-centered eroticism of the seductive and celebratory aspects of *Lemonade*.)[15]

Where Black women commentators heard and saw calls for resistance and joyous celebration of Black femme-inine women, even if compromised in complex ways, apparently fragile conservative white men with disproportionate access to media and power heard and saw indecency and an inappropriate politicization of a sports entertainment space.[16] As in the aftermath of Janet Jackson and Justin Timberlake's 2004 Super Bowl performance, white men, the "dominant viewing public," were framed as "the victim of the ... woman of color whose performance ... threatens the social fabric of white heteronormativity and public decency."[17] White male commentators complained, too, about the Katrina-inspired imagery, but their concern was not for the exploitation of Black trauma (as it was for Wallace and Kehrer), but rather that Beyoncé was antipolice and, for them, the questioning of such institutions was unpatriotic. The interpretation depends on the sociopolitical situation of the listener; as Nina Sun Eidsheim writes, "listening is never neutral, but rather always actively produces meaning; it is a political act."[18] These conservative responses come from a place of white privilege (an aspect of systemic white supremacy) and not only do they not acknowledge Beyoncé's critique, they divert attention away from Black Lives Matter: the media conversation became about the propriety of the performance rather than about the issues Beyoncé raised. With hindsight, this, together with the NFL's framing of the performance (to be discussed further herein), could be seen as indicators of what was to come later in 2016 with the lamentable presidential electoral success of racist dog-whistle politics. *Saturday Night Live*'s parody of this shocked white response—a trailer for the horror movie *The Day Beyoncé Turned Black*—reveals an underlying truth: Beyoncé's video and her 2016 Super Bowl show made clear her support for the Black Lives Matter movement and her take, in Black History Month, on Black history and civil-rights struggles in a way that even white audiences could not miss. Musicologist Lauron Kehrer, in an article that offers a sharp analysis of Beyoncé's use of samples of queer musicians from New Orleans, sees the trailer as playing on Beyoncé not hitherto being known for an unapologetically Black stance, but Julia Cox's chapter in this volume, "Beyoncé's Mixed-Media Feminism," as well as an earlier contribution by Anne Mitchell, show that in fact Beyoncé's politics manifested in her output prior to *Lemonade*.[19] The question becomes which spectators (accidentally or deliberately) missed the cues before February 2016. And part of the answer is that although Beyoncé is a global superstar, the predominantly white, middle-aged male audience members of the Super Bowl were largely not Beyoncé's audience and, furthermore, they did not want to hear these politics. They did not want to listen.[20] As a comparison, the responses to Lady Gaga's 2017 Super Bowl performance—which opened with Gaga's mash-up of "God Bless America" (Irving Berlin) and "This Land Is Your Land" (Woody Guthrie's protest song, more recently adopted for anti-Trump rallies)—showed that most people were apparently unaware of the political message. Indeed, despite the song's calls for inclusivity at time when Trump's high-profile restrictions on inbound travel from Muslim countries were still in force, many claimed Gaga avoided criticism.[21] Gaga's subversive statement was not missed by everyone, as the journalistic citations attest, but there was no outcry, and, in stark contrast to the reaction to Beyoncé, commentators did not claim she was unpatriotic. This may seem particularly surprising since Gaga had already protested Trump's election in 2016, outside Trump Tower no less, but it also speaks to the extent of white privilege and how racism shapes the reception and policing of Black bodies perceived as always dissenting and unruly.

What appeared to conservative white men to be indecent, unwholesome, and unpatriotic about Beyoncé's performance was the call to viewers to "get in/formation" about race politics, following clues embedded in the lyric, the costume, and the choreography. It seems conservative commentators found (perhaps find) Beyoncé's *raising* these issues in this environment—in which the issues are already present, although white audiences may (pretend to) be oblivious to them—to be more outrageous and inappropriate than the issues themselves. In confronting willfully ignorant white viewers with the nation's history of white supremacy, Beyoncé becomes a killjoy, as recently described by Sara Ahmed.[22] Beyoncé getting in formation to give information, to disrupt the production and maintenance of racial ignorance, however imperfectly, slays the white fantasy of a postracial United States.[23] Had Beyoncé ignored racial politics—as she arguably did in her turn as the Super Bowl headline act in 2013—she might have embodied diversity for the Super Bowl's primarily white audience without controversy, enabling them to feel "good, ... to relax and feel less threatened," to draw on Ahmed again.[24] But she did not. Instead, white men posited Beyoncé's performance, her brown-skinned, Black body, as the cause of tension, and the loss of a "shared atmosphere" of entertainment.[25]

The white responses to "Formation" that followed Beyoncé's 2016 Super Bowl performance are best understood in the context of systemic patriarchal white supremacy. White people who think of racism as individual prejudice rather than a dominant structuring principle of US and European cultures, institutions, and systems, become outraged when their mistaken but all-too-common belief in a colorblind, postracial era—a belief that maintains white supremacist systems—is disrupted in the spaces felt, fantasized, or pretended to be equal.²⁶ American football is one such space, held up on the one hand as integrated, but continuing to be, in fact, like many sports, "a perpetuator of racial differences and a vehicle for widespread racism."²⁷ The history of racism in the NFL includes a period of racial exclusion from the field (1934–46), when Black players were barred from the playing field altogether, and continues with today's integration but with positional discrimination.²⁸ As Ahmed notes of a different context—that of universities—Black or brown people in white-dominated organizations embody diversity; the organization may put them on display as visible proof of the "overcoming of institutional whiteness," but the price for the organization's ongoing commitment is that they be grateful for being included and will not rock the boat.²⁹ They are expected "not to speak about anything that exposes the conditions of [the institution's] commitment. As such, a condition of commitment becomes a demand to use happy words and not to use unhappy words."³⁰ The demand for the oppressed person's happiness—their display of acquiescence to the dominant values—is itself oppressive.³¹ Anything that indicates unhappiness—however justified—becomes a point of controversy, and, as with Ahmed's killjoy figure, the person voicing the problem becomes the problem.³²

Arguably, the NFL's framing of Beyoncé's performance on their YouTube channel boosts the idea of violence against white men playing out in the half-time show. The full-length video is called "Coldplay's FULL Pepsi Super Bowl 50 Halftime Show Feat: Beyoncé & Bruno Mars!"³³ The NFL also uploaded a video clip excerpting the performances by Bruno Mars and Beyoncé, "Beyoncé and Bruno Mars Crash the Pepsi Super Bowl 50 Halftime Show."³⁴ This curious and revealing word choice is distant from the more straightforward language of the full video and suggests that Beyoncé and Mars, who had each headlined in previous years, were uninvited guests when, of course, their part in the show, including the dance-off, was meticulously planned, rehearsed, and paid for. The title language for the 2016 excerpt not only crashes Beyoncé and Mars into Coldplay's performing space, it knocks Coldplay out of the title space (although they remained in the performing space: the clip ends with all the musicians performing together). "Crash" evokes barriers and violence. "Crash" suggests Mars and Beyoncé do not belong in that space. And the crash here is produced not by Coldplay, Beyoncé, or Mars, but by the NFL. The implication that Beyoncé and Mars do not belong imagines the space they "crashed" into as a white space,[35] a space articulated and constituted from an institutionally white perspective, is a sporting with Black and white bodies that (if unconsciously) feeds into the racist white fear of displacement and loss of white privilege and power.

This is the institutional context of Beyoncé's 2016 Super Bowl performance. It is also the context for NFL quarterback Colin Kaepernick's subsequent decision, starting six months after Beyoncé's performance, to take a knee during the national anthem to protest police killings of Black people, a decision that cost him his athletic career.[36] Beyoncé's performance arguably set the stage for Kaepernick's peaceful protest, and her celebrity leadership on Black Lives Matter was implicitly recognized when she was invited to present the Sports Illustrated Muhammad Ali Legacy Award to Colin Kaepernick in November 2017.[37] Neither Beyoncé or Kaepernick used "unhappy" words; nonetheless, their embodied and visual protest of systemic oppression spoke loudly. The sound of "Formation" is celebratory and joyful; likewise, Beyoncé's performance could be read as a celebration of Black political organizing in Black History Month. As Emily Lordi's chapter in the present volume points out, "Formation" articulates "countless forms of labor that are available to everyday people" and that are crucial to Black Lives Matter: information gathering, witnessing, and organizing. Although Beyoncé's capitalist messaging supports the dominant economic values, her performance, although problematic in some ways, was not an assertion of agreement with the dominant racial politics, and that was what made her performance a subject of international conversation.

Beyoncé's performance, and that of Mars, sonically claimed a place in a site of national and cultural importance. Gayle Wald has argued that the act of Black musical performance in significant sites "constitutes the use of sound to render these places/spaces more hospitable, 'making room' for black presence."[38] Such performances, she continues, "reveal sonic reflection as an important means of collective self-recognition."[39] Beyoncé has continued to sonically inhabit other significant cultural spaces. In 2018 Beyoncé was the first Black woman to headline at Coachella—appending the judgment "Ain't that 'bout a bitch" to her midshow acknowledgment of the fact—and, even before her performance, reporters and fans renamed the event Beychella. Although the annual Coachella festival has had a primarily white audience, Beyoncé's *Homecoming* documentary, like her Beychella performances, puts Black women front and center. There were some parallels to her 2016 Super Bowl performance: the Chi-Lites' "Are You My Woman (Tell Me So)"/ "Crazy in Love" hook accompanied her walk down the steps to the main stage after the introduction. She performed with DRUMLine Live, a touring group drawing on the marching band tradition of historically Black colleges and universities (HBCUs); the staging, costumes, and, importantly, the sounds alluded to HBCU culture. In addition to fresh arrangements of her own songs, including "Formation," Beyoncé performed part of "Lift Every Voice and Sing," the Black national anthem, which calls for the people to "march on till victory is won."[40] Perhaps most significant, she followed up her final performance with the announcement that she would establish a second scholarship program, this time for HBCU students.

This brief narrative is an example of the way in which Beyoncé is thoroughly engaged with and paradigmatic of many of the central issues both in the United States and the wider world today, musically *and* politically. It exemplifies the range of concerns of the present volume. Yet, as is doubtless already clear, Beyoncé's is no simple relationship with society. Though the contributions to this volume are generally enthusiastic in their examination of Beyoncé, the contributors do not shy away from examining more controversial aspects of her work to date; the volume as a whole is, in the broader sense, critical. The authors consider the questions of Beyoncé's appropriation of other cultures and of the broader politics of borrowing, authorship, and ownership that are in play in her work, alongside questions of sexualization, race, the "authenticity" of image, and fan's video responses. Thus, these chapters contribute to pop-cultural debates on the status of intertextuality, originality, and online fan culture, as well as to debates about the sexualized and racialized bodies of women.

Beyoncé's work ethic is spectacular, both literally and figuratively, as Emily J. Lordi reminds us. The way in which Beyoncé is constructed—both the discourse she constructs around herself and the constructions that are made of her—is the focus of Lordi's and Lisa Colton's contributions, and Will Fulton examines the way Beyoncé constructs her music. In addition, Eduardo Viñuela points out in passing that career ambition is part of the motivation for Beyoncé's Carmen Brown in *Carmen: A Hip Hopera* (2001).[41]

Lordi's interest concerns itself with the ways in which Beyoncé's relationship with work changes throughout her career. The racialized ethics of hard work, inherited from 1960s and 1970s soul music, impel Lordi's reflections on Beyoncé's shift from an "independent woman" and "survivor" working (and playing) harder than anyone else (in which she both subscribes to the values of neoliberal economics and reveals the sheer effort involved in so doing) to a rejection of that ethic on *Beyoncé* (2013), and even more so on *Lemonade*, in favor of what Lordi terms an "aesthetic of easeful imperfection," even if Beyoncé can choose this path only after the point at which she already rules the world. Lordi perceives Beyoncé as beginning to perform resistance to neoliberal ideas of work and entrepreneurship of the self (the brand Beyoncé). The question of what can be heard (and felt) in Beyoncé's vocal performances underpins much of Lordi's reading, and it is this same vocal tactility that is at the heart of Colton's chapter, in which Colton engages with questions of authority through a reading of Beyoncé's vocal performances on *I Am . . . Sasha Fierce* (2008). Indeed, it is precisely the way in which Beyoncé's body *sounds*, which is to say *makes* sound and *re*-sounds, that is vital, especially because—to be sure, occasionally seemingly licensed by lyrical content—the question of what Beyoncé's voice has to say is marginalized, if not sometimes erased, by corporeal, fleshly readings of her as a physical object. Beyoncé, Colton argues, both through vocal and studio production, refutes such readings of Black women's voices in more general terms, her performances physically—that is *vocally*—symbolizing power and control. These constructions are vital too, if differently figured, for Jaap Kooijman and Viñuela.

Where Lordi and Colton think through Beyoncé's vocal labor, Fulton scrutinizes Beyoncé's authorship, her creative work process, and her workplace. Beyoncé's collaborative mode of studio practice has been undervalued and little understood. Although some critics have read Beyoncé as artistically weak in comparison with artists and producers who more obviously mirror the model of the singular Romantic genius, others have seen her as aesthetically marginal to her own success, aside from her physical glamour (an intersection that recurs in Lisa Colton's chapter). Fulton reconsiders Beyoncé's collagist creative practice through a close reading of the writing and production of "Hold Up" and "Don't Hurt Yourself" (both 2016). This wide-ranging examination reveals much not only about the nature of this approach to song writing, but also about the ways in which race, gender, and genre intersect with such judgments and, in turn, how those judgments inform practical questions of, inter alia, copyright.

The cultural work of reading Beyoncé's performances on screen unites Cox's, Kooijman's, Tinsley's, and Viñuela's contributions. Cox traces the origins of *Lemonade*'s more activist Beyoncé to her turn to feminism in "***Flawless" (2013). "***Flawless" couples unconventional song structure with some unconventional, even disorienting, sonic and performative practices, allowing Beyoncé to disrupt some of the tropes she had hitherto been associated with—respectability politics, for example—and to explore her own journey of feminism. Cox finds that in "***Flawless," Beyoncé's use of archival broadcast footage of her early band Girl's Tyme on *Star Search* in 1993 and audio sampling of Chimamanda Ngozi Adichie, together with Beyoncé's decision to eschew verse-chorus conventions, constructs a personal narrative quest that "merges Beyoncé's ... interiority with cultural memory." Cox details the contradictions that remain throughout the visual song, finding a lack of commitment to collective power and a personal feminism divested of radical elements, so that in the end it stops short of radical transformation and structural change. It is important to note that what Beyoncé has to say—what she *means*, in at least two senses—is not singular and fixed, but complex and mobile. A similar refusal to allow readings of Beyoncé to collapse into the uniform—and an insistence that feminism is never "simply" feminism—characterizes Tinsley's rich, Black femme-inist reading of "Sorry" (2016), one which stresses and celebrates the "no-men-allowed love between Black Southern women" that recurs throughout *Lemonade*. The situatedness of Tinsley's text in the South, in a Texas *palpably* bordered by Louisiana, enables what Eve Sedgwick terms a reparative reading that looks to find a Black, queer women's wholeness from the fragmentary, insisting that "Sorry" (and *Lemonade* more broadly) makes it possible to imagine ways of performing Black femme identity/ies in ways otherwise hardly available in mainstream representations. Tinsley deliberately eschews a focus on the limitations of Beyoncé's work in favor of the "fight to extract sustenance from a popular culture largely uninterested in the survival of marginalized—including Black and queer—communities." This glorious, reparative, Black, queer, femme-inist reading of "Sorry" is decidedly erotic, in Audre Lorde's sense.[42] Tinsley's writing rings with the joy of life and love as she pieces together "fragmented images of Black femme power . . . to create images of Black/queer/women's wholeness." Tinsley delights in what she identifies as ratchet femme carrying Beyoncé to a Black-woman-centered paradise, in which Beyoncé embraces an aggressive femme identity with an all-femme party. Tinsley's vibrant chapter pulses with love for this Black femme-ininity.

Beyoncé in and on film is the subject of Kooijman and Viñuela's chapters. Each author examines Beyoncé's roles in films (Kooijman: *Dreamgirls* [2006] and *Cadillac Records* [2008]; Viñuela: *Carmen: A Hip Hopera* [2001]) and how, through the parts she took in them, she is interpolated into and interpellated in a history of stardom wherein any reading of Beyoncé necessitates reading her, too, in relationship with Nina Simone (Kooijman), Etta James (Kooijman), Diana Ross (Kooijman), and Dorothy Dandridge (Viñuela) even if, too, it is very particular versions of these prototypes that are made available by Beyoncé's own performance of stardom.[43] Viñuela focuses on the way in which a particular *gitanismo* intersected with her star persona as she embodied a peculiarly un-Carmen-like Carmen in *Carmen: A Hip Hopera* (2001). Here Beyoncé adopts Carmen's agency—the same narrative of empowerment, according to Viñuela's argument, that later underpins "Single Ladies" and "Run the World (Girls)" (2011)—but while aspiring to a capitalist model of success unrecognizable within the nineteenth-century context of Carmen's "gypsyness" and marginalizing any sense of genuine rebellion against societal mores. Nonetheless, Viñuela argues, at this critical juncture in Beyoncé's passage from membership in Destiny's Child through to becoming a solo artist in her own right, the independence Carmen figures is a significant part of enabling Beyoncé symbolically to make that transition. The same sort of connection between the Hispanic and the "Oriental," stabilized through the figure of the gypsy, Viñuela contends, makes possible Beyoncé's success in the global marketplace, here figured through her crossover into the Latin market, with the release of a vinyl album of Spanish-language versions of tracks from *B'Day* (2006).

The re-presentation of stars and reinterpretation of their work by fans is a staple of contemporaneous online life, and indeed there are online responses almost instantly in the form of blog posts (Lordi), dance videos (Mary Fogarty Woehrel), fans' reaction videos (Melissa Avdeeff), and sign-language interpretations, all presented with varying degrees of facility and professionalism (Áine Mangaoang), raising, once again, questions of authority and authorship, questions sometimes directed toward Beyoncé. Woehrel considers the shifting readings of Shane Mercado's performance of Beyoncé's "Single Ladies (Put a Ring on It)" (2008) choreography as he blurs the distinction between professional dancer and fan, just as the choreography itself is judged differently according to how audiences construct its relationship with Bob Fosse's "Mexican Breakfast" routine: Beyoncé the serious artist was condemned for the borrowing, while Beyoncé the Fosse fan is lauded. It is significant, too, that the work of Beyoncé's choreography team is elided: authorship of choreography is automatically attributed to Beyoncé.

The final two chapters in this volume consider radically different ways in which online communities have responded to and, in a sense, remediatized aspects of Beyoncé's work. Mangaoang examines the production of sign-language versions of numerous tracks, considering the various modes in which the work has been undertaken, the ethics of such approaches, and what such videos may have to say about what Beyoncé means in a multimodal context, while simultaneously stressing the important ways in which this cultural practice poses a challenge to the audist, phonocentric approaches that continue to characterize the majority of examinations of musical practice. The videos are often in "home mode," made in an intimate, domestic space. Those same spaces are central to the video for Beyoncé's "7/11," the reception of which, as exemplified through the phenomenon of YouTube reaction videos, is the focus of Avdeeff's chapter, which tracks the wide-ranging responses of YouTubers—from unbridled fandom, through confused bemusement, to refusal and rejection—to imagery that evokes the "best slumber party ever" through the privacy and intimacy of the safe space of teenage girls' bedrooms intertwined with the fun and silliness of pre-drinks in a single, extended *faux* selfie.

Beyoncé's performance of parenthood, although a subject of several recently published articles, is not under consideration in this volume.[44] We realize this with some surprise, for we have collaborated on this volume and our previous collection of essays on Lady Gaga in the throes of our own intense parenting years with our respective partners. Melanie and Han's daughter, Asha, arrived while we were preparing the Lady Gaga volume; and during the process of developing the present text, Martin and Kate's daughter, Alice, was born. This book is for Alice, though it's not obvious she'll know what to do with it for a few years yet. Since neither of us has plans to extend our families any further, Melanie and Martin expect to be cautious in developing any further collaborative projects(!).

MARTIN IDDON is Professor of Music and Aesthetics at the University of Leeds. He is editor (with Melanie L. Marshall) of *Lady Gaga and Popular Music: Performing Gender, Fashion, and Culture* and author of *New Music at Darmstadt: Nono, Stockhausen, Cage, and Boulez*; *John Cage and David Tudor: Correspondence on Interpretation and Performance*; alongside various other monographs and edited volumes.

MELANIE L. MARSHALL is Lecturer in Music at University College Cork. She is editor (with Martin Iddon) of *Lady Gaga and Popular Music: Performing Gender, Fashion, and Culture* and (with Linda L. Carroll and Katherine A. McIver) of *Sexualities, Textualities, Art and Music in Early Modern Italy*.

NOTES

Emily J. Lordi's chapter appears in a slightly different form in *Black Camera* 9/1 (2017). We are grateful to be able to reprint it here.

1. See Edward Barsamian, "Bruno Mars Channels Run D.M.C. for the Super Bowl," *Vogue*, February 7, 2016, https://www.vogue.com/article/bruno-mars-versace-super-bowl-performance-outfit-celebrity-style.

2. Beyoncé's costume was by Dsquared2. Of Beyoncé's costume, the designers Dean and Dan Caten said, "We . . . wanted to create something where she resembles a warrior leading her female posse who fall into formation and take Super Bowl 50 at half-time!" (Dsquared2, "Super Bowl 2016: Beyoncé in DSquared2," corporate announcement, February 8, 2016, https://www.dsquared2.com/experience/en/d2-life/superbowl-2016-beyonce-in-dsquared2/).

3. Mars and his dancers' slick moves between each other and across the stage did not elicit similar audience responses. The X choreography superficially resembled the kinds of moves of marching bands, although that resonance may owe to the performing space being not on the stage, but on the sports field. In this regard, Beyoncé worked with marching bands from historically Black colleges and universities in her Coachella 2018 performance, captured in *Homecoming: A Film by Beyoncé*, dir. Beyoncé Carter-Knowles with Ed Burke (Netflix, 2019, 237 minutes).

4. In truth, "Uptown Funk" surely shares more with Detroit's rather less hip Was (Not Was) than it does with Minneapolis's Prince, with or without his New

Power Generation. Beyoncé's 2013 Super Bowl set included "Crazy in Love"; the sample is heard for the first time just over one minute into the performance. *Lemonade* has a thematic link to the earlier song. Tinsley observes that "Don't Hurt Yourself" from *Lemonade* echoes the video of "Crazy in Love" but rather than being crazy in love, the grown-up woman is now *"questioning the point* of her long-term relationship" (Tinsley, *Beyoncé in Formation*, 26).

   5. Alicia Garza, "Black Lives Matter Co-founder to Beyoncé: 'Welcome to the Movement,'" *Rolling Stone*, February 11, 2016, https://www.rollingstone.com/politics/politics-news/black-lives-matter-co-founder-to-beyonce-welcome-to-the-movement-162647/. On the history of Black Lives Matter, see Ransby, *Making All Black Lives Matter*, which includes the radical origins of the movement in the work of Black women activists.

   6. Beyoncé and her husband, Jay-Z, are rumored to have donated their own money to pay bail for protestors (Jessica Glenza, "Jay Z and Beyoncé Bailed Out Protestors in Baltimore and Ferguson, Activist Says," *Guardian*, May 18, 2015, https://www.theguardian.com/music/2015/may/18/jay-z-beyonce-baltimore-ferguson-protests-bail-money). Wesley Lowery also cites rumors that Beyoncé may have met with DeRay McKesson, an activist who traveled to Ferguson to join the protests, in her offices in New York prior to donating money together with her husband, Jay-Z (Lowery, *They Can't Kill Us All*, 158).

   7. Chris Roberts, "Black Lives Matter's Alicia Garza: Beyoncé, the Patriarchy, and (Why She Isn't Voting for) Hillary Clinton," *SF Weekly*, February 12, 2016, http://www.sfweekly.com/news/black-lives-matters-alicia-garza-beyonce-the-patriarchy-and-why-she-isnt-voting-for-hillary-clinton/. In the same interview, Garza said, "We're trying to impact culture and to impact policy. . . . You can't do one without the other."

   8. Harris, "Interlude F," 157.

   9. Olutola, "I Ain't Sorry," 100.

   10. Dianca London, "Beyoncé's Capitalism, Masquerading As Radical Change," *death and taxes*, February 9, 2016, https://archive.is/9yusZ.

   11. Wallace, "Critical View," 195. Olutola also discusses colorism in reference to the Super Bowl performance ("I Ain't Sorry," 106–7). On Beyoncé's acknowledged use of work by queer New Orleans artists, see Kehrer, "Who Slays?"

   12. bell hooks, "Moving beyond Pain," *bell hooks Institute Blog*, May 9, 2016, http://www.bellhooksinstitute.com/blog/2016/5/9/moving-beyond-pain.

   13. Ibid.

   14. Olutola, "I Ain't Sorry," 105–8.

   15. Tinsley has also recently published a monograph on *Lemonade*: *Beyoncé in Formation*.

   16. See, for example, Rudolph Giuliani interviewed on Fox News (video clip embedded in a tweet by *FOX & Friends*, February 8, 2016, https://twitter.com

/foxandfriends/status/696707685639540736, and embedded in Niraj Chokshi, "Rudy Giuliani: Beyoncé's Halftime Show Was an 'Outrageous' Affront to Police," *Washington Post*, February 8, 2016, https://www.washingtonpost.com/news/arts-and-entertainment/wp/2016/02/08/rudy-giuliani-beyonces-half-time-show-was-an-outrageous-affront-to-police/). For conservative sports commentator Jeff Crouere, Beyoncé's performance was, by implication, unpatriotic ("NFL and Beyonce Promote Divisive Message," *Townhall*, February 13, 2016, https://townhall.com/columnists/jeffcrouere/2016/02/13/nfl-and-beyonce-promote-divisive-message-n2118892).

17. Fleetwood, *Troubling Vision*, 131.

18. Eidsheim, *The Race of Sound*, 24. See also Black, "Abolitionism's Resonant Bodies."

19. Kehrer, "Who Slays?," 82–83. On the concept of being unapologetically Black and its relation to Black Lives Matter, see Ransby, *Making All Black Lives Matter*, 97–100. Anne M. Mitchell discusses Beyoncé's politics in "Beyoncé."

20. Rob Tornoe asserts that "demographically, viewers of the NFL tend to be wealthier, whiter, older and more male than America as a whole" ("NFL to Colin Kaepernick: We're Cool with Crime, but Opinions Are Bad for Our Brand," *Forbes*, August 6, 2017, https://www.forbes.com/sites/cartoonoftheday/2017/08/06/nfl-ravens-to-colin-kaepernick-were-cool-with-crime-but-opinions-are-bad-for-our-brand-unpatriotic/).

21. Trump's first high-profile immigration and travel exclusions came into force in January 2017 and were still in place during the performance. For contemporaneous news coverage, see Alice Vincent, "This Land Is Our Land: How Lady Gaga Sang an Anti-Trump Protest Song at the Super Bowl without Anybody Noticing," *Daily Telegraph*, February 6, 2017, https://www.telegraph.co.uk/music/what-to-listen-to/land-land-lady-gaga-sang-anti-trump-protest-song-super-bowl/ (the *Telegraph* is a right-leaning, conservative—and broadly pro-Conservative—British newspaper), and Chris Willman, "Gaga Meets Guthrie: Why 'This Land Is Your Land' Still Skirts the Line between Patriotic Anthem and Political Broadside," *Billboard* February 6, 2017, https://www.billboard.com/articles/news/7678208/lady-gaga-super-bowl-halftime-woody-guthrie.

22. Ahmed, *Living a Feminist Life*, 36–40. When feminists raise issues to do with oppression and discrimination, it is common for institutional systems to label the feminist as the problem rather than address the problematic issues.

23. On various forms and functions of racial ignorance, see Sullivan and Tuana, *Race and Epistemologies*.

24. Ahmed, "Embodying Diversity," 44.

25. Ibid., 49.

26. See, for example, Chokshi, "Rudy Giuliani."

27. Brown, "Portrayal of Black Masculinity," 218. On color blindness and whiteness in sports, including the NFL, see Leonard, *Playing While White*.

28. Levy, *Tackling Jim Crow*; Thomas G. Smith, "Outside the Pale."
29. Ahmed, "Embodying Diversity," 41.
30. Ibid., 46.
31. Ibid., 48–49.
32. Ahmed, *Living a Feminist Life*, 39; Ahmed, "Embodying Diversity," 48–49. Ahmed's discussion of "being the problem" is also pertinent here: Sara Ahmed, *On Being Included: Racism and Diversity in Institutional Life* (Durham: Duke University Press, 2012), 141–71, especially 152–57. Ahmed traces the idea back to W. E. B. Du Bois.
33. NFL, "Coldplay's FULL Pepsi Super Bowl 50 Halftime Show Feat: Beyoncé & Bruno Mars!," February 11, 2016, https://youtu.be/c9cUytejf1k.
34. NFL, "Beyoncé and Bruno Mars Crash the Pepsi Super Bowl 50 Halftime Show," February 11, 2016, https://youtu.be/SDPITj1wlkg.
35. It bears repeating that the land that became the United States was not a white space originally, of course; it was a Native American space. White folks *crashed* it, stole it, and then brought stolen Black people into the space against their will. The people who have been erased, pushed out, are Native Americans.
36. Tim Daniels, "Aaron Rodgers Says Colin Kaepernick Isn't on NFL Team 'Because of His Protests,'" *Bleacher Report*, August 30, 2017, https://bleacherreport.com/articles/2730440-aaron-rodgers-says-colin-kaepernick-isnt-on-nfl-team-because-of-his-protests. See also Les Carpenter, "Kaepernick, Activism and Politics: The NFL Doesn't Know How to Stop This Row," *Guardian*, August 23, 2017, https://www.theguardian.com/sport/2017/aug/23/colin-kaepernick-impact-nfl-blacklist-anthem-protests. It is significant, too, that Kaepernick's position of quarterback is a role that has been particularly subject to positional discrimination and is racially marked as white. On this, see Leonard, *Playing While White*, especially 5, 18–20.
37. The award recognizes "individuals whose dedication to the ideals of sportsmanship has spanned decades and whose career in athletics has directly or indirectly impacted the world" ("Sports Illustrated Muhammad Ali Legacy Award," *Sports Illustrated*, accessed October 1, 2018, https://www.si.com/specials/muhammad-ali-sportsman-legacy-award/index.html). See also Michael Rosenberg, "Colin Kaepernick Is Recipient of 2017 Sports Illustrated Muhammad Ali Legacy Award," *Sports Illustrated*, November 30, 2017, https://www.si.com/sportsperson/2017/11/30/colin-kaepernick-muhammad-ali-legacy-award.
38. Wald, "Soul Vibrations," 691.
39. Ibid.
40. Perry explains the significance and history of the anthem in *May We Forever Stand*. Beyoncé described her motivation for using the anthem in "Beyoncé in Her Own Words: Her Life, Her Body, Her Heritage," *Vogue*, August 6, 2018, https://www.vogue.com/article/beyonce-september-issue-2018.

41. *Carmen: A Hip Hopera*, dir. Robert Townsend (MTV, 2001, 98 minutes).
42. Lorde, "Uses of the Erotic."
43. *Dreamgirls*, dir. Bill Condon (DreamWorks/Paramount, 2006, 130 minutes); *Cadillac Records*, dir. Darnell Martin (TriStar, 2008, 109 minutes).
44. In this regard, see, for instance, Chatman, "Pregnancy, Then It's 'Back to Business'"; Jolly, "Birthing Baby Blue"; Moss, "Beyoncé and Blue."

BIBLIOGRAPHY

Ahmed, Sara. "Embodying Diversity: Problems and Paradoxes for Black Feminists." *Race, Ethnicity and Education* 12, no. 1 (2009): 41–52.

———. *Living a Feminist Life*. Durham, NC: Duke University Press, 2017.

———. *On Being Included: Racism and Diversity in Institutional Life*. Durham, NC: Duke University Press, 2012.

Black, Alex W. "Abolitionism's Resonant Bodies: The Realization of African American Performance." *American Quarterly* 63, no. 3 (2011): 619–39.

Brown, Drew D. "The Portrayal of Black Masculinity in the NFL: Critical Race Theory and the Images of Black Males." In *Black Athletic Sporting Experiences in the United States: Critical Race Theory*. Edited by Billy J. Hawkins, Akilah R. Carter-Francique, and Joseph N. Cooper, 217–46. New York: Palgrave Macmillan, 2017.

Chatman, Dana. "Pregnancy, Then It's 'Back to Business': Beyoncé, Black Femininity, and the Politics of a Post-feminist Gender Regime." *Feminist Media Studies* 15, no. 6 (2015): 926–41.

Eidsheim, Nina Sun. *The Race of Sound: Listening, Timbre, and Vocality in African American Music*. Durham, NC: Duke University Press, 2019.

Fleetwood, Nicole. *Troubling Vision: Performance, Visuality, and Blackness*. Chicago: University of Chicago Press, 2011.

Harris, Tamara Winfrey. "Interlude F: 'Formation' and the Black-ass Truth about Beyoncé and Capitalism." In *The Lemonade Reader*. Edited by Kinitra D. Brooks and Kameelah L. Martin, 155–57. New York: Routledge, 2019.

Jolly, Natalie. "Birthing Baby Blue: Beyoncé and the Changing Face of Celebrity Birth Culture." In *The Beyoncé Effect: Essays on Sexuality, Race and Feminism*. Edited by Adrienne Trier-Bieniek, 143–54. Jefferson, NC: McFarland, 2016.

Kehrer, Lauron. "Who Slays? Queer Resonances in Beyoncé's *Lemonade*." *Popular Music and Society* 42, no. 1 (2019): 82–98.

Leonard, David J. *Playing While White: Privilege and Power on and off the Field*. Seattle: University of Washington Press, 2017.

Levy, Alan H. *Tackling Jim Crow: Racial Segregation in Professional Football*. Jefferson, NC: McFarland, 2003.

Lorde, Audre. "Uses of the Erotic: The Erotic as Power." In *Sister Outsider*, 53–59. Berkeley, CA: Crossing, 2007.
Lowery, Wesley. *They Can't Kill Us All: The Story of Black Lives Matter*. London: Penguin, 2017.
Mitchell, Anne M. "Beyoncé as Aggressive Black Femme and Informed Black Female Subject." In *The Beyoncé Effect: Essays on Sexuality, Race, and Feminism*. Edited by Adrienne Trier-Bieniek, 40–54. Jefferson, NC: McFarland, 2016.
Moss, Sonia R. "Beyoncé and Blue: Black Motherhood and the Binds of Racialized Sexism." In *The Beyoncé Effect: Essays on Sexuality, Race, and Feminism*. Edited by Adrienne Trier-Bieniek, 155–76. Jefferson, NC: McFarland, 2016.
Olutola, Sarah. "I Ain't Sorry: Beyoncé, Serena, and Hegemonic Hierarchies in Lemonade." *Popular Music and Society* 42, no. 1 (2019): 99–117.
Perry, Imani. *May We Forever Stand: A History of the Black National Anthem*. Chapel Hill: University of North Carolina Press, 2018.
Ransby, Barbara. *Making All Black Lives Matter: Reimagining Freedom in the Twenty-First Century*. Oakland: University of California Press, 2018.
Smith, Thomas G. "Outside the Pale: The Exclusion of Blacks from the National Football League, 1934–1946." *Journal of Sport History* 15, no. 3 (1988): 255–81.
Sullivan, Shannon, and Nancy Tuana, eds. *Race and Epistemologies of Ignorance*. Albany: State University of New York Press, 2007.
Wald, Gayle. "Soul Vibrations: Black Music and Black Freedom in Sound and Space." *American Quarterly* 63, no. 3 (2011): 673–96.
Wallace, Alicia. "A Critical View of Beyonce's 'Formation.'" *Black Camera* 9, no. 1 (2017): 189–96.

1

Beyoncé at Work, Making Beyoncé

ONE

Surviving the Hustle

Beyoncé's Performance of Work

EMILY J. LORDI

For all the questions she raises, one thing is clear: Beyoncé has worked hard to become Beyoncé. "I'm not gon' give up, I'm not gon' stop, I'm gon' work harder," she sang on *Destiny's Child*'s "Survivor," repeating a similar sentiment on her solo "Formation": "I see it, I want it, I stunt, yellow bone it/I dream it, I work hard, I grind till I own it." The daughter of the famously enterprising Mathew and Tina Knowles clearly learned a great deal from her parents' work ethic and acumen, just as she received formative if paradoxical training in the art of creative independence from her mogul husband, Jay-Z.[1] Over the years she has regendered James Brown's soul-era self-designation as the "hardest working man in show business" to become pop music's most ambitiously perfectionistic star, an artist whose departure from the groups Girl's Tyme and Destiny's Child can seem inevitable not only because of her superior vocal and dance skills, but also because she worked harder than her peers—"harder than probably everybody I know"—to develop them.[2] As she discloses in a 2009 documentary, when she is in the zone of rehearsing a show, she can go for hours without eating or using the bathroom; she must therefore be reminded to give her dancers and other crew members periodic breaks.[3] In terms of spectacular work ethic, her closest analogue might be Michael Jackson, the wunderkind who practiced hardest on Sundays in the service of God and whose sessions ended only when he could no longer move.[4] But Beyoncé is probably unrivaled among stars of her generation (save Prince) in her attention to *every detail* of a performance, concert, documentary, or music video, whether lighting, choreography, costumes, or stage design. And her stamina in concert—where she presents at least two hours of rigorous dancing and actual (not lip-synched) singing that stop for nothing but a series of rapid costume changes—is an unremarked yet phenomenal aspect of her art.

That brand of take-no-prisoners hard work acquired a distinctive racial politics in Beyoncé's parents' generation. As I have argued elsewhere, the discourse of soul that arose in the late 1960s and early 1970s marked soul as the aesthetic and moral reward for racialized forms of struggle and labor, thereby serving to recuperate Black struggle into a narrative of racial redemption: what does not kill one makes one stronger, gives one soul.[5] This is the logic that allows James Brown to claim "hardest working man" as a badge of honor, and it has been mobilized, across the late twentieth and early twenty-first centuries, by figures as diverse as Brown, born into extreme poverty to become the "godfather of soul"; Jay-Z, who describes his quintessentially hip hop sojourn "from the bottom of the bottom to the 'Top of the Pops'"; and Beyoncé herself, whose expressed ambition to work harder transforms the role of would-have-been victim into that of survivor. But if working hard to become a survivor is the millennial version of earning the right to claim soul, then what are the gendered and sociopolitical meanings of this development? Namely, what is the political value of Beyoncé's work ethic at a historical moment when neoliberal discourse privatizes success and failure as metrics of personal resilience and hard work, a national moment marked by such deep suspicion of the public good that social services are thought to betoken a nefarious socialist agenda?[6]

It is in this context that political scientist Lester Spence determines to "knock the hustle" lionized by the neoliberal turn in politics and supported by hip hop discourse since the 1980s. According to Spence, Ronald Reagan's dramatic tax cuts, decreased support for public housing, and reduction of unemployment benefits shifted bipartisan views of the US government from a social good to a problem and engendered a neoliberal cult of the enterprising individual that hip hop has helped to bolster.[7] "We turn to people like Jay Z, Ace Hood,... Napoleon Hill and other prominent black entertainers," Spence writes, for models of the neoliberal "hustle": the incessant work of personally developing human capital in a bid for economic success.[8] As if to supplement Spence's male-dominated account of the hustle,[9] Beyoncé—whose

2008 track "Diva" reminds us that "a diva is a female version of a hustla"—models a specifically gendered version of the hustle throughout the late 1990s and early 2000s. As the lead singer of Destiny's Child, she interpellates her fans as "independent women" who "sacrifice and work hard" to "get what [they] want," kicks her no-account boyfriend to the curb in "Bills Bills Bills," and declares herself a "survivor" whose setbacks, as I've noted, only spur her to "work harder." This valorization of work profoundly informs her first four solo albums as well: *Dangerously in Love* (2003), *B'Day* (2006), *I Am... Sasha Fierce* (2008), and *4* (2011). But something changes in 2013 with her release of the visual album, *Beyoncé*. That album, which she recorded and filmed in secret before releasing it in December of 2013, is a pivotal moment in Beyoncé's evolving artistic philosophy and performance of creative and vocal labor.

This chapter reads Beyoncé's singing practices, visual productions, and comments on her own music (for instance, in her 2013 behind-the-scenes docu-advertisement for *Beyoncé*) to theorize her changing conceptions of artistic labor in relation to neoliberal theories of work. I argue that, although her career is initially shaped by a spectacular performance of hard work and perfectionism that peaks with her 2011 album *4*, her 2013 album *Beyoncé* "knocks her own hustle," advancing an aesthetic of spontaneity and imperfection that rejects the incessant labor that neoliberalism demands and that her own œuvre had long celebrated. In other words, the album resists the logic that would frame her as pop music's poster girl for a conservative ideology that sees all success as a sign of hard work and failure as a failure of will. Of course, Beyoncé's rejection of the hustle is enabled by years of her own (and others') hard work; it is her luxury, as a global pop star, to take a break. If her rearticulation of work as play is not especially democratic (the album is called *Beyoncé* for a reason), then her release of "Formation" in 2016 aims to resolve that contradiction by articulating several forms of labor that are available to everyday people: information gathering ("get information"), organizing ("get in formation"), dancing, and even being still (form a line and just *be* there, to witness or calibrate next moves). Without completely rejecting Beyoncé's own gendered version of post-civil-rights Black entrepreneurialism ("I dream it, I work hard, I grind till I own it"), "Formation" imagines the power of manifold forms of work to challenge the system that requires women of color to hustle to survive in the first place.

"RUN THE WORLD (GIRLS)"

From Destiny's Child's self-titled debut album (1998) to Beyoncé's fourth studio album *4* (2011), Beyoncé meticulously constructed a diva persona that was equal parts fabulousness and exposure of the work required to be so fabulous. In the words of her work-hard-play-hard dance club anthem "Get Me Bodied," "a little sweat ain't never hurt nobody"—a truth the civic potential of which First Lady Michelle Obama exploited by using the song "B'Day" to popularize fitness routines for US children. But Beyoncé's hard work has not always or often been fun, exactly. She could "do" humor and satire in the tradition of comic entertainers, but hers was, like Lucille Ball's or Josephine Baker's, the "zany" labor of late capitalism, which, as theorized by Sianne Ngai,[10] dissolves the boundaries between work and play in a way that is both mesmerizing and overwhelming: Beyoncé plays a frantic tear-stained fifties pinup-housewife in the video for "Why Don't You Love Me"; she gamely rides a bucking bull prop that throws her at the end of "Suga Mama."

In a prescient and important set of essays, Daphne Brooks reads this frenetic mode of performance—specifically as Beyoncé enacts it on her 2006 album *B'Day*—as registering not only late-capitalist duress but the specific "emotional and material stress of post-millennium and post-Katrina [Southern] life."[11] Central to Brooks's reading is B'Day's Southern bayou iconography and the artist's performance of work. The album stages Beyoncé's declaration of independence from her manager-father and her seizure of control over multiple forms of work: "romantic, sexual, and physical as well as monetary."[12] Here, as Brooks writes, "the 'Independent woman' of Destiny's past has morphed into a production Svengali,"[13] a role that Beyoncé asserts in the album's first moments by roll-calling a series of sounds into "Déjà Vu": bass, hi-hat, 808 drum machine, even "Jay," who enters as beckoned on the lead verse. According to Brooks, "Déjà Vu" registers Black women's emotional and technical labor by establishing Beyoncé's control over this production and by foregrounding the vocal work the song demands: as Beyoncé's voice "escalates to ... sky-scraping ranges, one is reminded of how hard, in fact, the singer is working here—and how much effort [and stamina] it takes to dash ... through these wordy-verses ... at breakneck speed."[14] In short, Beyoncé at once announces her control over her music and performs its excessive demands. An ode to a haunting lover as well as to a musical past,

"Déjà Vu" revives sounds from the soul and disco eras—a fuzzy bass and hyped-up Donna Summer hook. But here Beyoncé begins to turn the soul era's valorization of Black (vocal) labor into a *critique* of the demands shouldered by Black working women. In that way, *B'Day* presages her rejection of those demands seven years later.

To extend Brooks's analysis of Beyoncé's gendered performance of labor into the years after *B'Day*'s release is to see how her particular brand of hardworking vocal virtuosity—if not the sociopolitical investments signaled through *B'Day*'s bayou imagery—intensifies on her next two albums, *I Am... Sasha Fierce* and *4*. Tracks such as "Halo," "Countdown," "Love on Top," and "I Care" showcase Beyoncé's continual growth as a vocalist, along with her unabated desire to kill it every time. "Love on Top," from *4*, ends with a house-wrecking church trick in which Beyoncé keeps modulating the chorus a half-step higher, a tiered-wedding-cake of modulations that proves she deserves a lover who "gives [his] all," as she is clearly doing now. That this vocal track is composed of a "patchwork of takes that couldn't possibly coexist" is a sly insider's joke that Beyoncé exposes through her music video, which features a routine of early 1990s dance moves so rigorous that one could not actually sing while performing them.[15] *4* also includes a less conventional but no less climactic—and more sincere—performance of emotional labor, as Beyoncé croons and swoons along with a guitar solo at the top of her range on "I Care," the understated title of which Rich Juzwiak jokingly noted by stressing the album's overwhelming expression of care.[16]

There is much to value in Beyoncé's thirteen-year performance of labor, both for how it registers Black women's frenetic work and dispossession, as Brooks argues with respect to *B'Day*, and for how it regenders the discourse of the hustle while intervening in sexist discourses of Black women's performance. That is, Beyoncé's performance of labor overturns the remarkably durable cultural narrative that depicts Black women as natural, unthinking divas while attributing their innovations to the male producers and other male industry figures who "discover" and otherwise shape them. A fifteen-minute video montage on YouTube that collates "Beyoncé's bossiest moments"—by which the filmmakers mean not instances of excessive aggression but bosslike behavior one might wish to emulate—reminds us that the racial dimensions of this labor are as logistical as they are ideological. In one clip, Beyoncé responds to a video of a stage rehearsal: "I hate all that ugly blue light. I'm a black girl, you can't put blue lights on black girls. . . . I cain't trust them," she mutters, "They don't know what they're doing."[17] This comment, one imagines, encodes years of such indignities: insensitive questions, hairdressers who can't do Black hair, the specific strains of working with "experts" who lack the skills needed to portray Black artists in the best possible light. This behind-the-scenes moment reveals what Beyoncé's own meticulously self-directed documentaries tend to veil: the racist conditions that require her to work doubly hard as a Black woman, to ensure not only that she and her ideas are taken seriously, but also that they are properly executed by people whose racial sensibility and know-how she can trust. Ultimately, Beyoncé's performance of labor exposes the raced and gendered *necessity* of seizing power within disempowering working conditions, while recentering her own agency and therefore encouraging us to locate her genius in her performative choices.[18]

Yet for all that is laudable about Beyoncé's spectacular work ethic, the social context in which it unfolds should curb our enthusiasm about its implications. This is because what aligns her with the contemporary rappers Spence studies and separates her from her soul predecessors—those artists who had popularized, secularized, and politicized Black performative labor—is a neoliberal context in which "competition and market-oriented behavior [become] the guiding principles of governments and the standard by which to judge individuals, populations, and institutions."[19] Beyoncé's work ethic is easily conscripted into this view, which sees "the perfect human being . . . [as] an entrepreneur of his own human capital."[20] Indeed, one moment in her documentary *Life Is but a Dream* (2013) supports the privatization of personal development, failure, and success with particular candor. While pregnant and preparing for her rigorous 2011 Billboard Awards performance of "Run the World (Girls)," she explains, she became acutely aware that "women have to work much harder [than men do] to make it in this world." Although she notes the emotional and economic injustice of that system, Beyoncé proceeds to present her own "lean in"–style philosophy of female empowerment through personal perseverance. She concludes, "At the end of the day, it's not about equal rights; it's about how we think. We have to reshape our own perception of how we view ourselves. We have to step up as women and take the lead and reach as high as humanly possible. That's what I'm gonna do, that's my philosophy, and that's what 'Girls' is all about."

In a shrewd feminist critique of neoliberalism, especially as it affects pop musical aesthetics, Robin James theorizes resilience as a gendered form of labor, one that "normalizes the sexist, racist damage traditional white supremacist patriarchy inflicts on white women and people of color as the ultimately innocuous damage that they are individually responsible for overcoming."[21] "Run the World (Girls)" would seem to epitomize James's paradigm, insofar as it asks women to believe they run the world, or could, and thus posits a "fake it till you make it" approach to global patriarchy. But a closer listen reveals that even this anthem registers contradictions that Beyoncé's own commentary on it elides. The song celebrates working women, mothers, and "college grads"—but, ideally, women who are all three, in addition to being extremely wealthy: "Boy you know you love it how we smart enough to make these millions, strong enough to bear the children, then get back to bidness." Such lyrics suggest that the song's celebration is really for Beyoncé herself who, sure enough, titled her first postpartum concerts in May 2012 "Back to Business." Indeed, the song is driven by the tension between Beyoncé and other women. The syntax of the chorus—"Who run the world/Girls"—creates a loop that makes "girls" both the subject of a phrase and the answer to a question. It therefore hails "girls who run the world" (few though they may be), while also imagining a world in which (all) the people "who run the world" could be (who?) "girls." The objection that we do not live in that world misses the point, which is to fancifully hitch description (there are some powerful women out here) to prophecy (female world domination).[22] In short, the song both interrogates Beyoncé's representative status and makes a mythic ideal of her success. That the backing voices on "Run the World" are not a chorus of female singers but multiplied tracks of Beyoncé herself serves to simulate community in the form of a sonic echo chamber and so again reflects the tension between the singer's own exceptional status and the people her anthem aims to inspire if not to represent.

The tension in "Run the World" between Beyoncé and her fans better prepares us for the revision she enacts two years later, when she proceeds to knock—or, at least, to radically revise—the hustle that had been central to the creation of her own (and the Knowles family's) empire. Whatever her *actual* feelings and covert strategies, with the release of *Beyoncé* she *performs* a refusal to keep working so hard to stay on top and, in that way, repudiates industry metrics as the determinants of her artistic worth. This move is crucial to her transformation from pop star to serious artist—two roles she will link with that of Black activist in 2016.

She controlled the narrative about the meaning of *Beyoncé* as surely and shrewdly as she had roll-called her musicians into "Déjà Vu." In the five short videos she released on YouTube concurrent with the album itself, she explains that the album reflects her attempt to let go and embrace imperfection. Looking relaxed and minimally made up in a white T-shirt and jeans, she expresses her new belief that what matters are not the trappings of success but the affective experience of professional "respect," interpersonal "impact," and familial connection: gazing into her husband's eyes and hearing her daughter say "Mommy."[23] Discussing how hard she worked to become "Beyoncé," she explains that the trophy display in her opening video "Pretty Hurts" represents the excessive cost of that work: "The trophy represents all of the sacrifices I made as a kid, all of the time that I lost being on the road, in the studios, as a child. And," she smiles, "I just wanna blow that shit up."[24] The video enacts that fantasy. Playing the role of "Miss Third Ward," Beyoncé trains and primps for a pageant along with other starving, unhappy women before wreaking havoc on her trophy case.

As Natalia Cecire writes, "Pretty Hurts" "announces what emerges as the whole album's preoccupation: Bildung, the making of Beyoncé and *Beyoncé*."[25] In Cecire's reading, the album is about "the spectacle of occluded labor" behind Beyoncé's acts of creation, the herculean work behind the *work*. But Beyoncé, in her commentary, figures work as something more akin to play, and in this sense does not so much hide her labor in plain view as reframe it. In the *Beyoncé* documentary, she explains that the music and videos alike were animated by the ideal of "being in the moment and embracing mistakes and effortlessness. . . . It's really just about fun and art and, you know, creativity that is instant. Whatever comes into your head in that moment, you can't plan it. It's just something so refreshing about that."[26] Her vocal and physical performances bear this point of view out by rejecting some of her signature forms of hard work. Instead of the labored performance of perfection, Beyoncé presents subtler, less intensive vocals on this album, which features drunken sex ("Drunk in Love"), awkward dancing (ditto), the humor and erotics of desire ("Waterfall"). In the documentary, she describes filming scenes on Houston streets without knowing what would happen and recording songs simply when so moved; she narrates (and cinematically enacts) her process of suddenly rising to the microphone to sing the first verse of "Partition," a scene that underscores her skill as a lyricist as well as her boldness as a woman and artist.

It is because *Beyoncé* as a whole refigures work as play that "Pretty Hurts" is not, in my view, the album's most representative song or video but rather its antithesis, a dramatization of the kind of performance that the rest of *Beyoncé* will go on to reject. In the video's staged pageant performance, Beyoncé-the-contestant moves to the microphone and meekly sings in the exceedingly "pretty" sound that had made her famous. Here is the ideal sonic image to which she has had to conform—the vocal achievement we hear in "Halo" and that reaches its peak in the voice-guitar duet on the bridge of "I Care" and the out-choruses of "Love on Top" (even as that song's audible suturing of takes hints at the ideal's impossibility)—and that the remainder of *Beyoncé* resists. There are very few hard-to-sing lines on this album, and Beyoncé rarely stretches or strains. She hews to Frank Ocean's limited range on her duet with him, "Superpower," and does the same with Drake on their duet, "Mine." Her choice of collaborators is apt, since both Drake and Ocean represent the flawed and moody vibe (one arguably popularized by Kanye West) that Beyoncé plumbs on this album. Regendering these male artists' sullen introspection, she dispels the mirage of a flawless marriage by divulging postpartum details and fears about her relationship: "I'm not feeling like myself since the baby, are we gonna even make it?/Oh, cause if we are, we're taking this a little too far." The marriage recovers, but not gracefully, with "Drunk in Love," whose uncharacteristically meandering video shows Beyoncé and Jay-Z dancing aimlessly on the beach.[27] Taken together, these moments suggest that the album's representative sentiment is not "pretty hurts" but "I woke up like this," from "Flawless." Crucially, "this" is not always beautiful (as one sees in the basement-grunge-battle video for "Flawless"), although it is worthy of celebration. Overall, *Beyoncé* presents a vocal and visual style that is less concerned with being "flawless" than with being versatile. In place of the feminine ideal of excessive work made to look easy, Beyoncé advances an aesthetic of easeful imperfection.

In relinquishing certain forms of painful or limiting work, she eschews the neoliberal model that posits the development of human capital as the point of all work and hard work as the key to success. But, of course, it is only because she "runs the world" that she can do this: it is her very success that allows her to disavow the hard work that has (partly) enabled it. As she states in the *Beyoncé* documentary, "I've done so many things in my life, in my career, that at this point I feel like I've earned the right to be me and to express any and every side of myself."[28] She has "earned the right" to approach her artistic process this way, to take this risk; she has earned the capital and the clout to gather her creative friends in the Hamptons while she records the new music that serves as her "outlet" during her intensive early period of mothering.[29] Artistically, it is only because she has developed "the finest set of ears, the sharpest musical mind, of anyone in her pop generation" that her "play" will *be* so artful.[30] The fact that this work looks and sounds "easier" than her earlier powerhouse performances, then, does not make it more democratic. In fact, Beyoncé's refiguration of work-as-play can seem acutely *un*available to fans who are themselves faced with the choice to either hustle or drown.

By 2013, it is not only Beyoncé's personal luxury but also a commercial necessity to conclude, as she does in "Haunted," "Perfection is so 'eh.'" Her perennial performance of perfection had likely become bad for business, less relatable to her core audience of Black women and less hip amid the work of younger stars like Drake, Frank Ocean, and Rihanna who made a brand of failure and ennui. So it is not that her new approach to this album resists market logic; on the contrary, her decision to surprise-release the album as a "gift" to her fans (albeit not a free one) represents a brilliant marketing move at a moment when anticommercialism sells and earns respect from establishment critics. None of Beyoncé's four prior solo albums had sold as many copies in the first week as did *Beyoncé*. It was downloaded more than any album in the history of the iTunes store up to that point and was nominated for five Grammys (of which it won three), including Album of the Year. But the fact that Beyoncé's strategic self-definition yielded commercial and critical success does not negate the fact that her performative approach to and discursive representation of *Beyoncé* offered an alternative to the neoliberal ethics of hard work that had shaped her career and, in so doing, presaged her developing political imagination as it manifested three years later, on *Lemonade*.

"IN FORMATION"

Although *Lemonade* maintains *Beyoncé*'s more experimental and less polished vocal, compositional, and choreographic aesthetic, the album represents a new moment in Beyoncé's conception of work. Its imagery and lyrics represent and extend several forms of labor to Black women and other culture workers on the frontlines of the Black Lives Matter movement. In the surprise-release video for "Formation," which debuted on February 6, 2016, Beyoncé drives and dances through the Dirty South and invokes Hurricane Katrina through a shot of a drowning police car; the flood is not represented as a historical event but an ever-present disaster that coexists alongside demands that police "stop shooting us." In part because of this visual imagery, and in part because the song's lyrics celebrate Beyoncé's "Jackson Five nostrils" and "hot sauce in my bag swag," Beyoncé's call for ladies to "get in formation" departs from her earlier shout-outs to "Independent Women," "Single Ladies," and "Girls" who "Run the World" in that it hails a markedly *Black* female constituency. (In fact, each word of the first line of "Formation," in which she addresses rumors that she and Jay-Z belong to a satanic secret society, is uniquely Black and Southern: "Y'all haters corny with that Illuminati mess.") She sought to represent this particular imagined community the day after the video's release, storming the field of the 2016 Super Bowl Halftime Show with a crew of natural-haired Black women dancers dressed in Black Panther regalia.

Taken as a whole, *Lemonade* is a cinematic and sonic Afrodiasporic journey from betrayal to redemption in which the "work" consists in the gathering of a multivalent Black female "we." Beyoncé performs this work by gathering Black musical and visual history: invoking soul tracks, work songs, and dancehall rhythms and alluding to Julie Dash's *Daughters of the Dust*, Michael Jackson's "Black or White" video, and Beyoncé's own plantation scenes in the video for "Déjà Vu." In this regard, her album reflects the anthologizing impulse of Toni Cade Bambara's *The Black Woman* (1970) and the collage aesthetic of Toni Morrison's coedited documentary archive *The Black Book* (1974), both of which enact what Bambara terms an epochal "turning away from the larger society" in an effort to "get basic with each other."[31] This work of gathering resounds with special urgency through Amiri Baraka's iconic Black Arts poem "SOS" (1969), in which Baraka calls "all black people" to "come in, come on in."[32] In a shrewd reading of the poem, Philip Brian Harper notes that "What is striking ... is not that it 'calls' black people in this nationalistic way but that this is *all* it does; the objective for which it assembles the black populace is not specified in the piece itself."[33] What strikes Harper is not the poem's emergency assembly but the fact that Baraka has nothing for Black people to do once they get there.

Whereas for Harper this indirection indexes the challenges of the Black Arts "nationalist agenda,"[34] *Lemonade* shows that a lack of specificity about what it means to "get in formation" can be fruitful; when the aim of doing so is to celebrate Black community and femininity and to protest antiblack violence, it makes sense not to prescribe what that should look like. As noted earlier, the wordplay of the chorus ("get in formation," "get information") sets equal value on information gathering, organized protest, and social dance. Everyday people have accordingly transposed the iconography and ethos of "Formation" into myriad forms of work. The week after *Lemonade*'s release, in April 2016, fifty Black women in Chicago donned Black Panther uniforms that recalled those of Beyoncé and her Super Bowl dancers. Blocking Lakeshore Drive, they called for the firing of the local police officer, Dante Servin, responsible for killing twenty-two-year-old Rekia Boyd in 2012, as well as for the prioritization of public education, Chicago State having just laid off hundreds of employees in a budget crisis.[35] Joining such grassroots activist efforts was the sustained intellectual labor that Beyoncé's album both inspired and embodied. As Brooks notes, the "wealth of online criticism from voices often barred from media conversation about art, is one of the greatest gifts Beyoncé continues to give us all."[36] One such gift was the "Lemonade syllabus," a document that echoes the Black Arts Movement's demands that people learn Black (women's) history before commenting on Black (women's) art. Of course, part of this intellectual labor was also about getting paid. This was itself in keeping with "Formation," the lyrics to which valorize monetary compensation—"the best revenge is your paper"—just as Beyoncé had done since the late nineties. That the album was released by and generated profits for Tidal, the streaming company of which Beyoncé is one of approximately twenty "artist-owners," consolidated that "revenge."[37] To the extent that the company was then largely associated with Jay-Z, the success of *Lemonade* also displayed Beyoncé's continued ability to assist him or "Upgrade U," while subversively mobilizing male capital to the project of gathering a Black female "we."

But there is something else, too, which goes beyond familiar forms of hustling, direct action, inquiry, and critique. When the film begins, Beyoncé appears bereft by her lover's betrayal; she swan dives onto a city street that opens up into an ocean. Here is the deep internal space of what Elizabeth Alexander calls "the black interior," a wild, private creative resource that speaks through dreams.[38] Everything is quiet in Beyoncé's underwater world, as it is in the video's first image of her still, breathing body. This first view of the artist—her hair in cornrows and her body covered in a fur coat—reflects what Ralph Ellison might have called a studied hibernation: "a covert preparation for a more overt action."[39] But what does it mean to hibernate not underground, as Ellison's narrator does, but in plain view? The image serves, in part, to register Ellison's own insight about the synonymy of Black invisibility and hypervisibility. But Beyoncé's hibernatory stillness additionally exploits white fears of a once enslaved Black populace quietly seething and primed to retaliate while maintaining opacity if not privacy in public through the shelter of costume, stillness, and breath.

In a blog post published within hours of the "Formation" video's release, Zandria Robinson describes Beyoncé as calling for a *collective* stillness, for a way of being in a formation that is not yet active, a lying-in-wait. Robinson especially ascribes this latent social energy to those on the margins of the margins: poor, Black, Southern, gender-queer, trans, disabled people such as Beyoncé invokes through the voice of murdered gender-queer comedian Messy Mya.[40] Through her moments of haunting stillness, Beyoncé proposes a kind of work that looks nothing like hustling and still less like conventional forms of leadership. Insofar as her call to "get in/formation" inspires but does not explicitly guide or direct, it refuses the model of Black male charismatic leadership that Erica Edwards critiques in favor of the non-hierarchical vision of Black Lives Matter.[41] Rejecting even the spirited hustle of Black female empowerment, Beyoncé offers an image that more closely resembles meditation or prayer. This represents her most marked departure from both the soul tradition of racially redemptive work and the neoliberal glorification of incessant productivity. And it poses a unique threat to the established order, because who can predict what comes next?

EMILY J. LORDI is Associate Professor of English at Vanderbilt University. She is author of *Black Resonance: Iconic Women Singers and African American Literature; Donny Hathaway Live;* and *The Meaning of Soul: Black Music and Resilience since the 1960s.*

NOTES

1. Tina Knowles ran one of the most successful salons in Houston and later joined forces with Beyoncé to launch a fashion line, House of Dereon; her father, Mathew Knowles, was a producer and manager for Beyoncé's own groups, from Girl's Tyme to Destiny's Child, among other acts. Beyoncé describes Jay-Z's influence in these terms in the 2013 HBO documentary *Life Is But a Dream*, dir. Ed Burke, Beyoncé Knowles, and Ilan Benatar (HBO, 2013, 90 minutes).

2. Beyoncé, "Beyoncé Self-Titled," part 2, "Imperfection," December 13, 2013, https://www.youtube.com/watch?v=cIv1z6n3X xo.

3. *What Happens in Vegas: Behind the Scenes of I Am . . . Yours*, dir. Nick Wickham (Columbia, 2009, 24 minutes).

4. King, "Don't Stop," 201–2; *Michael Jackson's Journey from Motown to Off the Wall*, dir. Spike Lee (Showtime, 2016, 110 minutes).

5. See Lordi, "Souls Intact."

6. Suspicions of Barack Obama's secret "socialist agenda" shaped conservative discourse about his presidency, whether because of his health-care reform or support for transgender bathrooms (Toby Harnden, "Barack Obama Reignites Fear of Socialist Agenda," *Telegraph*, October 27, 2008, http://www.telegraph.co.uk/news/worldnews/barackobama/3269668/Barack-Obama-reignites-fear-of-socialist-agenda.html; Paul Sperry, "Obama's Final Days Show His True Socialist Agenda," *New York Post*, June 20, 2016, http://nypost.com/2016/06/12/obamas-final-days-show-his-true-socialist-agenda/).

7. Spence, *Knocking the Hustle*, 20–21.

8. Ibid., 115.

9. From Spence's prefatory account of his own struggles as a tenure-track assistant professor with five home-schooled kids and one out-of-commission car to his critique of charismatic male prosperity gospel preachers and Black public intellectuals, Spence's study focuses almost exclusively on men. It is therefore unsurprising that the phrase he uses to represent everyday (Black) people's internalization of neoliberal ideology is Jay-Z's gendered quip (on Kanye West's 2005 "Diamonds from Sierra Leone (Remix)"): "I'm not a business man; I'm a *business*, man!" (Spence, *Knocking the Hustle*, 2).

10. Ngai, *Our Aesthetic Categories*.

11. Brooks, "All That You Can't Leave Behind," 196; see also Brooks, "Suga Mama, Politicized," *The Nation*, November 30, 2006, https://www.thenation.com/article/suga-mama-politicized/.

12. Brooks, "All That You Can't Leave Behind," 182.

13. Brooks, "Suga Mama."

14. Brooks, "All That You Can't Leave Behind," 194.

15. I am grateful to Martin Iddon for this insight and formulation.

16. Rich Juzwiak, "Beyoncé's Odes to Joy," *Village Voice*, June 29, 2011, https://www.villagevoice.com/2011/06/29/beyonces-odes-to-joy/.

17. video tube, "Beyoncé Shadiest/Top Bossiest Moments," December 12, 2016, https://www.youtube.com/watch?v=BMTnqQQOUiA.

18. These choices are, as Jody Rosen notes, remarkably eccentric. Stressing Beyoncé's identity as "a vocalist with truly weird and original melodic and rhythmic approaches," he notes that, if "the slippery rap-style syncopations [of] 'Say My Name' and the jarring timbral and tonal variations [of] 'Ring the Alarm' and '1+1' . . . sound 'normal' now, it's because Beyoncé, and her many followers, have retrained our ears" (Rosen, "Her Highness," *New Yorker*, February 20, 2013, http://www.newyorker.com/culture/culture-desk/her-highness).

19. Spence, *Knocking the Hustle*, 113.

20. Ibid.

21. James, 7. James argues that Beyoncé's 2008 song and video for *Diva* refuse "resilience discourse" by "outhustl[ing] the hustle" that is expected of her (125): "She doesn't *embody* damage; rather, she *wreaks* it" (118). Five years later, Beyoncé is no longer outhustling the hustle so much as she is rejecting it.

22. This objection was humorously and effectively made by YouTube personality Nineteen Percent in her video "Beyoncé—Run the World (LIES)," May 20, 2011, https://www.youtube.com/watch?v=p72UqyVPj54.

23. Beyoncé, "*Beyoncé* Self-Titled," part 2.

24. Ibid.

25. Natalia Cecire, "Beyoncé's Second Skin (Part 1)," *Works Cited*, May 23, 2014, http://nataliacecire.blogspot.com/2014/05/beyonces-second-skin-part-i.html.

26. Beyoncé, "*Beyoncé* Self-Titled," part 3, "Run 'N Gun," December 25, 2013, https://www.youtube.com/watch?v=UPmX4ASAcaE.

27. The beach video for "Drunk in Love" highlights the one form of labor that Beyoncé's comments on the making of *Beyoncé* reveal. Explaining that she gained approximately sixty pounds during her pregnancy, she divulges that "I worked *crazily* to get my body back. I wanted to show my body! I wanted to show that you can have a child and you can work hard and you can get your body back. . . . You could have your child and you could still have fun and you could *still* be sexy and still have dreams and live for yourself" (Beyoncé, "*Beyoncé* Self-Titled," part 4, "Liberation," December 30, 2013, https://www.youtube.com/watch?v=1b1loWJfxaA).

28. "*Beyoncé* Self-Titled," part 5, "Honesty," January 3, 2014, https://www.youtube.com/watch?v=LFXJGr7sYDk.

29. Beyoncé, "*Beyoncé* Self-Titled," part 4.

30. Rosen, "Her Highness."

31. Bambara, *Black Woman*, 7; Harris et al., *Black Book*.

32. Baraka, "SOS."

33. Harper, *Are We Not Men?*, 41.

34. Ibid.

35. "17 Arrested after Protesters Stop Traffic on Lake Shore Drive," *NBC Chicago*, April 30, 2016, http://www.nbcchicago.com/news/local/Protesters-Block-Lake-Shore-Drive-to-Disrupt-NFL-Draft-Town-377690751.html.

36. Daphne A. Brooks, "How #BlackLivesMatter Started a Musical Revolution," *Guardian*, March 13, 2016, https://www.theguardian.com/us-news/2016/mar/13/black-lives-matter-beyonce-kendrick-lamar-protest.

37. According to the Tidal website, other "artist-owners" include such industry leaders as Nicki Minaj, Lil Wayne, Jack White, Madonna, and Rihanna, "Tidal Owners," accessed August 10, 2017, https://support.tidal.com/hc/en-us/articles/203055651-Who-owns-TIDAL.

38. Alexander, *Black Interior*, x.

39. Ellison, *Invisible Man*, 113.

40. Zandria Robinson, "We Slay, Part I," *New South Negress*, February 7, 2016, accessed August 10, 2017, http://newsouthnegress.com/southernslayings/. I am attentive to criticisms that Beyoncé's engagements with queer and other marginalized populations are appropriative insofar as they obscure the labor and lives of her "sources." Because *Lemonade* features countless producers, filmmakers, and Black women celebrities like Serena Williams, I predict her future work will bring yet more visibility (and compensation) to other artists and collaborators.

41. Edwards, *Charisma*. I am grateful to Stephanie Li for her assistance with this formulation.

BIBLIOGRAPHY

Alexander, Elizabeth. *The Black Interior*. St. Paul, MN: Graywolf, 2004.
Bambara, Toni Cade. *The Black Woman: An Anthology*. New York: Mentor, 1970.
Baraka, Amiri. "SOS." In *The LeRoi Jones/Amiri Baraka Reader*. Edited by William J. Harris, 218. New York: Thunder's Mouth, 1991.
Brooks, Daphne A. "'All That You Can't Leave Behind': Black Female Soul Singing and the Politics of Surrogation in the Age of Catastrophe." *Meridians* 8, no. 1 (2007): 180–204.
Edwards, Erica. *Charisma and the Fictions of Black Leadership*. Minneapolis: University of Minnesota Press, 2012.
Ellison, Ralph. *Invisible Man*. New York: Vintage, 1995.
Harper, Philip Brian. *Are We Not Men?: Masculine Anxiety and the Problem of African-American Identity*. New York: Oxford University Press, 1996.
Harris, Middleton A., Ernest Smith, Morris Levitt, Roger Furman, and Toni Morrison eds. *The Black Book*. New York: Random House, 1974.
James, Robin. *Resilience and Melancholy: Pop Music, Feminism, Neoliberalism*. Winchester: Zero, 2015.

King, Jason. "Don't Stop 'til You Get Enough: Presence, Spectacle, and Good Feeling in *Michael Jackson's This Is It.*" In *Black Performance Theory.* Edited by Thomas F. DeFrantz and Anita Gonzalez, 184–203. Durham, NC: Duke University Press, 2014.

Lordi, Emily J. "Souls Intact: The Soul Performances of Audre Lorde, Aretha Franklin, and Nina Simone." *Women and Performance* 26, no. 3 (2016): 55–71.

Ngai, Sianne. *Our Aesthetic Categories: Cute, Zany, Interesting.* Cambridge, MA: Harvard University Press, 2012.

Spence, Lester. *Knocking the Hustle: Against the Neoliberal Turn in Black Politics.* Brooklyn, NY: Punctum, 2015.

TWO

"A Scientist of Songs"

Beyoncé, the Recording Studio, and Popular Music Authorship

WILL FULTON

Figure 2.1 shows a popular meme that circulated in February 2015, just as a tweet was widely shared that stated, "Beyonce: 27 writers and 19 producers, Kanye: 49 writers and 25 producers. Beck: 1 writer, 1 producer."[1] At the 2015 Grammy Awards, Beck won the Album of the Year award instead of Beyoncé, and Kanye West subsequently voiced his objection to the decision.[2] The meme and tweet present Beck as a solo auteur and Beyoncé as a pop construct, while the choice of images and design is indicative of a gendered positioning. Beck is pictured above Beyoncé with the wistful image of a Romantic genius, in a visage reminiscent of Ary Scheffer's 1847 *Portrait of Frédéric Chopin*, Wilhelm August Rieder's 1875 portrait of Franz Schubert, or Henri Lehmann's 1839 *Portrait of the Young Franz Liszt*. The image and the accompanying text cast Beck as a maker, confident in his considerable mastery of instruments and skills, in the tradition of male nineteenth-century European composers. In contrast, Beyoncé runs her hand through her hair with slightly pursed lips and stares into the camera. In this meme, she is presented as having "zero" skills either at instrumental performance or songwriting and for that reason needs extensive help from numerous creative forces to construct her album.

This binary positions a paradigm of artistry and authenticity against a disdainful example of manufactured pop artifice. The implication is that collaborative production is a sign of weakness, whereas solo songwriting and production are the marks of a "true" artist. In such a binary, to play

Fig. 2.1. Popular meme (creator anonymous) circulating after 2015 Grammy Awards. Image from Tahnee Cadrez, "Why the Artistry Argument between Beck & Beyoncé Is a Stupid One," A Girl Mad as Birds . . . , February 13, 2015, accessed August 10, 2017, http://tahneesucks.tumblr.com/post/110879139611/why-the-artistry-argument-between-beck-beyonce.

instruments and compose original melodies is creative, while to rely on excessive technology, studio musicians, digital sampling, and outsourced ideas from producers is indicative of a lack of artistic talent. Although Beck has participated in his fair share of sampling and collaborating with producers during his career,[3] in this positioning, his image is employed to shame, by comparison, West and Beyoncé: notably, two prominent African American performers who engage in sampling and collaborative production practices. Although the popularity of ideas expressed in the meme is buoyed by early-twenty-first-century culture and revenue-per-click media, the ideas stem from the larger reception of African American musical production, one informed by earlier trends in copyright legislation and music journalism.

This chapter considers how Beyoncé's collagist creative practice—the collaging of outsourced sections in creating song recordings—challenges the sole artist model, as she participates in an innovative collaborative writing and production process in the recording studio. Contextualizing current popular music reception through a survey of music copyright history and popular music criticism, I argue that borrowing is systemic in popular music, but artistic "credit" is often misunderstood by fans. I address how views of popular music making have been shaped by trends in journalism like "rockism" and "poptimism." As Marla Kohlman has stated, intersectionality plays a critical role in the reception of Beyoncé, as a Black woman who is a "commoditized item to be consumed by the public gaze."[4] Although Beyoncé's practice of borrowing is akin to the practices of musicians deemed to exemplify rock artistry—such as the Beatles, the Beach Boys, and Led Zeppelin—racialized and gendered views of musical creativity and intersectional thinking in the critical reception of a female African American performer are distinctly shaped by historical factors.

Through an examination of the composition and production history of "Hold Up" and "Don't Hurt Yourself," two tracks from Beyoncé's *Lemonade* album (New York: Parkwood/Columbia, 2016), and drawing on published remarks by Beyoncé and several of her collaborators, including Jack White, Mike Will Made It, Diana "Wynter" Gordon, MNEK, and Diplo, I show how Beyoncé's process involves constructing songs through the synthesis of outsourced sections and reimagines pop songwriting by employing collagist processes in a way that reflects and reconciles pop music's complicated relationship with acts of borrowing. In order to examine how genre, race, and gender have an impact on reception, I consider the creative practices and reception of Led Zeppelin (an all-male white rock band) in comparison with those of Beyoncé (an African American female pop/R&B soloist) and how their assessments are shaped by racialized and gendered attitudes about music making. These creative practices and the complex issues related to popular music composition and copyright law are then revealed in the examination of Beyoncé's "Don't Hurt Yourself" (2016), a track that samples Led Zeppelin's recording "When the Levee Breaks" (1971).

THE PROBLEM OF AUTHORSHIP AND THE LEGACY OF COPYRIGHT

The problem of authorship in popular music has been examined by Dave Headlam, Robert Middleton, Lars Eckstein, and Keith Negus, among others.[5] Central to authorship issues in popular music is the critical lauding of originality and authorial intent for singer-songwriters (either performing as solo artists or working in bands) within a culture in which borrowing is virtually systemic. Further, as Susan McClary, Sheila Whiteley, Vaughn Schmutz and Alison Faupel, and Marion Leonard have shown, the meritocracy and artistic autonomy are often the focus of male performers' reception, while women (with Madonna a common example) earn fewer accolades as songwriters and producers and are often depicted as dependent rather than autonomous.[6]

Prior to the eighteenth century, borrowing was a widely accepted aspect of Western musical culture. The assessment of creative genius, however, in terms of the originality of the lone nineteenth-century composer—with Beethoven, Chopin, and Wagner as common models—and the resultant power shift toward composers and away from performers, was a focus of the concurrent explosion of music journalism, one shaped by new legislation:

> The early history of music copyright also reflects a trajectory in which initial concerns about unauthorized copying and distribution of completed works later came to shape conceptions on the creation side such that copying in creation became increasingly disfavored during the nineteenth century and subject to increasingly sacralized views of musical creativity.... In contrast, as was the case with Western art music when it was a living and vibrant musical tradition, living musical traditions often involve interchange, reuse, borrowing, improvisation, and other uses of existing works that may be inconsistent with sacralized conceptions of creativity.[7]

Artistic works in the precopyright/preprivatization model, an era that overlapped with the implementation of copyright laws in the twentieth century, relied considerably on appropriation of parts of other creative works: "Whether we are talking about Dada, Cubism, Futurism, Surrealism, Situationism, or Pop Art, creators across artistic movements have long acknowledged the centrality of appropriation in their creative practices. Collage was an essential method used to create literary works like T. S. Eliot's *The Waste Land*, Kathey Acker's *Blood and Guts in High School*, William Burrough's *Naked Lunch*, James Joyce's *Ulysses*, and Marianne Moore's poetry. In the world of audio, collage practices played a key role in the development of avant-garde music, as well as the birth of hip hop."[8]

But just as twentieth-century artistic movements were thriving as a result of free appropriation of elements from other creative works, lawyers were working on behalf of copyright holders (both individuals and corporations) to secure intellectual works as privately held property. The current era of copyright and intellectual commodity could be described as a privatization model, wherein copyright controllers (generally companies rather than individual creators) retain control of the creative works. The institution of copyright laws, specifically the US copyright acts of 1909—which protects written works—and of 1976—which, among other media, protects sound recordings—transformed popular music making into a corporate-controlled process. At the same time, the dominance of mass-marketed popular music created within the public imagination the perception of industry practice as an artistic norm.

Music composition copyright considers the textual qualities of the work (melody, harmony, and lyrics) yet ignores performative elements. Consider the significance for the production of popular music forms rooted in African American folk music, in which what Cheryl Keyes calls performers' "timbral signatures" and other elements are paramount. Rhythms, drum patterns, synthesizer patches, vocal harmonies, pitch bends, electric guitar timbres, instrumental and vocal techniques, and instrumental arrangements are not covered by copyright and therefore fair game. These features commonly fall under the category of influence in critical reception. They might colloquially be described as performers' trademarks, but the law would not regard them as such. In many ways, the situation made it easy for musical techniques developed by individuals or in communal music-making settings such as folk traditions (the product of collective inter-influence) to be freely exploited while protecting the interests of publishing companies (for compositions) and later record labels (for digital samples).

Although artistic works are acts of cultural expression and praised for their individual creation, as Simon Waxman states, culture is "fundamentally a process of collective plagiarism": "Culture, in other words, is a social phenomenon. It is not the creation of one or another artist, but of many doing somewhat similar things. Under certain economic arrangements, a sturdy defense of artistic copyright may encourage the production of cultural artifacts, but it also discourages the repetition and adaptation that make cultures themselves. . . . [Thus] the property regime . . . continues to slowly, subtly privatize collective life for the benefit of the few."[9]

Popular music historically has thrived on all types of borrowing, including interpolation, lyrical troping on folk songs, sampling, and quotation. Borrowing has often been negatively associated in fan reception with hip hop sampling,[10] but many of the standard bearers of popular music artistry—including the Beatles, the Beach Boys, the Rolling Stones, and Led Zeppelin among a wide range of others—have faced litigation for borrowing from other compositions.[11] In addition to musical borrowing, music videos are often homages to well-known films (evident in the videos of Madonna, Tom Petty, and a great many others),[12] and album iconography is regularly inspired by previous artworks. To pay homage or to be inspired or influenced by a prior work are viewed positively within reception, whereas to take, sample, or plagiarize are viewed negatively. Originality and singular artistry, as represented by Beck in the 2015 meme image, is ideal (an "artist" is welcome to be inspired by, or pay homage to, other works). Derivative, sampled, borrowed, and otherwise aided creative elements are often deemed to be less creative.[13]

Yet because most fans don't consider the implications of copyright law on the creative process, the concept of credit is vague and malleable. Fans can choose to defend their favorite performers for infringing copyright or find fault with performers who legally sample for lacking "talent." Fan perception of the music business, and the differences between influence, homage, and theft, can be both arbitrary and weighted by gendered and racialized associations with the performer and the performer's musical style.

TWO PLAGIARISM CASES IN FAN RECEPTION: LED ZEPPELIN AND BEYONCÉ

Consider, for example, fan reactions to respective accusations of appropriation by Led Zeppelin and Beyoncé. In 2013, singer-songwriter Jake Holmes made a legal claim that Led Zeppelin's "Dazed and Confused" (Atlantic,

1968) was plagiarized from his song of the same name that was recorded in 1968 and therefore infringed copyright. It would be hard to argue that Led Zeppelin's guitarist Jimmy Page did not plagiarize in this case: the title, melody, harmony, and some of the verses are the same, and the band settled out of court with Holmes. Yet some fans' online responses to the story show the way in which, even in the face of blatant plagiarism, a musician can be defended:

> This is BS [that] paige [sic] should be sued. They sound completely different. any retard could figure out that they arent [sic] the same song. As for the other guy he's just trying to make a quick buck. Nice timing @$$hole!! (bs23666)[14]
>
> "HE PLAYED AN 'A' NOTE AND THAN [sic] A 'C' JUST LIKE MY SONG! I DEMAND MONEY!"—Some Guy that failed at music. (derpdragon)[15]
>
> dude technically pagey could get off by saying zepps [sic] version is a dub and slap a "dazed and confused taken from jake holmes" sticker on this crap and its [sic] all good (liberationarmy)[16]

Although fan allegiance is clearly at work here, it is evident that these commentators aren't aware of what's at stake, what it means to plagiarize a song in popular music. It's not an issue of artistic fairness or "credit where credit is due," but an issue of copyright ownership and therefore money. Led Zeppelin's catalog has generated well over a billion dollars in revenue for various parties. The income derived from the recording and composition of the band's "Stairway to Heaven" alone was estimated in one article at $566 million, $12 million of which is publishing income.[17] "Dazed and Confused" likely similarly earned tens of millions of dollars (in related concert revenue, album sales, radio royalties, and DVD music video income), yet Holmes is perceived by some fans as opportunistic for his claim.

In contrast, consider reaction to a claim made against Beyoncé's "XO" by songwriter Ahmad "Javon" Lane. I offer no stance on whether Beyoncé indeed profited from the songwriter's ideas, but the two songs sound little alike. Though several Beyoncé fans offered comments in her defense, the tone of the majority of fan comments on the online story is revealing:

> I have heard both songs matter of fact is she got her idea from that song.... Of [sic] the subject, Beyonce is so full of herself now.[18]

> My how the mighty have fallen! Never would have thought that people would wake up and see this woman for who she is ... she is just an imperfect, average looking woman that made it with the help of her daddy.[19]
>
> Beyonce is a burlesque dancer in the United States. She is a stripper, that sings in her lounge act.[20]

These responses to the claim against Beyoncé are clearly gendered and more personal than those relating to Led Zeppelin's case. Jake Holmes is "just trying to make a quick buck" for his claim, while the claim against Beyoncé is a "matter of fact" that allows fans to "wake up and see this woman for who she is," which one commenter describes as a "stripper," who another says is "full of herself." In order to understand this climate of fan reception, it is necessary to consider the ways in which music criticism has shaped how popular music performance is perceived by a general audience.

BLACK MUSIC, GENDER, AND CRITICAL RECEPTION

The reception of Black music has always been shaped by critical monitoring. Beginning in the 1960s, the rise of rock critics followed the mold of jazz criticism, and critics were highly influential. As Frith notes, critics "functioned as rock ideologists" who helped to form "the values and assumptions of rock culture."[21] Frith explains the critical perception of Black music in the dawn of the 1970s:

> The only black musicians to be accepted as rock "artists" ... [were] Jimi Hendrix and Stevie Wonder, and for a while Sly Stone. ...
> If the blues tradition was too natural to be art, black pop—soul—had become, by the end of the 1960s, too artificial. Record companies marketed soul as a package. ... [It] was black artists that had come to symbolize show business. By the 1970s *Rolling Stone* was reviewing Motown Records in these terms: "Tom travesties," "opportunistic commercial album making of the worst sort." "What happened to the days when black music was black," asked the *New Musical Express*, "and not this vacuous Muzak and pretentious drivel."[22]

A largely white base of critics had developed a litmus test for "authentically" Black music even as the majority of white rock performers were mimicking African American performance techniques.[23] Portia Maultsby terms this the "politics of race erasure" in Black popular music reception and finds that a mainstream (largely white) music critic's "critique of the performance aesthetic is often predicated on the writer's cultural perspective and familiarity (or lack of) with the cultural codes and musical values defined and affirmed among African Americans."[24] Meanwhile, in addition to the reception of the Beatles (and later the Beach Boys) as high art, Bob Dylan was a "catalyst" for a change in popular music, as his "emergence from the folk mainstream brought his personal and poetic visions to a wider audience."[25] Folk traditions (many rooted in African American styles) were widely adopted by rock performers and were considered authentic, whereas pop music, R&B, and disco were increasingly deemed artificial.

This critical reception of Black music helped shape the "disco sucks" backlash in the late 1970s (culminating in the violent destruction of records at the 1979 Disco Demolition Night), as well as how rock audiences reacted to the ascendancy of Michael Jackson, Prince, Whitney Houston, Mariah Carey, and then Beyoncé to positions as prominent pop artists at certain points of their respective careers. Although Jackson and Prince incorporated new wave and rock sounds and styles to challenge the post-disco positioning of Black music, women performers were often conceived in terms of what Frith describes as soft soul and disco's "artificiality."[26]

The positioning of pop artifice versus rock authenticity has been pejoratively termed "rockism," a "knee-jerk backlash against producer-powered idols who didn't spend years touring dive bars."[27] In this positioning, post-Motown and post-disco dance pop music (and that which is most directly based in concurrent R&B) is judged as frivolous: "Over the past decades, these tendencies have congealed into an ugly sort of common sense. Rock bands record classic albums, while pop stars create 'guilty pleasure' singles."[28] Race and gender likely play a role in critical perception as well: "Rockism isn't unrelated to older, more familiar prejudices—that's part of why it's so powerful, and so worth arguing about. The pop star, the disco diva, the lip-syncher, the 'awesomely bad' hit maker: could it really be a coincidence that rockist complaints often pit straight white men against the rest of the world? Like the anti-disco backlash of 25 years ago, the current rockist consensus seems to reflect not just an idea of how music should be made but also an idea about who should be making it."[29]

An extremely (and likely intentionally) polemic example of post-disco and rockist positioning is rap-rock/country performer Kid Rock's misogynist reaction to Beyoncé, whose success he claims to be "flabbergasted" by: "Beyoncé, to me, doesn't have a fucking 'Purple Rain,' but she's the biggest thing on Earth. How can you be that big without at least one 'Sweet Home Alabama' or 'Old Time Rock & Roll'? People are like, 'Beyoncé's hot. Got a nice fucking ass.' I'm like, 'Cool, I like skinny white chicks with big tits.' Doesn't really fucking do much for me."[30] Here Rock denotes the quality of what he perceives as major works that would qualify as deserving praise for an artist, respectively mentioning the *rock* ballad of one African American pop musician and band (Prince and the Revolution) and two groups common on classic rock stations (Lynyrd Skynyrd and Bob Seger and the Silver Bullet Band); the lead performers are all male. Beyoncé, in contrast, is not viewed as a maker, producer, or progenitor of real music but a pop object praised only for her "nice fucking ass." Rock's assessment has been shaped by the positioning of rock authenticity against pop artifice, an opposition that has often been gendered and racially charged.

Consider columnist Roger Friedman's incendiary *Fox News* exposé "Beyonce Takes Credit for 'Writing' Songs": "Vanity Fair finally puts a solo African-American on its cover, and doesn't do any fact checking. Beyonce Knowles, who's full of sass and has a striking voice, actually thinks she's a songwriter.... In fact, not one of the songs listed under Beyonce's name on the BMI Web site is written solely by her. They are usually credited to a list of songwriters. The list comprises the *actual* writers, and then a few people who've 'tweaked' the song with a rap or by adding samples."[31]

Friedman begins his diatribe by first positioning Beyoncé as an "African-American" who has not been "fact check[ed]" and is "full of sass" (an obviously gendered and racialized description) before describing her as deluded ("she actually thinks she's a songwriter") and distinguishing her from "actual" songwriters: he employs racial and gender positioning in order to assist in discrediting her.

Even in cases in which women are compared with women, the debate over artistry often centers on who writes or who does not write their music. The prizing of singer-songwriters over nonwriting performers further sets the standard for composition as talent. In response to the online post

"Why Beyonce Is Overrated," commenter Rachelle Kebaili offered this assessment: "Well here's MY opinion. Yes, Beyoncé has a great voice and is a great performer. BUT, she is a made/created artist. She doesn't write her music. She is NOT a singer/songwriter and she should maybe be glad about that with some of her ridiculously idiotic lyrics. That said she's NOT Adele and will NEVER be Adele. Adele is an artist that sings with heart and writes her own lyrics. She's real, honest, and authentic. That's what people want. Not some fake, studio made artist."[32] This perception of Adele's singer-songwriter authenticity versus a "fake, studio made" artist is further emphasized by the perception that Adele comes from a singer-songwriter tradition, while Beyoncé is seen as a product of post-disco pop manufacturing. Adele is perceived as having rock authenticity.

The flipside to this "rockist" critical stance has been called "poptimism," termed so by critics' defense of rock's artistic merits in the growing early-twenty-first-century acceptance by critics of pop as worthy of critical praise (notably, as rock becomes less popular and less impactful in popular music culture).[33] If rockists err in praising rock out of attachments to archaic views of musical authenticity, Saul Austerlitz argues, poptimists "privilege the deliriously artificial over the artificially genuine."[34] The concern is that critics become "cheerleaders for pop stars" during a period in which the revenue-per-click online media advertising creates a potentially dangerous vacuum for new artists and ideas: "Click culture creates a closed system in which popular acts get more coverage, thus becoming more popular, thus getting more coverage. But criticism is supposed to challenge readers on occasion, not only provide seals of approval."[35] The polarized media conversation about Beyoncé becomes a discourse about the discourse, a meta-debate, one fed by revenue feeds. This conversation generally downplays her contribution to the production and songwriting of her creative works in the recording studio.

BEYONCÉ IN THE RECORDING STUDIO

Historically, neither music production in the recording studio nor the culture of popular music has been egalitarian in terms of gender, and remarkably little has changed in the early twenty-first century. Although women had a critical impact on the sound culture of popular music in countless ways and several Black female producers (including Sylvia Robinson, Patrice Rushen, and Missy Elliot) had a significant impact on musical style within the recording studio, the primary "territory which women are expected to inhabit" was "that of singer."[36] Further, Tricia Rose notes that women "are in general not encouraged in and often actively discouraged from learning about and using mechanical equipment. This takes place informally in socialization and formally in gender-segregated vocational tracking."[37] As a result of this and other factors, recording studio control rooms are historically both white- and male-dominated spaces, and the contribution of women producers is sometimes regarded as suspect.[38]

As is the case with Beyoncé's work as a producer, the legitimacy of her publishing credits is often questioned. The doubts are in part due to her assumed participation in what is pejoratively referred to as the "write a word, get a third" practice, in which established recording artists or other powerful industry figures receive songwriting credit for little or no participation in traditional compositional features of melody, harmony, and lyrics.[39] This practice is not new, and was already common enough in 1955 that Elvis Presley can be heard in a recording casually stating to a group of fellow artists that he "asked for a piece of that song."[40] For Beyoncé, criticism of her description of herself as a songwriter (rather than cowriter) is seen as her dishonestly taking credit for the work of others.

Beyoncé contributed to songwriting within Destiny's Child, and more and more throughout her solo career, which began in 2005. Her contributions included cowriting sessions in the studio with others exchanging lyrical ideas, a practice documented in a filmed recording studio session for the song "Upgrade U" in 2006.

The album documentary footage shows Beyoncé, Sean Garrett, and Angela Beyince trading lyrical ideas for verses while the instrumental track for "Upgrade U" plays in the background. Such visual representation may be curated to highlight Beyoncé's contribution to songwriting, but her creative partners (including Jack White, Mike Will Made It, MNEK, Diplo, and others quoted here) consistently describe her as orchestrating and rewriting song ideas throughout the collaborative creative process. Although single songwriters occasionally contribute complete compositions, Beyoncé has increasingly preferred several writers and producers with markedly different styles to offer parts that are then synthesized into one song.

It is not surprising to note that Beyoncé herself is conscious of how borrowing and synergism benefit her art, as well as of the ambiguities about how much borrowing is acceptable, as is evident in a revealing conversation with her then-creative director Frank Gatson after a Broadway performance of *Chicago*:

BEYONCÉ: Ain't nobody gon' want us to go to they shows, Frank.
GATSON: Why?
BEYONCÉ: 'Cause we gon' take everything! (laughs)
GATSON: Everybody does that, though.
BEYONCÉ: No, everybody does . . . but we go and meet everybody, and say, 'hey, great show!' and steal it (laughs).[41]

Gatson is surely correct that creative professionals continually mine elements in other works to incorporate or influence their own, but Beyoncé's concern shows that she is self-aware about her process of borrowing and how it may be perceived negatively. Her self-conscious synthesis of material from numerous sources likely led to her developing a collagist method of producing and cowriting songs (particularly evident on *Beyoncé* and *Lemonade*) and can be seen as a curated collecting and troping of ideas from various sources, a creative process that both replicates communal music making for the age of privatization and reflects the synergism of pop music borrowing. Far from the "write a word, get a third" participation, her creative process is marked by a distinct method of collecting and merging different ideas, while adding her own lyrics, melodies, and harmonies throughout. The process is clearly demonstrated in the composition and production histories of "Hold Up" and "Don't Hurt Yourself."

"HOLD UP"

The composition and production history of Beyoncé's "Hold Up" reveals both how her collagist process relies on outsourced input from multiple sources, as well as how technology and the litigious copyright environment have affected the creative process. While listening to the Yeah Yeah Yeahs' 2003 song "Maps," which features the chorus "Wait, they don't love you like I love you," Ezra Koenig (then of Vampire Weekend) tweeted "what if it was 'hold up' instead of 'wait'?" in October 2011.[42] Three years later, Koenig was in the studio with producer Diplo crafting song ideas for Diplo's MIDI tracks (originally intended for Vampire Weekend or Diplo's project Major Lazer). He decided to try his tweeted lyric concept ("hold up, they don't love you like I love you") in a new melody to a two-bar looped ostinato of Andy Williams's 1963 recording "Can't Get Used to Losing You" and recorded a demo track of the vocal.

While Koenig's melody and rhythm are completely distinct from the phrase in "Maps," he felt obligated to credit the share writer's credit and tweeted in 2016, "of course, i made sure the YYY's were credited."[43] Whether this was owing to a sense of altruism or to the tweet three years earlier, it is arguable that such a credit is also the product of a litigious copyright climate. This is particularly true considering that the Yeah Yeah Yeahs did not credit an earlier popular song with a similar lyric phrase "He Don't Love You (Like I Love You)," which was recorded by Tony Orlando and Dawn, Dolly Parton, and several others. In a twenty-first-century songwriting climate, lyric troping (an old tradition in the preprivatization model of folk music that produced many orphaned works referred to as traditional) is staged on social media within Koenig's Twitter post, which then inspired a new pop composition.

Diplo developed the track with German reggae producer Jr Blender, who contributed guitar and drum programming, sent the track to Beyoncé with Koenig's chorus in the basic melodic arch of the final version, and Beyoncé chose it. At this point, it was likely one of dozens considered for inclusion on an untitled album. In keeping with the practice of many prominent recording artists, Beyoncé considers as many as eighty songs for inclusion during album production and can work on a song for years before it surfaces.[44] According to collaborator Mike Will Made It, Beyoncé would refer to this stage—a demoed MIDI track and chorus—as an "idea" for a song.[45] At that point, as Diplo describes it, "I put their song together and a couple writers wrote on it. It's kind of like how Beyoncé does it, she's sort of like a orchestrator, that's why she's a producer on the record."[46]

This part of the process sets Beyoncé's recording and compositional style (particularly for the *Beyoncé* and *Lemonade* albums) apart from most past and contemporary approaches to pop music composition, although it shares similarities with Kanye West's recent techniques. Rather than relying on one verse, melody, and structure throughout the song (which is still the most common form for pop songwriting), "Hold Up" involves a different approach for each of the three verses, a technique of collagist songwriting that benefits from a number of outsourced collaborators. Further, although these verse ideas are offered at separate times by independent collaborators (who may never meet), they are connected within the final song into a cohesive narrative trajectory that merges biographical details about Beyoncé (including references about, or interpreted to be about, her marriage) and story elements that may have had an entirely different meaning for the contributor who offered it.[47]

At different recording sessions, she met with producer Emile Haynie, British singer-songwriter MNEK, and producer and songwriter MeLo-X. During her sessions with Emile (who provided additional drum programming), she revealed that she was looking for lyric ideas for the track, and he played her some of Father John Misty's music. She expressed interest in Misty's music and asked Emile to see whether Misty would write some lyrics. He returned a demo recording of a vocal lyrics and melody (what became the first verse and refrain), although Misty states that he was completely "in the dark" and reportedly shocked that she incorporated his verse until shortly before the album's release: "[I] recorded a verse, melody and refrain that, unbelievably—when you consider how ridiculous my voice sounds on the demo—ended up making the record."[48]

Later, at a different session, she called in songwriter-producer MeLo-X (a collaborator since 2014 whom Beyoncé had effectively discovered online).[49] He recalls that

> I heard the track and was very excited about it because I'm Jamaican. And anything that sounds anywhere near Jamaica is kind of my lane, I would say. I heard the track and I worked on some song ideas and wrote some stuff for it.... It was pretty much, maybe fifty percent complete when I heard it, and I just wrote a bunch of things from my perspective and my tone of voice or how I would sing it if I was an ill reggae artist, like Barrington Levy singing on that track. And wrote a bunch of ideas and melodies and things like that.[50]

In contrast with John Misty's country-rock-styled first verse, MeLo-X heard the track in a reggae context and considered a Barrington Levy chat-like performance for a verse. The second verse shows his influence, and a completely different idea of what the melodic and lyrical style of the song should be. The studio sessions involved listening to other music suggested by MeLo-X that strengthened the song's reggae connection as well: "I would bring up classic dancehall songs. And classic reggae tunes and we would vibe off of shit like that. I was kind of like putting her onto some shit maybe she didn't know about and she would put me onto artists and music she was into. It helped with the direction as well."[51]

He also added harmonies and layers to the chorus: "I kind of put a bunch of ideas down. A bunch of harmonies, a bunch of different layers, and she kept a lot of that in. In the second chorus you can hear my vocals under hers coming in. It's cool that she kept that. I was just putting that there to create a vibe. I had like in my mind, I was thinking of Bob Marley and his backup singers, he had his wife, and how they would harmonize to a lot things that he did. So I took to that approach with the background vocals that I did."[52] These parts added to the track as layers, MeLo-X imagines dancehall chat for his second verse, and then the Wailers' I-Threes singers cooing backup vocals for chorus harmonies, while John Misty's significant country-twanged contribution is offered on a taped demo that he himself thought little of.

At another session, Beyoncé invited British singer and songwriter MNEK to offer ideas. He recalls that "I went to her studio, and she played me stuff she was working on.... She'll hear what an artist does, she'll hear what a writer does, and she'll interpret it and make it her own, [and] blend it with her vibe.... She played me the chorus of 'Hold Up,' and she was just like, 'Do your thing, do what you got to do' ... and I was like, 'OK let me try to do some stuff to it and do something around it.'"[53] MNEK reacted to what he heard, which was by his description the track and chorus (not the other verses). She may not have had the Misty and Melo contributions yet, or else she was considering his ideas separately. He recalls taking it back to his studio: "I came up with a few ideas. I came up with the one section, in the middle eight, that's just like [singing] 'I-i-i-it's such a shame to let this good love go to waste.'"[54]

Asked whether he met any of the other writers, MNEK says, "The process was more remote than that. That's the thing. The way she works[,] ... she pieces together stuff and she pieces together, you know, Diplo's going to work on the track; she's going to send it to me to do a melody idea. That's the process. And it worked because she's overlooking everything, saying 'I like this, I like that, this is how this should sound, this is how that should sound.' It's all coming out of the process."[55]

When the parts of the record are mixed, only Beyoncé and engineer Stuart White participate in the process; what gets added or subtracted (including parts offered that were rejected in the final mix) determines what the song becomes for the audience. Digital studios and software platforms like Pro-Tools allow for nonlinear editing, as well as a virtually unlimited number of tracks. Beyoncé can reorder the parts of a song in modular sections, and she is known to layer between fifty and one hundred vocal tracks to any given song.[56] Interpolations of Soulja Boy Tell'em's "Turn My Swag On" (Santa Monica: Interscope, 2008) and Beyoncé's own "Countdown" (New York: Columbia, 2011) were incorporated into the song during production. Each interpolation quotes a song with a specific meaning for listeners. "Countdown" connects the song's narrative to Beyoncé's running lyrical thread about herself and (her own) marriage. Meanwhile, the Soulja Boy quotation, which occurs at the end of the song, is an expensive add-on in a sense (in terms of publishing clearance and writer's share for the interpolation), for it occurs for approximately twenty seconds at the song's end. But within the song's collage, the incorporation of the well-known ode of self-appreciation offers the song a wry yet upbeat ending while subtly reinforcing her engagement with hip hop culture by quoting a popular hood anthem.[57]

As producer Mike Will Made It describes Beyoncé's "Formation," "She takes ideas and puts them with her own ideas, and makes this masterpiece.... It's really a process to make one of these great songs. It's layers. Layers and layers and layers."[58]

Beyoncé mines for ideas throughout the process, adding lyrics and vocal arrangements throughout, and creates something that benefits from multiple creative impulses yet is synthesized into a cohesive narrative.

"DON'T HURT YOURSELF"

This process and similar authorship issues are reflected further in the production of "Don't Hurt Yourself," Beyoncé's collaboration with Jack White. White produced the basic instrumental track, playing guitar and bass, with a rhythm section featuring Raconteurs members Patrick Keeler (drums) and Mark Watrous (Hammond organ), as well as layered operatic vocalise from Ghanaian vocalist (and frequent White collaborator) Ruby Amanfu. Amanfu's vocal operates as part of the instrumental texture and is edited and mixed to have the quality of a sample. At this stage of the production, it was not made clear to all involved that the track was intended for Beyoncé; Amanfu was pleasantly surprised to find out what the track was used for.[59] White added what he terms "a sketch of a lyrical outline," some of which (his vocal performance in the first chorus) Beyoncé kept in the final track.

Further production occurred during a second set of sessions. Derek Dixie, Beyoncé's tour musical director and multi-instrumentalist, provided additional drum programming. Jon Brion was called in to create a string arrangement based on MIDI orchestrations by Eric Gorfain, and more than thirty string players added tracks at a separate session (which is audible only subtly in the final mix). Beyoncé added her own lyrics while listening to the parts, took others away, listened to Amanfu's vocalise and White's vocal with her own, and continually reconceived the track, influenced by discussions with Dixie or other collaborators. She called on singer-songwriter Diana "Wynter" Gordon, who recalls that (in addition to her work on several other tracks) she "came in on the Jack White song and helped finish it."[60]

Gordon's primary lyrical contributions were likely to the second, syncopated verse ("I am the dragon, breathing fire"), although she contributed ideas that were incorporated into other parts of the final product as well. By Gordon's description, during the whole process, Beyoncé considers the ideas offered by contributors in a nonlinear fashion, and the song is the result of a type of modular construction:

> Beyoncé is a scientist of songs. I've never seen anyone work the way she works. She definitely changes the song structures. She can take two songs, say, "I like two lines, I like the melody then let me use that for a verse and a bridge and write the whole middle." It's more of a collaboration. You never know what she'll like. I came to her with a bunch of songs and she was like, "I like that verse, I like the idea." But she definitely doesn't take things as is, at least not from me.[61]

The climactic choruses of "Don't Hurt Yourself" feature a sample of John Bonham's iconic drum introduction from Led Zeppelin's "When the Levee Breaks" that is retriggered on a MIDI sequencer (likely by Dixie) in a new rhythmic pattern to match Keeler's syncopated live-drum pattern. The usage sample is a valuable example of modern copyright practices.

Led Zeppelin recorded their cover of African American singer-guitarist "Memphis" Minnie (née Lizzie Douglas) Lawlars's 1929 song in 1971. Like

Beyoncé, Led Zeppelin continually mined for influences from various styles, and one recorded song may reflect several influences. Thus Minnie Lawlars's folk-blues song, originally recorded with solo acoustic guitar and vocal, is reimagined in Led Zeppelin's recording as a bombastic, psychedelic hard-rock electric blues. As Led Zeppelin begins the song—a heavy, loping solo drum ostinato (recorded in a cavernous space) precedes a heavy blues riff—they were possibly influenced by a similar drum introduction of a Funkadelic recording, played by Ramon "Tiki" Fulwood.[62] Funkadelic's psychedelic recording "Good Old Music" was featured on the group's eponymous debut (Detroit: Westbound, 1970) and would have been available to Led Zeppelin at the time of the "Levee" recording. Led Zeppelin's iconic "Levee" drum introduction has been sampled numerous times, including earlier recordings by the Beastie Boys, Björk, and Enigma, but the sample was not legally cleared in these cases. (Like songwriting copyright disputes, sample infringement cases have become increasingly common in the early twenty-first century.)

Although the use of Minnie Lawlers's lyrics may have been enough in some cases for the song to be considered a full cover version (to which her publishers would retain full copyright), Zeppelin and manager Peter Grant were able to negotiate significant cowriting credits for the four Led Zeppelin band mates. The band did make notable changes to the song's melodic phrasing and added lyrics as well. Minnie Lawlars shares writing credit on the song's copyright with the four members of the band. In contrast, although Lawlars's publishers participate in some remuneration for the song's phenomenal marketplace success, she is not credited on the compositional copyright for "Don't Hurt Yourself." The implicit argument of Led Zeppelin's publishers, who have a majority share of the song's copyright, is that because the lyrics are not contained in the sampled section, it is only Led Zeppelin's intellectual property that is represented.

It is arguable, however, that Led Zeppelin's recording and composition could not have existed without Lawlars's lyrics. Memphis Minnie's lyric is about the hardship caused by the Great Mississippi Flood of 1927 and "a person [who] is desperate about having to leave home to find work elsewhere," namely Chicago.[63] Erin Sweeney Smith has posited that Led Zeppelin's fixation on the mythologized African American South and its imagined characters was an important part of the recording's conception (the band incorporated lyrics and other elements from numerous Southern blues themes into a considerable portion of their repertoire, and the group clearly drew inspiration from blues as well as other sources).[64] Had Memphis Minnie's song been recorded by a less powerful or less business savvy artist, or if her publishers and estate had better representation, Led Zeppelin's version may have been registered as strictly a cover (without shared copyright). Therefore, the removal of her name from the copyright on the sampling Beyoncé recording suggests that a recorded song is perceived as a series of components (written by different creators), rather than a single ontological whole. Both Led Zeppelin's and Beyoncé's recordings are directly informed by similar synergistic thinking about sonic tropes and ideas and by recording studio practices of mining and synthesizing ideas into recordings.

Beyoncé's very sampling of Led Zeppelin is itself a show of industry power, as few artists could get permission to draw from Led Zeppelin or pay the royalty advances. Beyoncé and her collaborators may have chosen to do so in part because of the intertextual meaning the iconic sample carries about hard rock and sonic bombast for listeners. The sampling of the Led Zeppelin song serves to enhance sonic impact during the choruses: it is not audible during most of the track. The extent to which the performance of a bass drum, snare drum, and high-hat recontextualized into a new rhythm constitute a portion of the compositional copyright is arguable. Like the removal of Lawlars's name, it is not a case of an ethical, moral context of copyright and "credit where credit is due," but a case in which majority shareholders and financially endowed creatives have greater control. Like the interpolation of Soulja Boy's "Turn My Swag On" in "Hold Up," the use of Led Zeppelin serves as an expensive add-on for "Don't Hurt Yourself," as well as an intertextual reference to its source.

CONCLUSION

Beyoncé's songwriting and production process in the recording studio consists of the synthesis and troping of ideas developed by diverse creators. The final recordings represent not the work of one solo auteur, but the curated collage of the product of several writing and production sessions. As Beyoncé adds lyrics, melodies, and harmonies throughout, she serves as coauthor, orchestrator, and producer in her mining of the ideas of multiple contributors. As shown in her aforementioned exchange with Gatson, she is well aware of how her own art benefits from appropriation of diverse influences, and she hones a process of music creation for recordings that both satisfies a litigious copyright climate and imbues each record with the benefit of multiple lyricists and melodists.

This collagist process, and Beyoncé's awareness of it, is clearly exhibited on Beyoncé's "Sorry (original demo)," a recording included on the 2019 rerelease of *Lemonade*. The demo version, which does not include the word *sorry* in the lyrics, features only lyrics and melodies used in the concluding section of the final album version. The demo also includes several lyric sections that were unused in the final version, such as the original chorus ("young, wild, and free") and a completely different instrumental track. As both the listed songwriters and coproducers differ between the original demo and the final version, Beyoncé clearly synthesized component elements of multiple compositional ideas to create the final recording.

If the product of this process is unique in that it juxtaposes different melodic and rhythmic offerings into one fluid idea, it also recreates the communal troping on songs that produced repertoires of folk and classical music in an era before each melodic phrase was subject to a copyright infringement litmus test. Alex Ross argues, "T. S. Eliot famously commented, in 1920, that 'immature poets imitate; mature poets steal,' and added that the 'good poet welds his theft into a whole of feeling which is unique.' This is what Bach does in the Passacaglia and Fugue; it's what Shakespeare does throughout his plays. These days, though, we seem to want geniuses who play by the rules and give due credit to their colleagues; we want great art executed in the manner of a scholarly paper, with painstaking acknowledgments and footnotes."[65] Ross could be describing the credits to Beyoncé's *Lemonade* album here, which feature dozens of contributors' names on several songs, and detailed clearance information for every sampled sound (as well as hundreds of creatives and laborers who contributed to the album's film component). In the era of privatization, every part of the composition must be accounted for.

The reception of Beyoncé's music has been shaped by several factors, including latter twentieth-century popular music criticism (retroactively and reductively understood as rockism), the converse of early-twenty-first-century (poptimist) celebration of pop music, reactionary post-disco reception of commercialized Black music as artifice, revenue-per-click media, and controversy culture. In the age of diminishing returns for musicians, due in great part to the weakening of intellectual property resulting from file sharing and the subsequent waning of retail music, Beyoncé's decision to hire so many writers and producers in the process of making an album could be seen as a positive contribution to the profession, rather than a weakness in her creativity. In a popular music context where there are fewer revenue streams for songwriters and producers, it is arguable that the music world needs collaborative models, not solo auteurs.

Though Beyoncé likely participated in "write a word, take a third" publishing negotiations at various points in her career, her work on *Beyoncé* and *Lemonade* reflects an innovative creative process in which she is active throughout both in composition and production. She participates in a collagist process of outsourcing ideas while navigating a litigious copyright climate and crafting song recordings imbued with the communal inter-influence of preprivatized music making. She is also the head of a corporation that controls her music (Parkwood Entertainment) and co-owner of the Tidal streaming music service, and she is far from passive in the process of privatizing intellectual property on her own behalf.

Beyoncé has managed to assert power in the music industry and consolidate control of her musical works more than any other Black female performer, and as a result has become the standard bearer for Black female empowerment in music while receiving the brunt of racialized and gendered views of post-disco, producer-dependent pop artificiality. Although Beyoncé's producing and cowriting credits serve to continually assert her control over her music, she makes no attempt to present a sacralized creative process or to position herself as solo auteur. Instead, her process highlights a range of collaborators making music in concert with a "scientist of songs."

WILL FULTON is Associate Professor of Music at LaGuardia Community College, City University of New York. He is coauthor of *Camp Lo's Uptown Saturday Night*.

NOTES

1. See, for instance, Wildfire Radio's tweet, February 10, 2015, accessed August 10, 2017, https://twitter.com/wildfire_radio/status/565175734915043328.

2. Laura Stampler, "Kanye Says Beck Should Have Given Beyoncé His Grammy," *Time*, February 9, 2015, http://time.com/3700870/2015-grammy-awards-kanye-beck-beyonce/.

3. For example, see Beck's breakthrough second album *Odelay* (Santa Monica, CA: Geffen, 1996), which is produced by hip hop producers the Dust Brothers and features dozens of samples.

4. Kohlman, "Beyoncé as Intersectional Icon?," 27.

5. Headlam, "Does the Song Remain the Same?"; Robert Middleton, *Studying Popular Music*; Eckstein, "Torpedoing the Authorship"; Negus, "Authorship."

6. McClary, *Feminine Endings*; Whiteley, *Women and Popular Music*; Schmutz and Faupel, "Gender and Cultural Consecration"; Leonard, *Gender in the Music Industry*.

7. Arewa, "Creativity, Improvisation, and Risk."

8. McLeod and DiCola, *Creative License*, 1.

9. Simon Waxman, "'Blurred Lines' Ruling Makes Influence Illegal," *Al Jazeera America*, April 4, 2015, http://america.aljazeera.com/opinions/2015/4/blurred-lines-ruling-makes-influence-illegal.html.

10. See McLeod and DiCola, *Creative License*.

11. Gavin Edwards, "The Beatles' 5 Boldest Rip-Offs," *Rolling Stone*, December 23, 2015, http://www.rollingstone.com/music/news/beatles-5-boldest-rip-offs-20151223; Elizabeth Flock, "Without Chuck Berry, These 10 Famous Rock Songs Would Not Exist," *NewsHour*, March 20, 2017, http://www.pbs.org/newshour/art/without-chuck-berry-10-famous-rock-songs-not-exist/; and Headlam, "Does the Song Remain the Same?"

12. Vernallis, *Experiencing Music Video*; Aly Semigran, "The 12 Best Music Videos Inspired by Movies: Kanye West, Ariana Grande and More," *Billboard*, November 30, 2018, http://www.billboard.com/articles/news/list/7525539/best-movie-music-videos-kanye-west-fade.

13. McLeod and DiCola, *Creative License*; McLeod and Kuenzli, *Cutting across Media*.

14. bs23666, July 1, 2010 (12:47 a.m.), comment on "Jimmy Page Sued over 'Dazed and Confused,'" *UltimateGuitar.com*, June 30, 2010, https://www.ultimate-guitar.com/news/general_music_news/jimmy_page_sued_over_dazed_and_confused.html.

15. derpdragon, June 30, 2010 (11:59 a.m.), comment on "Jimmy Page Sued over 'Dazed and Confused,'" *UltimateGuitar.com*, June 30, 2010, https://www.ultimate-guitar.com/news/general_music_news/jimmy_page_sued_over_dazed_and_confused.html.

16. liberationarmy, June 30, 2010 (5:38 p.m.), comment on "Jimmy Page Sued over 'Dazed and Confused,'" *UltimateGuitar.com*, June 30, 2010, accessed August 10, 2017, https://www.ultimate-guitar.com/news/general_music_news/jimmy_page_sued_over_dazed_and_confused.html.

17. Joe Bosso, "How Much Is Stairway to Heaven Worth," *MusicRadar*, June 23, 2008, http://www.musicradar.com/news/guitars/how-much-is-stairway-to-heaven-worth-161369.

18. Id rather not, June 13, 2015, comment on "You Stole My Song! Beyoncé Sued for $7 Million by Background Singer for Stealing 'XO'—Read the Documents," *Radar Online*, June 13, 2015, http://radaronline.com/exclusives/2015/06/beyonce-knowles-sued-7-million-lawsuit-copied-song-xo-background-singer/. Accessed February 14, 2017.

19. albertabatchelor, June 23, 2015, comment on "You Stole My Song! Beyoncé Sued for $7 Million by Background Singer for Stealing 'XO'—Read the Documents," *Radar Online*, June 13, 2015, http://radaronline.com/exclusives/2015/06/beyonce-knowles-sued-7-million-lawsuit-copied-song-xo-background-singer/. Accessed: February 14, 2017.

20. Yes, I'm That Leah, June 13, 2015, comment on "You Stole My Song! Beyoncé Sued for $7 Million by Background Singer for Stealing 'XO'—Read the Documents," *Radar Online*, June 13, 2015, http://radaronline.com/exclusives/2015/06/beyonce-knowles-sued-7-million-lawsuit-copied-song-xo-background-singer/. Accessed: February 14, 2017.

21. Frith, "Rock and Popular Culture," 309.

22. Frith, *Sound Effects*, 21–22.

23. Ronald Radano examines the assessment of Black music in terms of authenticity in "On Ownership and Value." Radano focuses on an earlier period, however, in which largely white commentators shaped views of Black folk idioms like the blues as intrinsically authentic, and not post-1950s views of soft soul, disco-related R&B, and other forms of Black pop as veering from this authenticity model.

24. Maultsby, "Politics of Race Erasure," 60–61.

25. Barker and Taylor, *Faking It*, 168.

26. Valuable critiques of race and gender issues in rock music criticism can be found in McDonnell and Powers, *Rock, She Wrote*, and Brooks, "Write to Rock."

27. Kelefa Sanneh, "The Rap against Rockism," *New York Times*, October 31, 2004, http://www.nytimes.com/2004/10/31/arts/music/the-rap-against-rockism.html.

28. Sanneh, "The Rap."

29. Ibid.

30. Kid Rock quoted in Patrick Doyle, "The Killer inside Kid Rock," *Rolling Stone*, February 26, 2015, http://www.rollingstone.com/music/features/the-killer-inside-kid-rock-20150226.

31. Roger Friedman, "Beyonce Takes Credit for 'Writing' Songs," *Fox News*, October 18, 2005, http://www.foxnews.com/story/2005/10/18/beyonce-takes-credit-for-writing-songs.html. Emphasis added.

32. Rachelle Kebaili, undated comment on Lincoln Fiske, "Why Beyoncé Is Overrated," *Thought Catalog*, February 4, 2013, http://thoughtcatalog.com/lincoln-fiske/2013/02/why-beyonce-is-overrated/.

33. Eric Weisbard, *Top 40 Democracy*.

34. Saul Austerlitz, "The Pernicious Rise of Poptimism," *New York Times Magazine*, April 4, 2014, https://www.nytimes.com/2014/04/06/magazine/the-pernicious-rise-of-poptimism.html.

35. Ibid.

36. Frith, *Sound Effects*, 155.

37. Rose, *Black Noise*, 57.

38. Jennifer Swann, "Even Missy Elliott Doesn't Get Credit for Her Own Songs—and She's Not Alone," *TakePart*, February 3, 2015, http://www.takepart.com/article/2015/02/02/missy-elliott-produces-her-own-music.

39. For more on this process, see de Laat, "Write a Word," 225–56. Because there are royalties for radio play only for songwriters (and not performers) in the United States, performing recording artists have long sought ways to share in publishing copyright. Major label recording artists such as Mariah Carey and Beyoncé tend to refrain from public acknowledgment of this practice, but late soul singer Sharon Jones described it well: "Don't think I'm going to be stupid enough to get out here and sing and not get anything. I don't ask for a lot of publishing. But I sing them songs, I come up with certain hooks; I bring those stories to life. Give those songs to somebody else; they wouldn't sell like that. My voice alone is a trademark. Here at Daptone, if you write a song for me, you know I'm going to get some publishing" (quoted in Michael Glitz, "Sharon Jones Made It the Hard Way," *Huffington Post* blog, May 13, 2010, http://www.huffingtonpost.com/michael-giltz/sharon-jones-made-it-the_b_574755.html).

40. During the recording session released as *Million Dollar Quartet*, Presley introduces "Is It So Strange" by telling Jerry Lee Lewis and Carl Perkins, "old Faron Young wrote this song, sent to me to record. He didn't want to give me none of it, he wanted all [of it]." Audible on "Is It So Strange," *Elvis Presley: The Million Dollar Quartet* (Memphis: Sun Records, 1990).

41. "Beyoncé Shadiest/Top Bossiest Moments," posted by video tube, December 12, 2016, https://www.youtube.com/watch?v=BMTnqQQOUiA.

42. Ezra Koenig, Twitter post, April 25, 2016 (11:05 a.m.), https://twitter.com/arzE/status/724660587523805184.

43. Ibid.

44. Beyoncé describes the process with respect to her self-titled 2013 album: "When I started picking the songs that I gravitated towards—because I recorded about 80 songs—it was the songs that were more effortless for me that stuck around [over the two-year recording process]" (Stacey Anderson, "Beyoncé Recorded 80 Songs for Visual Album," *Rolling Stone*, December 30, 2013, http://www.rollingstone.com/music/videos/beyonce-recorded-80-songs-for-visual-album-20131230). See also Paul Watson, "DJ Swivel: Recording Beyoncé's 4," *Sound on Sound*, October 2011, http://www.soundonsound.com/people/dj-swivel-recording-beyonces-4.

45. After Will sent Beyoncé a track and freestyled chorus for what would become "Formation," she told him "I like that 'Formation' idea" (Mike Will quoted in John Seabrook, "How Mike Will Made It," *New Yorker*, July 11, 2016, http://www.newyorker.com/magazine/2016/07/11/how-mike-will-made-it).

46. Diplo, "Beats 1 Story: Diplo on Beyoncé," *Beats 1*, November 5, 2016, https://itunes.apple.com/gb/post/idsa.809845a4-17d3-11e6-b614-89fa981356d7.

47. Several Beyoncé contributors, including producer Mike Will Made It, singer-songwriter MNEK, and Diana "Wynter" Gordon explain how the meaning of lyrics can be reinterpreted and recontextualized by Beyoncé. See Marc Hogan, "Beyoncé's *Lemonade* Collaborator MNEK Talks Lending 'Hold Up' a Key Line," *Pitchfork*, April 28, 2016, http://pitchfork.com/news/65132-beyonces-lemonade-collaborator-mnek-talks-lending-hold-up-a-key-line; Jessica Goodman, "Diana Gordon interview: The 'Becky with the Good Hair' Scribe Opens Up about New Music," *Entertainment Weekly*, August 2, 2016, http://ew.com/article/2016/08/02/diana-gordon-interview; Seabrook, "How Mike Will Made It." One notable example provided by producer Mike Will Made It is how a freestyled lyric by a member of Rae Strummurd with a sexual connotation—"OK ladies, now let's get in formation"—became the chorus for Beyoncé's feminist Black-power anthem.

48. Father John Misty quoted in Sarah Grant, "Father John Misty: 'I Went Crazy' on Beyonce's 'Lemonade,'" *Rolling Stone*, April 26, 2016, http://www.rollingstone.com/music/news/father-john-misty-i-went-crazy-on-beyonces-lemonade-20160426.

49. MeLo-X states that posting remixes of Beyoncé's music online led to them working together and that he was virtually unknown in the music industry beforehand (Matthew Strauss, "Beyoncé's *Lemonade* Collaborator MeLo-X Gives First Interview on Making of the Album," *Pitchfork*, April 25, 2016, http://pitchfork.com/news/65045-beyonces-lemonade-collaborator-melo-x-gives-first-interview-on-making-of-the-album/).

50. MeLo-X in Strauss, "Beyoncé's *Lemonade* Collaborator MeLo-X."

51. Ibid.

52. Ibid.

53. MNEK in Hogan, "Beyoncé's Lemonade Collaborator MNEK."

54. Ibid.

55. Ibid.

56. See Steve Jennings-X, "Beyonce Runs Her World: Inside the Recording of 4," *Mix*, August 1, 2011, http://www.mixonline.com/news/profiles/beyonce-runs-her-world/366291. See also Watson, "DJ Swivel."

57. There is a sizable body of scholarship on the importance of cultural memory and troping in African American musical forms, ranging from hip hop sampling to quotations in jazz improvisation. See, for example, Perchard, "Hip Hop Samples Jazz"; Monson, "Doubleness"; and Chang, "Records That Play."

58. Will quoted in Seabrook, "How Mike Will Made It."

59. See Alex Gale, "'Lemonade' Backup Singer Ruby Amanfu Talks Beyonce, Jack White and Racism," *Billboard*, April 30, 2016, http://www.billboard.com/articles/news/7350347/lemonade-backup-singer-ruby-amanfu-talks-beyonce-jack-white-and-racism.
60. Gordon in Goodman, "Diana Gordon interview."
61. Ibid.
62. See Hoskyns, *Led Zeppelin IV*.
63. Fast, *In the Houses of the Holy*, 165.
64. Smith, "Race, Gender, and the Phantasmagoric South."
65. Alex Ross, "The Unoriginal Originality of Led Zeppelin," *New Yorker*, April 14, 2016, http://www.newyorker.com/culture/cultural-comment/the-unoriginal-originality-of-led-zeppelin.

BIBLIOGRAPHY

Arewa, Olufunmilayo B. "Creativity, Improvisation, and Risk: Copyright and Musical Innovation." *Notre Dame Law Review* 85, no. 5 (2001): 1833–38.
Barker, Hugh, and Tuval Taylor. *Faking It: The Quest for Authenticity in Popular Music*. New York: Norton, 2007.
Brooks, Daphne A. "The Write to Rock: Racial Mythologies, Feminist Theory, and the Pleasures of Rock Music Criticism." *Women and Music* 12 (2018): 54–62.
Chang, Vanessa. "Records That Play: The Present Past in Sampling Practice." *Popular Music* 28, no. 2 (2009): 143–59.
de Laat, Kim. "'Write a Word, Get a Third': Managing Conflict in Songwriting Teams." *Work and Occupation* 42, no. 2 (2015): 225–56.
Eckstein, Lars. "Torpedoing the Authorship of Popular Music: A Reading of the Gorillaz' 'Feel Good Inc.,'" *Popular Music* 28, no. 2 (2009): 239–55.
Fast, Susan. *In the Houses of the Holy: Zed Zeppelin and the Power of Rock Music*. New York: Oxford University Press, 2001.
Frith, Simon. "Rock and Popular Culture." In *American Media and Mass Culture: Left Perspectives*. Edited by Donald Lazere, 309–22. Berkeley: University of California Press, 1987.
———. *Sound Effects: Youth, Leisure, and the Politics of Rock and Roll*. New York: Pantheon, 1981.
Headlam, Dave. "Does the Song Remain the Same: Questions of Authorship and Identification in the Music of Led Zeppelin." In *Concert Music, Rock, and Jazz since 1945: Essays and Analytical Studies*. Edited by Elizabeth West Marvin and Richard Herrman, 313–63. Rochester, NY: University of Rochester Press, 1995.
Hoskyns, Barney. *Led Zeppelin IV (Rock of Ages)*. Emmaus, PA: Rodale, 2006.
Kohlman, Marla. "Beyoncé as Intersectional Icon? Interrogating the Politics of Respectability." In *The Beyoncé Effect: Essays on Sexuality, Race and Feminism*. Edited by Adrienne Trier-Bieniek, 27–39. Jefferson, NC: McFarland, 2016.

Leonard, Marion. *Gender in the Music Industry: Rock, Discourse and Girl Power.* New York: Routledge, 2007.

Maultsby, Portia M. "The Politics of Race Erasure in Defining Black Popular Music Origins." In *Issues in African American Music: Power, Gender, Race, Representation.* Edited by Portia M. Maultsby and Mellonee V. Burnim, 47–65. New York: Routledge, 2017.

McClary, Susan. *Feminine Endings: Music, Gender, and Sexuality.* Minneapolis: University of Minnesota Press, 1991.

McDonnell, Evelyn, and Ann Powers, eds. *Rock, She Wrote: Women Write about Rock, Pop, and Rap.* Medford, NJ: Plexus, 2014.

McLeod, Kembrew, and Peter DiCola. *Creative License: The Law and Culture of Digital Sampling.* Durham, NC: Duke University Press, 2011.

McLeod, Kembrew, and Rudolf Kuenzli, eds. *Cutting across Media: Appropriation Art, Interventionist Collage, and Copyright Law.* Durham, NC: Duke University Press, 2011.

Middleton, Robert. *Studying Popular Music.* Philadelphia: Open University Press, 1990.

Monson, Ingrid. "Doubleness and Jazz Improvisation: Irony, Parody, and Ethnomusicology." *Critical Inquiry* 30 (1994): 283–313.

Negus, Keith. "Authorship and the Popular Song." *Music and Letters* 92, no. 4 (2011): 607–29.

Perchard, Tom. "Hip Hop Samples Jazz: Dynamics of Cultural Memory and Musical Tradition in the American 1990s." *American Music* 29, no. 3 (2011): 277–307.

Radano, Roland. "On Ownership and Value." *Black Music Research Journal* 30, no. 2 (2010): 360–70.

Rose, Tricia. *Black Noise: Rap Music and Black Culture in Contemporary America.* Hanover, NH: Wesleyan University Press, 1994.

Schmutz, Vaughn, and Alison Faupel. "Gender and Cultural Consecration in Popular Music." *Social Forces* 89, no. 2 (2010): 685–707.

Smith, Erin Sweeney. "Race, Gender, and the Phantasmagoric South in Led Zeppelin and Memphis Minnie's 'When the Levee Breaks.'" Paper presented at the Society of American Music Conference, Little Rock, March 9, 2013.

Vernallis, Carol. *Experiencing Music Video: Aesthetics and Cultural Context.* New York: Columbia University Press, 2004.

Weisbard, Eric. *Top 40 Democracy: The Rival Mainstreams of American Music.* Chicago: University of Chicago Press, 2014.

Whiteley, Sheila. *Women and Popular Music: Sexuality, Identity, and Subjectivity.* New York: Routledge, 2000.

THREE

"Singing All the Time"
Constructions of Cultural Identity in Beyoncé's I Am . . . Sasha Fierce

LISA COLTON

In a relatively little-known hit by Plastic Operator (*Different Places*, 2007), lead singer Pieter Van Dessel bemoans the danger of his girlfriend's public vocality: "She gets all the attention at the party: she's singing all the time," before reflecting that "As long as she's careful, it is okay."[1] Historically, the reputations of women whose voices are on display have been tainted by the cultural association of an open mouth with the availability of a woman's sexual body; a lack of moderation in speaking has frequently been seen as both causal and symbolic of women's weak morality and of their tendency toward sexual promiscuity. Women marginalized by traditional power structures—notably women of color—have been especially prone to reductive assessments of their character within Western culture, and it is easy to find such assessments in the reception of nonwhite female singers, even in popular music, a field in which they are often highly successful.[2] The continued media fetishization of Black, female bodies is driven by deep-rooted historical circumstances and associated beliefs, in which the dominant gaze has long been not only male but also colonial.[3]

"Do you think of yourself primarily as a singer, or a dancer, or a performer?" Steve Kroft asked Beyoncé on *60 Minutes*. "I think I'm an entertainer. I don't know; I think it's hard to say because I love to act, and I love to dance, but my favorite thing to do is just to stand there and perform and sing," she replied.[4] Of the many pop vocalists whose job it is to "sing all the time," Beyoncé stands out as a woman who refuses to limit her utterances. A powerful performer with presence and range, her voice is recognizable both for its distinctive style and as a result of a substantial string of group and solo hits. During the same period in which her voice has become ubiquitous in popular culture, Beyoncé has also—like several women identified as "disruptive divas" in music of the 1990s—mixed personal creativity with political and social engagement.[5] As collaborative songwriter, arranger, and producer, Beyoncé maintains her authority over how her voice is displayed, and she has attempted to build a reputation of Christian morality and of personal control over her strongly sexualized image. In this chapter, I will show that, despite Beyoncé's attempts to regulate her media identity, her own vocality remains construed and constructed according to markers of gender, ethnicity, and class. These socionormative matrices allow her authority over the meaning of her voice, but *only so far*.

Positioning Beyoncé's voice within an intertextual frame—one replete with diverse signifiers—deepens the impact of her music in ways that repeatedly emphasize cultural identity. As Valerie Smith has articulated, such aspects of identity are "discursively produced and never fixed, always involving negotiations of gender, sexuality, race, and class."[6] By singling out Beyoncé's voice as the central pillar of her songs, I wish to reconnect its musical sound to previous readings of the singer's music in which the visual aspects of her singing, dancing body are more often the analytical source material. Such approaches, which are common to the way in which women musicians have been treated in academic literature and the media more widely, serve to redress the neglect of women musicians but too often ultimately do so by examining them as objects of a male "gaze," in which their looked-at bodies are separate from the significance of their utterances. For an artist like Beyoncé, whose back catalog contains many songs offering permission for audiences to admire her "bootylicious" body, it is arguably more challenging to move beyond the primarily visual: the way in which she controls her identity cannot simply be disentangled from the way in which she controls her *image*.[7] The final part of this chapter takes the sonic analysis of her music and assesses the extent to which the meaning of her songs is then supported or subverted by the way in which they are constructed for visual consumption, either in video or live performance. Although Beyoncé's physical presentation is not the primary focus of my analysis, the dominance of video in the marketing and commercial consumption of popular music more generally means that the visual context is a relevant final lens through which Beyoncé's vocality passes to her listeners.

Although academic engagement with Black-identified genres, artists (including some female musicians), and performance practices has been growing, significantly less work has been done on these topics than on the music or practices of white musicians.[8] Where attention is paid to hip hop or soul, for example, or to its individual artists, discussions tend to focus emphatically on the visual, the gestural, or the lyrical; the musical dimensions are largely overlooked. Scholarship on Beyoncé has generally followed this pattern.[9] Writers, notably Aisha S. Durham, have provided critical assessments of the significance of class, race, sexuality, and gender in Beyoncé's video and stage performances.[10] Indeed, the stimulus for such work has been that even for this global superstar, it has been possible to argue that "academic literature has failed to fully theorize the cultural significance of Beyoncé."[11] Even so, Durham's research, which emanates from media and cultural studies perspectives, excludes much close examination of the strictly musical. Like other writers, Durham reads Beyoncé as "an iconic body," one through which questions of power, feminism, and commercial value are played out in a highly visual, public sphere. The voice is no distraction from the view of these lenses, but shifting the focus from image to voice—by definition the most intimate of instruments—might make it possible to *hear Beyoncé's body* anew.

In the present study, I focus my analysis on four tracks from *I Am... Sasha Fierce* (2008): "Diva," "Single Ladies (Put a Ring on It)" (hereafter "Single Ladies"), "Ave Maria," and "Halo." This album presented two sides of the singer in a complementary two-disc set: the first, a short collection of ballads, draws on the subjective, emotional experience of romantic love; the second disc embraces more energetic hip hop and electronic dance music elements and acts as a vehicle for the singer's alter ego (Sasha Fierce), a character more outwardly attuned to female empowerment.[12] Aspects of songs on *I Am... Sasha Fierce* seem to relate closely to Beyoncé's efforts to be both highly vocal (presence within the track, range, virtuosity) and independent from common tropes of the provocative female artist, such as being sexually explicit. In order to consider the relative stability of markers of personal identity within the vocal content and style and the musical settings in which the voice is placed, I will consider primarily musical evidence. I will demonstrate that not only what she sings but how she sings it, and how her voice is framed within the broader musical text (from instrumentation to musical production), allows, indeed demands, readings that are not constrained by the competing claims made for Beyoncé's public—and private—image.[13]

HEARING BEYONCÉ'S BODY

What are the musical signifiers of Beyoncé's body in her music? Above all, Beyoncé's corporeal *musical* presence is signaled through her voice, whose technical agility, dramatic range, tessitura, timbre, and blend of speech and song are extensive. As Nina Eidsheim has argued, although the physical aspects of Black and white voices are indistinguishable from one another, listeners of the past two centuries have continued to describe Black voices with racially inflected language.[14] In a similar vein, it is important to recognize that the differences between male and female voices are not biologically but culturally determined and that the identification of a performer's gender from registral and timbral vocal qualities is one that relies on social conditioning of the listener as much as on that of the speaker or singer.[15] Sonic markers of difference can be perceived, often subconsciously, through the verbal and timbral aspects of language, speech, and song. The perception of difference is possible *not* because of actual differences in anatomy, but because of the ways in which voices are learned and developed. Training practices within popular music (in contrast to classical opera) seek to emphasize the distinctive qualities of individual voices, which are closely connected to notions of authenticity for the listener.[16] In short, Beyoncé's voice can be heard to reflect her gender, ethnic, and class identity not because of innate physical properties, but rather because of the signifiers of identity that are highlighted through its stylistic presentation in recording and performance: decisions about vocal delivery, melody, rhythm, pitch, accompaniment, lyric, musical quotation, and the treatment of her voice production all contribute to this framing.

My analysis begins by examining the first of these properties, the stylistic aspects of Beyoncé's own musical line. There are four main modes of vocal delivery on *I Am . . . Sasha Fierce* (see table 3.1), none of which is unique to Beyoncé as an artist but which, combined, evoke a range of genres and styles that are important for the perception and signification of what Beyoncé's

Table 3.1. Modes of Beyoncé's vocal delivery on *I Am . . . Sasha Fierce*.

Mode	Distinguishing features	Key examples
1	Spoken delivery, with minimal melodic inflection (rap)	Only brief appearances on this album
2	Pitched reciting tone in the middle of her range as the focal point of a disjointed melodic line that often departs from the reciting tone for notes at the third, fifth, or octave before return	"Diva"
3	Smoother melodic line, comprising high levels of internal repetition and mainly syllabic delivery	"Single Ladies"
4	Smooth melodic line with ample room for improvisation and embellishment	"Broken-Hearted Girl"; "Halo"; "Disappear"

sound means, what its sonic identity *is*. These modes are not only musically distinct from one another; they also encode aspects of the singer's identity through their performance: they are themselves intertwined with a wide range of contrasting popular music genres. Identifying the primary mode of an individual vocal line, or in some cases the way in which a song moves between the four, can be connected to—indeed cannot wholly be separated from—the broader signifying gestures of Beyoncé's body that accompany her voice (including scoring, production, image, and dance). Beyoncé's collaborative role in song writing ranges from adjusting lyrics from others' previously written songs to much more detailed involvement in arrangement and production; the actual responsibility that she has for melodic or textural aspects of her songs is impossible to disentangle from the final product. But the common melodic features in table 3.1 suggest that her collaborators write for and with her in ways that draw on a consistent set of stylistic patterns. It is arguably Beyoncé's range of modes across the album, in combination with how her voice is framed in arrangement and production, that provides her unique quality as an artist; she is not only "singing all the time" but also singing in diverse ways, sometimes within a single track.

The first mode, which derives explicitly from rap, is rarely found in extended sections on the album in question; it is more prominent within later work such as "7/11" (*Beyoncé*, 2014). Mode 2 is found across Beyoncé's group and solo output, before and since *I Am . . . Sasha Fierce*. Mode 2 moves from recitation on a single pitched note to alternation with harmonically consonant pitches (thirds, fifths, and octaves) and is a recognizable feature

Ex. 3.1. "Check On It" (mode 2).

Ex. 3.2. "Telephone" section featuring Beyoncé (mode 2).

of Beyoncé's vocal style. Beyoncé's hit "Check On It" (2005; see example 3.1) provides a useful archetype.

Example 3.2 is taken from Beyoncé's contemporaneous performance in Lady Gaga's "Telephone," in which her initial recitation on F leads to a line in which leaps on the words "Leave *my* girls *no* faster" serve to underline her authority within the group.[17] A brief departure from the mode in bars 5–6 of the example evokes the melodic properties of telephone technology and, with the cadence approached from a tone below, gives a modal or even non-Western flavor to the recitation.[18]

The limited melodic range associated with modes 1 and 2, and their tendency to avoid scalic, consecutive notes, is typical of 1990s R&B (see, for example, Missy Elliot's Bhangra-influenced "Get Your Freak On," 2001). The adoption of mode 2 over mode 1 offers the stridency of rap with a more pitch-based, potentially femininized sound. In this form of address, women's voices are used to project assertive claims and judgments in a style not dissimilar to the stereotypical "sassy" tone used in the provocative speech style associated with confident and witty Black women and camp gay men. A blend of modes 2 and 3 was also a defining feature of the creative output of Destiny's Child; in "Survivor" (2001), for example, there is a clear distinction between the tuneful verses in mode 3 and the chorus in mode 2. Mode 3 is more conjunct, so its rhetorical strength is built from short and repetitive material and a high density of text; a useful comparator here is the opening verse of "Dy-na-mi-tee" (Ms Dynamite, *A Little Deeper*, 2002), whose eight short lines are set to one repeated phrase heard four times, where each of the four statements has internal melodic repeats. Mode 3 is an efficient melodic frame, allowing pitch-based expression but without the luxury of melisma, improvisation, or larger-scale phrasing.

Finally, mode 4 is restricted to the R&B ballads found on disc 1, tracks that act as a location for intricate melodic decoration and display; it is a sound ubiquitous in the music of female artists like Whitney Houston, Mariah Carey, and Alicia Keys, whose vocal agility is a key part of their styles (such as Houston's cover of Dolly Parton's "I Will Always Love You," 1992). The virtuosity inherent in mode 4 requires the performance to appear simultaneously extemporized, controlled, and aesthetically beautiful. A style of performance associated with women taking their time to show skill, it can equally lead to perceptions of self-indulgence. The expressive potential of mode 4 derives from its heritage within blues, gospel, and soul genres, those most associated with slow jams; mode 4 is typically found setting lyrics that focus on emotional experience and interiority (e.g., Alicia Keys's "Fallin'," *Songs in A Minor*, 2001), and thus the sound world is one that lends itself to notions of personal authenticity.

Beyoncé's vocal display is a key part of her reputation as pop diva, a term with strong historical connections to opera, drama, and tragic heroism. Two songs from disc 2 stand out as worthy of consideration within this frame, and both explore a flexible, even virtuosic, range of modes. "Diva" is placed at the midpoint of disc 2 and serves as the most gangsta-rap-inflected track, in stark contrast with the ballads that feature on the first disc; it was released simultaneously as a single with "Halo" in order to highlight the contrasting personae of Beyoncé as represented on the album as a whole. The melodic style of "Diva" ranges moves between modes 1, 2, and 3, and backing vocals provided by "my ladies" suggest a female posse surrounding a strong gang leader. The lyrics include stuttering, nonsense syllables ("Na na na," "heh") akin to those found in the output of Lady Gaga, which function as vocal percussive anaphones to the sharp beats and offbeat finger clicks in the mix. At the beginning of the track, a highly processed cyborg voice is paired with Beyoncé's interrupting echo ("I'm a, I'm a, a diva (Hey)"). Even when Beyoncé's main lyric enters, the backing includes a cluttered combination of these two vocal contributions, which also serve as short bridges.

The main verse material is likewise busy, including Beyoncé's own backing vocal sighs and contributions from other backing singers. The linguistic register is replete with urban, gangster-related slang and about hustlers, typically men who raise private wealth through business on the fringes of the law (gambling, pimping women, selling drugs). In the song, Beyoncé self-identifies with this masculine culture, indicating that the term *diva* is the "female version of a hustler" in the lyrics. The character is redolent of Patricia Hill Collins's "Black Bitch" archetype, understood through behavior that is "aggressive, loud, rude, and pushy."[19] In a CBS interview on December 13, 2006, for example, Beyoncé summarized her Sasha Fierce character as "too aggressive, too strong, and too sexy."[20] Rhyme words in the initial verse material are pinpointed by departure from the reciting tone to a note a fifth or octave above it (mode 2, "Stop the *track*, let me face *facts*"), creating a bare harmony that foregrounds masculine aggression and the rhetorical authority of the words. Material at the extensive coda shifts between modes and contains some contrasting phrases that comprise repetitive, falling melodic lines.[21] Even within a restricted harmonic palette that avoids clear modality, the song's texture is complex: apart from upper string samples, most of the instrumentation is delivered by drums and a Roland TR-808, with the remainder of the space filled by the voices of Beyoncé as soloist, plus samples and overdubs of Beyoncé as backing singer(s), and her separate backing singers. The power of the song is thus conveyed through an artificial or forced dominance of Beyoncé, whose omnipresent vocality is sometimes overwhelming.

The stand-out high-energy song from *I Am . . . Sasha Fierce* is "Single Ladies," a song whose forthright attitude was closest to the enormously popular "Crazy in Love" (released from her debut album *Dangerously in*

Love, 2003). As in "Diva," Beyoncé's own voice is both the soloist and used as backing vocals, incorporating layered harmonies in response to the main refrain call. But where the concentrated sound and cultural frame of "Diva" presented a gritty, urban image of Beyoncé that was hard to believe (not least placed on the same album as so many ballads), "Single Ladies" speaks to a broader demographic. As Durham has noted, the song has a particular white-defined reception that foregrounds its subversion of gender stereotypes.[22] Covers and parodies have connected the meaning of the song to marginalized groups across middle-class America as well as to classical music (often justifiably criticized for the prevailing whiteness and masculinity of its oligarchy). "Single Ladies" was used, for example, in an episode of the musical theater show *Glee*, in which a young white football player and his teammates perform Beyoncé's signature dance on the field in a gesture of LGBTQ+ solidarity.

Some of the flexibility of the track for rearrangement stemmed from its use of participatory vocal and chant-inspired textures, including rousing antiphonal cries to all "single ladies" and extended passages texted only with "oh."[23] Such textures are found widely in African American inspired popular genres from blues to hip hop, as well as in the music of Christian churches. Although antiphonal textures are not limited to music of Black origin, their cultural association with African music gives them significant connotative power, and the listening audience may hear them as such in spite of the ubiquity of call-and-response within popular music more generally. This type of racially inflected listening has been articulated by Eidsheim, who has outlined the way in which a variety of Black performers and white listeners have mapped the qualities of Black voices onto the early influence of singing spirituals, even though not all Black singers are experienced in the genre.[24] Instead, assumptions about Black bodies and experiences affect what listeners expect to hear in a song: Beyoncé's body is signaled through call-and-response more than would be the case for a white performer.

HEARING BEYONCÉ'S SUBJECTIVITY: LYRIC, ALLUSION, AND INTERTEXTUALITY

Beyoncé voices aspects of her class mainly through the lyrical conventions of hip hop. The history of class as experienced or defined by various social groups in the United States is important for a full understanding of how

Beyoncé's voice is perceived by her audiences.[25] In the United States and Europe, class is traditionally a marker of position within society, with status primarily signified by wealth (either inherited or earned through climbing educational and social hierarchies). But the historical position of Black communities living in these countries is one in which their members were legally restricted or prevented from owning certain types of property, and they were—during the period in which slavery was legal—also treated as commodities themselves. The ongoing, disproportional economic marginalization of Black communities raises the significance of their wealth in the social hierarchy. It occurs in two ways: first, the connection between abject poverty and strong morality is a common cultural trope (the nineteenth-century notion of the "humble poor," which served to patronize working-class men and women in relation to the socially superior middle class); second, dominant groups within Black communities use material wealth to signify power and control over their social environment. For Black women, the control of the body, as their most contested property, is essential for social respectability.

As a genre stemming from economically disadvantaged Black urban communities in 1970s New York, hip hop has continued to offer opportunities for political resistance through verbal reference to property and, by extension, to the opportunities for education and for social control that might result from it.[26] Although the racist notion that Black communities were held in poverty by their innate lower intelligence was successfully refuted in the work of W. E. B. DuBois, the relationship between ethnicity, education, and economic status is one that remains highly charged in contemporary debate.[27] Material signs of social status are commonly found in R&B lyric and associated images, which are usually indicative of social power and, by extension, control in human relationships. Reference to the possession of cars, weapons, drugs, or women is a commonplace of hip hop.[28] For women, demonstrating chastity remains uppermost in social status, and vocal performance can be a risky business; Black women experience pressures and stereotypes in diverse ways, because perceptions about the sexuality of Black performers have been colored by their role in genres such as blues (whose authenticity is tied to lived experience) and Motown, in which groups were carefully managed to portray a "clean" image.[29]

Class is part of Beyoncé's lyrical vocabulary and is associated with the performance of both typically masculine and typically feminine social power in Black communities. This aspect is expressed quite differently on the two

Table 3.2. References to wealth and material possessions on *I Am ... Sasha Fierce*.

Jewelry	"Single Ladies (Put a Ring on It)"	"If you liked it then you should have put a ring on it" evokes both expensive personal property and an engagement ring as a symbol of exclusive "ownership" in courtship.
Clothing and makeup	"Single Ladies (Put a Ring on It)"	Lip gloss, Deréon jeans (clothing line owned by Beyoncé)
	"Diva"	Stiletto shoes worn since fifteen
	"Video Phone"	References to her lover's appreciation of her bag and manicured nails
	"Radio"	Large sunglasses ("stunna shades")
Food and drink	"Single Ladies (Put a Ring on It)"	"Drink in my cup"
Technology	"Radio"	Ownership of radio
	"Video Phone"	Implied ownership of filming technology to allow her lover to view her
	"If I Were a Boy"	"I would turn off my phone/Tell everyone it's broken/So they'd think that I was sleepin' alone."
Transport	"Radio"	Convertible car with stereo ("When I get into my car," "I got my top back and my beat low")
	"Diva"	Reference to there being no passengers on her plane may be not be literal
Money	"Diva"	References to being "so sick and filthy with Benjis" is slang for being wealthy with currency. (Benjamin Franklin features on the $100 bill.)

discs (see table 3.2). On disc 1, class is underlined by constant affirmation of monogamy and commitment, as well as by drawing lyrical references from the tropes of religious texts. Beyoncé is drawn in tight control of her mind, body, and sexual behavior. On disc 2, *Sasha Fierce*, references to money, jewelry, property, her own clothing brand, and other possessions are found frequently, and these items are shown off through dance gestures and in the scenarios of video and live performances. The only material possession mentioned on *I Am ...* occurs in the fantasy-based "If I Were a Boy," in which she imagines herself a man, turning off his telephone to spend more time with his girlfriend.

"Single Ladies" includes an entreaty to her love *not* to treat her to further material possessions, only giving her his love; the impression is that she is economically independent, an image that continues the theme found in tracks by Destiny's Child such as "Bills, Bills, Bills" (1999) and "Independent Women" (2000).

Beyoncé's middle-class, suburban roots create a problem for any of her references to class to be taken at face value: she was raised by two working parents in Houston, Texas, and was home schooled after eighth grade by a tutor. Unlike hip hop artists such as the Notorious B.I.G. or Tupac Shakur, Beyoncé's upbringing was not the urban New York context in which wealth and property were paramount and opportunities for education were limited. It was her early success with Destiny's Child—a career path backed by her manager father—that resulted in Beyoncé's incomplete education, not her family's economic position. Beyoncé's music and performances contain several signifiers of class, and they pertain to understandings of the relationship between history, race, class, and gender. Durham, for example, identifies in "Check On It" visual and lyrical prompts that help to authenticate Beyoncé's Southern (rather than urban New York) hip hop persona.[30] She further identifies the challenge for Beyoncé of conveying a message of authority in which middle-class respectability has historically been one "conferred by men," an aspect that is found in the often misogynist lyrical tropes of hip hop.[31]

In addition to direct lyrical reference to money and possessions, I would suggest that allusions to classical music and to Christian devotional song are indicative of Beyoncé's identity. I would go further: ethnicity and class are signaled not only by what she sings but how she sings it. In "Ave Maria" and "Halo," intertextual references to previous song traditions are delivered through mode 4, a ballad style that underlines Beyoncé's ethnic and socio-economic subjectivity.

Musical indicators of class are highly charged in their ability to emphasize meaningful aspects of songs, especially in styles that are inflected by association with particular ethnicities. The very period in which slavery was most politically contested—the late eighteenth and early nineteenth centuries— was also the time in which the canon of Western art music was being constructed in Europe. It goes almost without saying that the classical canon was predominantly founded on the work of white European men. Although one of the major projects of the later twentieth century was to challenge notions of canon in relation to its exclusion of marginalized groups, any popular song that draws deliberately on classical music works in dialogue with the power dynamics of classical music's past.

It is with class and classical heritage in mind that the significance of the track "Ave Maria" merits attention. "Ave Maria" is essentially a reworking of the song "Ave Maria! Jungfrau mild!" by Franz Schubert (1797–1828). The original work is a Christian song that, since its composition in 1825 (catalogued as D. 839), has been used as part of broader devotional and nonliturgical contexts such as religious ceremonies and concert music. Beyoncé's "Ave Maria" appears on *I Am . . . Sasha Fierce* as a gentle ballad, sandwiched between "Broken-Hearted Girl" and "Satellites."[32] The original prayer "Ave Maria" (Hail Mary), in honor of the Virgin Mary, has been part of Roman Catholic devotional practice since at least the eleventh century and takes as its basis scriptural text from the Gospel of St. Luke, "Hail, the Lord is with thee." Musical settings of the Ave Maria prayer have been common since the thirteenth century; the versions by Charles Gounod (1859, a melody that overlays J. S. Bach's Prelude in C from *Das wohltemperierte Klavier*) and Schubert (originally published as *Ellens Gesang III. Hymne an die Jungfrau*) are the best known and most regularly performed. Schubert's version inspired Beyoncé's: Beyoncé wrote her "Ave Maria" in collaboration with Amanda Ghost, for both artists had walked down the aisle to the original work at their weddings. Neither Beyoncé's nor Schubert's Ave Maria contain the whole prayer; instead, both draw on the incipit and set it in a vernacular song context, with Schubert's taking its remaining lines from a German translation of Walter Scott's *The Lady of the Lake*. The common resetting of the whole Latin prayer within Schubert's original music, however, has led to the popular misconception that the German composer composed his Lied with the full Latin text. It is this version—the complete Latin prayer with Schubert's music—that Beyoncé and Ghost seem to have had in mind in creating the track.[33]

Beyoncé's appropriation and performance of Schubert's "Ave Maria" is one that thus evokes classical music, as well as a European, Roman Catholic heritage: two stubbornly white, patriarchal contexts. Beyoncé's "Ave Maria" opens with a gentle, acoustic texture reminiscent of Christian praise bands. Amplified acoustic guitar and piano play the simple chordal accompaniment that suggests not only Schubert's setting but also feel-good anthems such as "You'll Never Walk Alone."[34] Gentle percussion enters midverse with synthetic but tactile low drum and finger clicks, giving a swaying, gospel feel. The

Latin text serves as a verse-end refrain within what is, for the most part, a standard thirty-two-bar song form. "And then I hear this voice inside: [saying] *Ave Maria*" closes both verse one and verse two before a bridge whose lyric suggests more of a secular than a religious context; the bridge then moves to a section setting the refrain once more, closing the short song with a repeat of the refrain in a soprano register, an octave above where it has been sung at verse endings. The song frequently draws on Christian, textual phraseology, such as "I found heaven on earth, you are my last, my first," which recalls the name of Jesus depicted as "Alpha and Omega" in the Book of Revelation, while simultaneously surely evoking, if more quietly, Barry White's "You're the First, the Last, My Everything." This symbolism, while clearly biblical, departs from the Ave Maria prayer itself, glossing the original text and linking Beyoncé's personal religious identity with her marriage to Jay-Z. Simultaneously, however, it connects Beyoncé's personal religiosity with the broader Christian church and with nineteenth-century concert music.

The connection with classical music is emphasized by the style of accompaniment and by the manipulation of the original melody (see examples 3.3a–c). The phrase "Ave Maria" is used not as an opening gesture, as in Schubert's Lied, but as a refrain, a structural marker. Initial presentations of the refrain are low in Beyoncé's chest voice, but the final declamations are an octave higher, requiring her more "classical" head-voice timbre. The Lied is transposed from B-flat Major up to C Major, a key associated in classical music with spiritual and bodily purity; the lilting use of sextuplet semiquavers in Schubert's piano line, in common time, is redrawn as a 12/8 ballad, recalling quasidevotional music such as the ubiquitous "Hallelujah" (Leonard Cohen), also in C Major, which has been covered by dozens of subsequent artists, including R&B musician Alexandra Burke (2008). Beyoncé's "Ave Maria" thus pays homage to "Hallelujah," a song whose poetic lyrics are self-referential to their own harmony as well as to an eclectic mixture of biblical and sexual imagery, creating a blend of sacred and secular references similar to those in Beyoncé's songs.

Melodic embellishment, written into Schubert's composition, appears extemporized by Beyoncé as in standard contemporary R&B performance practice, a feature strongly associated with female performers and their technical ability as divas. Although the original performance context of Schubert's "Ave Maria" would have been the salon or drawing room—a

Ex. 3.3a. Schubert, "Ave Maria," D. 839, op. 52, no. 6 (1825, published 1826).

Ex. 3.3b. Beyoncé et al., verse 1 refrain (transcribed from album).

Ex. 3.3c. Beyoncé et al., closing section (transcribed from album).

context recalled by the presence of voice and piano in Beyoncé's version—the Lied has been widely performed in the concert hall and is associated with performances by operatic divas such as Greek American Maria Callas and African American Jessye Norman, as well as an English version by contemporary pop diva Céline Dion (*These Are Special Times*, 1998). The Latin setting of Schubert's "Ave Maria" has also been recorded by popular female artists such as Barbra Streisand (*A Christmas Album*, 1967), and Gounod's related setting has been recorded by Karen Carpenter (*Christmas Portrait*, 1978). The presence of "Ave Maria" on *I Am* . . . therefore signals a variety of contexts that have had a long, sometimes problematic, relationship with racial or gender diversity and with the representation of female artists. As a prayer to the ultimate feminine icon of Christianity, the Virgin Mary, it serves to construct Beyoncé's identity as a pure, middle-class American woman. Some listeners would perhaps associate the song with Madonna's "Like a Prayer" (1989), whose video drew on Roman Catholic iconography and controversially depicted the star dreaming of kissing a Black male saint. Madonna's virginal identity was the focus of her representation from early work, notably "Like a Virgin" (1984). A possible reading would thus be that Beyoncé's performance is a reappropriation both of Madonna's earlier cultural reference points and perhaps also of her status as an iconic woman artist.[35]

There are other nods to Beyoncé's religious and ethnic identity in *I Am . . . Sasha Fierce*, especially on disc 1, which represents the more managed, clean-cut image of the artist. The hit song "Halo," for example, refers to angels, prayerfulness, and light in what is ostensibly a relatively clichéd contemporary popular song for an artist of any gender or ethnicity.[36] On the other hand, its opening statement, "Remember those walls I built? Well, baby they're tumbling down. And they didn't even put up a fight, they didn't even make a sound," is redolent of the walls that feature in the refrain material of well-known African American spiritual *Joshua Fit the Battle of Jericho*:

> Joshua fit the battle of Jericho,
> Jericho, Jericho,
> Joshua fit the battle of Jericho
> And the walls come tumbling down.

The song has been popularized through numerous performances and recordings by Black artists, such as Harrod's Jubilee Singers (1922), the Delta Rhythm Boys, the Golden Gate Quartet (1957), and Queen Mahalia Jackson (1958); white blues artists, such as Elvis Presley, also have recorded it. Although the precise compositional origins of *Joshua Fit the Battle of Jericho* are unclear, its lyrics speak of the oppression of Black people in the pre–Civil War United States and, as did many songs in its spiritual tradition, used biblical verses allegorically with political intent. In Beyoncé's "Halo," a steady, anthemic ballad, the verse builds through an orchestration that features piano, strings, solo cello, synthesized choir, and crisp percussive backbeats. As the verse moves through the bridge to the chorus, the texture builds with fuller synthesized sounds as well as duetting singer an octave below, presented relatively low in the mix. The refrain material presents Beyoncé's voice singing "Halo," as well as her own echoes of the same material in an antiphonal format, recalling a facet of traditional spirituals discussed earlier. In the second half of the song, the type of ornamentation found as a marker of virtuosity in mode 4 is increasingly present, decorating material with improvisation across an impressive pitch range.

CONCLUSIONS: FROM AUDIO TO AUDIOVISUAL

It would be remiss to ignore the effect that music video has on the final meanings of each of the songs discussed in detail in this chapter, although a comprehensive analysis of visual media lies beyond its scope. How does the visual presence of Beyoncé, typically positioned center stage in her videos, support or undercut the initial sonic and lyric meanings song? How are the narratives and the characterizations sculpted to draw attention to the various aspects of identity that Beyoncé is pushing in each song? Since the advent of MTV, and running alongside Beyoncé's own musical career, the place of video in establishing, marketing, and disseminating an artist's work has become central. Furthermore, as Durham and others have shown, Beyoncé's music videos and stage performances are sophisticated productions in which her personality, body, musicality, dance skills, and cultural capital are all on display.

There has been no official video for "Ave Maria," but it is instructive to watch live performances of Beyoncé singing it in concert. On international stage performances in 2009, Beyoncé stood under a spotlight, initially wearing a white leotard and white sleeved cape; between the bridge and the final, higher-octave "Ave Maria" refrain, an additional instrumental interlude created the opportunity for dancers to convert her costume into an elaborate veiled wedding outfit. After a passage that quotes "Angel" (Sarah McLachlan, *Surfacing*, 1997), the final section of Beyoncé's performance is a dramatic, classical-style performance of the Latin-texted Schubert Lied, abridged, accompanied by piano. The official video for "Halo" likewise plays with the virginal connotations of the color white and the singer's clothing and bedsheets, with Beyoncé and her male lover cast in a glowing light. The effect of both performances consistently asserts Beyoncé's engagement with earlier musical models in ways that support my initial analysis. It is perhaps safer for the artist to assert this disc's presentation as reflecting her genuine personality, in that it presents traditional markers of femininity and innocence common to a broad demographic. Beyoncé's song plays with the performance of purity as signified through the use of the "Ave Maria" material in "Halo," which is emphasized in the song's musical and visual framing on stage.

In the videos for "Single Ladies" and "Diva," Beyoncé is depicted as the leader of a group of nonwhite women, and both are shot largely in black and white. In "Single Ladies," the distinctive dance routine foregrounds the exaggerated shapes of the Black female body: high heels and high-cut leotards extend leg shapes and focus attention on the curves of the dancers' bottoms and breasts. The live performance at the 2009 Video Music Awards involved participation from a larger group of dancers, representative of various ethnicities, and thus portrayed a more diverse performance scenario than had the original video, or what might be understood from the musical style alone. "Diva" echoed the dancing triangle of "Single Ladies," but instead of being located in a plain studio, it was filmed in dimly lit locations in downtown Los Angeles, a setting associated with urban hip hop culture. In both videos, the absence of men reaffirms Beyoncé's chastity.

The album *I Am . . . Sasha Fierce* attempted to portray two sides of Beyoncé—the "good girl" on disc 1 and the assertive, empowered Fierce on disc 2; the Beyoncé/Sasha Fierce split persona served the singer well until 2010, when she formally merged the two sides of her character.[37] The mixed reception of the 2008 release was perhaps reflective of the commercial and marketing challenges of selling an album whose central performer emphasizes diverse cultural positions. Beyoncé begins by saying that she needs only love, but then she spends later tracks referring to the trappings of material wealth. She is a "female hustler," as well as a contemporary Virgin Mary. Her songs implicitly and explicitly claim to play with subjectivities variously chaste and deferential, but then assertive, dominant, and sexually mature.[38] The artistic voice that comes through from the album as a whole cannot be reduced to either of these stereotypes. Across all tracks, Beyoncé's pervasive vocality leaves little room for others in its textural presence, technical agility, and range of mode. It is not only the visual aspects of video that "signify subalterneity, and highlight identity as performance": intertextual and connotative musical references present Beyoncé as a contemporary artist with a broad, informed musical heritage.[39] Through the musical analysis and close consideration of intertextuality within Beyoncé's album, we can hear the crafting of subtler messages about Beyoncé, about women, and about women of color than we might expect from a commercially successful artist (and, indeed, than are available in her own Beyoncé/Sasha Fierce dyad). Beyoncé's vocality—and the way in which her voice is framed through songwriting, arrangement, and production—invites the listener to hear the full breadth of her cultural identity in powerful, nuanced ways.

LISA COLTON is Reader in Musicology at the University of Huddersfield. She is author of *Angel Song: Medieval English Music in History* and editor with Catherine Haworth of *Gender, Age, and Musical Creativity* and with Tim Shephard of *Sources of Identity: Makers, Owners and Users of Music Sources before 1600*.

NOTES

1. I draw on the use of *vocality* as defined by Dunn and Jones, who use the word in "all the voice's manifestations ... each of which is invested with social meanings not wholly determined by linguistic content" (*Embodied Voices*, 1).

2. The historical context for patronizing representations of nonwhite men and women in Western culture is explored in Said, *Orientalism*. Within film musicology, the ways in which signifiers of difference are frequently collapsed tougher in reductive representations of marginalized groups has been considered very effectively in Kalinak, "Fallen Woman." Sheila Whiteley goes further, articulating ways in which women artists are effectively obliged to "participate in making themselves commodities," an act that relies on reductive strategies, because such is the nature of the commercial market (*Sexing the Groove*, 178–79).

3. Netto, "Reclaiming the Body," esp. 149–51. The idea of a "dominant gaze" derives from studies lying outside of musicology, especially Berger, *Ways of Seeing*, and Mulvey, *Visual and Other Pleasures*.

4. Beyoncé interviewed by Steve Kroft for "Beyoncé—I Am ... Sasha Fierce/World Tour," *60 Minutes Special* (2009/10); accessed December 30, 2016, but no longer available.

5. Burns and Lafrance outline some of the prevailing features of such women (focusing on Tori Amos, Courtney Love, Me'Shell Ndegéocello, and PJ Harvey) in "Cultural Studies Approach," 1–3.

6. Smith, *Not Just Race*, xv.

7. The term *bootylicious* is traditionally credited to Snoop Dogg in his use of it in part of a song by Dr. Dre ("Fuck wit Dre Day," 1992), but it carried a different meaning. The now common definition (a positive portmanteau combining "delicious" with "booty" to praise the shape of a woman's backside) featured prominently in the Destiny's Child hit of the same name (written by Beyoncé and collaborators, released 2001) in which the lyrics refer repeatedly to a power game in which men are unable to cope with the "jelly" (wobbling backsides) of the three singers, including Beyoncé. On the contradictions between feminism and the manner in which Beyoncé draws attention physically and lyrically to her body, see Weidhase, "Beyoncé Feminism." See also Barrera, "Hottentot 2000," and Durham and Baez, "Tail of Two Women."

8. Important work on women artists, including women of color, includes Whiteley, *Women and Popular Music*, which includes discussion of Tracy Chapman

among predominantly white artist case studies. O'Brien, *She-Bop II*, was expanded in its second edition from an already balanced overview to include consideration of recent artists like Lauren Hill and Destiny's Child. Nevertheless, gender has tended to provide the initial frame for scholarly discussion. Stras's *She's So Fine* critiques twentieth-century girl groups with reference to gender, class, age, and ethnicity, and has much to inform understandings of the cultural heritage of artists like Beyoncé and Destiny's Child. An important study of the relationship between gender and popular music performed by Black musicians is Avery et al., "Tuning Gender."

9. The work of Hansen, "Empowered or Objectified?," is an important exception; his study of vocality in Beyoncé's "Partition" (2013) takes an impressively detailed analytical approach to aspects of production in particular, though it is far more visually focused than the present study.

10. See especially Durham, "Check On It"; Durham, *Home with Hip Hop Feminism*, esp. 81–100.

11. Durham, *Home with Hip Hop Feminism*, 82–83.

12. Beyoncé's employment of alter egos is explored in detail in Kumari, "Yoü and I."

13. The analysis of audiovisual media in relation to the presentation of conflicting artistic personae is especially important in contemporary pop, in which multiple significations and readings are possible, leading to potential fragmentation or contradiction. For relevant examples of such analysis, see Hansen, "Empowered or Objectified?," which draws on Hawkins and Richardson, "Remodeling Britney Spears."

14. See the summary discussion in Eidsheim, "Marian Anderson," 645–47.

15. Cusick, "On Musical Performances," and Schlichter, "Do Voices Matter?," esp. 43–44.

16. Eidsheim, "Race and the Aesthetics of Vocal Timbre," 340.

17. On the use of speech style delivery for authority, see Hansen, "Empowered or Objectified?," 171.

18. I acknowledge the limited evidence for Beyoncé's knowledge of music theory, as well as the problematic associations of modal melodic shapes with orientalism. But, in an interview after his performance with Beyoncé at the Grammy Awards (2004), Prince commented that he was surprised to find that she had a knowledge of scales, such as the mixolydian, and "Egyptian styles" ("Prince on Beyoncé," posted by Here4BeyonSLAY, April 24, 2010, https://www.youtube.com/watch?v=FfCIafZZx6I). For a fuller discussion of this song, see Colton, "Who's Calling?"

19. Collins, *Black Sexual Politics*, 123.

20. Cited in Kumari, "Yoü and I," 406.

21. The relative lack of melody, especially on an album with so many ballads, led Alex Petridis to comment that "The sonic trickery on the most experimental track,

Diva, isn't interesting enough to distract you from the absence of a tune" ("CD Review: *Beyoncé, I Am . . . Sasha Fierce*," *Guardian*, November 14, 2008, https://www.theguardian.com/music/2008/nov/14/beyonce-i-am-sasha-fierce).

22. Durham, *Home with Hip Hop Feminism*, 81.

23. On the ways in which call-and-response can be used to signify discussion between individuals or between communities, through song, see Khan, "Signifying the Monkey," 49–50.

24. Eidsheim, "Marian Anderson," 646.

25. On the importance of understanding the historical relationship between slavery, property, authenticity, and musicality, see esp. Radano, "On Ownership."

26. A history of hip hop lies beyond the scope of this study. See Forman and Neal, *That's the Joint*. For a critique of how hip hop has become the primary cultural object for the study of race and sexism, see Rose, *Hip Hop Wars*.

27. DuBois, *Philadelphia Negro*.

28. On the dominant themes of violence, misogyny, and possessions in songs by Black artists, see especially Avery et al., "Tuning Gender."

29. On the historical trope of musicality and female sexual impropriety, see especially LaMay, *Musical Voices*. On midcentury musicians, ethnicity, and popular music, see Stras, *She's So Fine*.

30. Apart from Beyoncé's own performance, including her experimentation with a range of hairstyles, Durham points out the authenticating presence of Houston rappers Bun B and Slim Thug (Durham, "Check On It," 8).

31. Durham, *Home with Hip Hop Feminism*, 89.

32. Songwriting credits for "Ave Maria" are paid to Beyoncé Knowles, Makeba Riddick, Tor Erik Hermansen, Amanda Ghost, Mikkel Eriksen, and Ian Dench.

33. The point is particularly supported by its performance in live shows, as is discussed at the end of this chapter.

34. "You'll Never Walk Alone" was written by Rogers and Hammerstein for *Carousel* (1945), and it has been covered frequently in popular song, notably by Gerry and the Pacemakers (1963).

35. I am grateful to Martin Iddon for this suggestion.

36. "Halo" has words and music by Beyoncé Knowles, Ryan Tedder, and Evan Bogart. Alex Petridis has criticized it as being derivative of Rihanna's hit "Umbrella" (2007) (Petridis, "*Beyoncé, I Am . . . Sasha Fierce*").

37. The story was widely reported; see, for example, Hillary Crosley, "Beyoncé Says She 'Killed' Sasha Fierce," *MTV News*, February 26, 2010, http://www.mtv.com/news/1632774/beyonce-says-she-killed-sasha-fierce/.

38. On the dichotomy of sexual stereotyping for women of color, see particularly Collins, *Black Sexual Politics*.

39. Baez and Durham, "A Tail of Two Women," 131.

BIBLIOGRAPHY

Avery, Lanice R., L. Monique Ward, Lolita Moss, and Dilara Üsküp. "Tuning Gender: Representations of Femininity and Masculinity in Popular Music by Black Artists." *Journal of Black Psychology* 43, no. 2 (2017): 159–91.

Barrera, Magdalena. "Hottentot 2000: Jennifer Lopez and Her Butt." In *Sexualities in History: A Reader*. Edited by Kim M. Phillips and Barry Reay, 407–17. New York: Routledge, 2002.

Berger, John. *Ways of Seeing*. London: Penguin, 1972.

Burns, Lori, and Mélisse Lafrance. "A Cultural Studies Approach to Women and Popular Music." In *Disruptive Divas: Feminism, Identity and Popular Music*. Edited by Lori Burns and Mélisse Lafrance, 1–29. London: Routledge, 2002.

Collins, Patricia Hill. *Black Sexual Politics: African Americans, Gender, and the New Racism*. New York: Routledge, 2004.

Colton, Lisa. "Who's Calling? Telephone Songs, Female Vocal Empowerment and Signification." In *Lady Gaga and Popular Music: Performing Gender, Fashion, and Culture*. Edited by Martin Iddon and Melanie Marshall, 67–81. New York: Routledge, 2014.

Cusick, Suzanne G. "On Musical Performances of Gender and Sex." In *Audible Traces: Gender, Identity, and Music*. Edited by Elaine Barkin and Lydia Hamessley, 25–49. Zurich: Carciofoli, 1999.

DuBois, W. E. B. *The Philadelphia Negro*. Philadelphia: University of Pennsylvania Press, 1899.

Dunn, Leslie C., and Nancy A. Jones. "Introduction." In *Embodied Voices: Representing Female Vocality in Western Culture*. Edited by Leslie C. Dunn and Nancy A. Jones, 1–13. Cambridge: Cambridge University Press, 1996.

Durham, Aisha S. "Check on It: Beyoncé, Southern Booty, and Black Feminism in Music Video." *Feminist Media Studies* 12, no. 1 (2012): 35–49.

———. *Home with Hip Hop Feminism: Performances in Communication and Culture*. New York: Peter Lang, 2014.

Durham, Aisha S., and Jillian Baez. "A Tail of Two Women: Exploring the Contours of Difference in Popular Culture." In *Curriculum and the Cultural Body*. Edited by Stephanie Springgay and Debra Freedman, 130–45. New York: Peter Lang, 2007.

Eidsheim, Nina Sun. "Marian Anderson and 'Sonic Blackness' in American Opera." *American Quarterly* 63, no. 3 (2011): 641–71.

———. "Race and the Aesthetics of Vocal Timbre." In *Rethinking Difference in Music Scholarship*. Edited by Olivia Ashley Bloechl, Melanie Diane Lowe, and Jeffrey Kallberg, 338–65. Cambridge: Cambridge University Press, 2014.

Forman, Murray, and Mark Anthony Neal. *That's the Joint: The Hip-Hop Studies Reader*. London: Routledge, 2012.

Hansen, Kai Arne. "Empowered or Objectified? Personal Narrative and Audiovisual Aesthetics in Beyoncé's Partition." *Popular Music and Society* 40, no. 2 (2017): 164–80.

Hawkins, Stan, and John Richardson. "Remodeling Britney Spears: Matters of Intoxication and Mediation." *Popular Music and Society* 30, no. 5 (2007): 605–29.

Kalinak, Kathryn. "The Fallen Woman and the Virtuous Wife: Musical Stereotypes in *The Informer, Gone with the Wind*, and *Laura*." *Film Reader* 5 (1982): 76–82.

Khan, Khatija Bibi. "Signifying the Monkey: Rhetorical Modes of Expressions in African American Music: The Case of KRS-One." *Muziki* 9, no. 1 (2012): 35–57.

Kumari, Ashanka. "'Yoü and I': Identity and Performance of Self in Lady Gaga and Beyoncé." *Journal of Popular Culture* 49, no. 2 (2016): 403–16.

LaMay, Thomasin K. *Musical Voices of Early Modern Women: Many-Headed Melodies*. Aldershot: Ashgate, 2005.

Mulvey, Laura. *Visual and Other Pleasures*. Bloomington: Indiana University Press, 1975.

Netto, Priscilla. "Reclaiming the Body of the 'Hottentot': The Vision and Visuality of the Body Speaking with Vengeance in *Venus Hottentot 2000*." *European Journal of Women's Studies* 12, no. 2 (2005): 149–63.

O'Brien, Lucy. *She-Bop II: The Definitive History of Women in Rock, Pop and Soul*. New York: Continuum, 2003.

Radano, Ronald. "On Ownership and Value." *Black Music Research Journal* 30, no. 2 (2010): 363–70.

Rose, Tricia. *The Hip Hop Wars: What We Talk about When We Talk about Hip Hop—and Why It Matters*. New York: Basic Civitas, 2008.

Said, Edward. *Orientalism*. New York: Vintage, 1979.

Schlichter, Annette. "Do Voices Matter? Vocality, Materiality, Gender Performativity." *Body and Society* 17, no. 1 (2011): 31–52.

Smith, Valerie. *Not Just Race, Not Just Gender: Black Feminist Readings*. New York: Routledge, 1998.

Spivak, Gayatri Chakravorty. "Can the Subaltern Speak?" In *Marxism and the Interpretation of Culture*. Edited by Cary Nelson and Lawrence Grossberg, 271–315. Urbana: University of Illinois Press, 1988.

Stras, Laurie, ed. *She's So Fine: Reflections on Whiteness, Femininity, Adolescence and Class in 1960s Music*. Farnham: Ashgate, 2010.

Weidhase, Nathalie. "'Beyoncé Feminism' and the Contestation of the Black Feminist Body." *Celebrity Studies* 6, no. 1 (2015): 128–31.

Whiteley, Sheila. *Sexing the Groove*. London: Routledge, 1997.

———. *Women and Popular Music: Sexuality, Identity and Subjectivity*. London: Routledge, 2000.

2

Beyoncé on Screen, Reading Beyoncé

FOUR

Beyoncé's Mixed-Media Feminism

Sounding, Staging, and Sampling Gender Politics in "***Flawless"

JULIA COX

Upon receiving the coveted MTV Vanguard Lifetime Achievement Award in September 2014, pop icon Beyoncé awarded fans with a performance.[1] Many were expecting a medley of her greatest hits, a musical Bildungsroman that showcased her evolution from girl-group ringleader to single lady to married, drunk, and in love. Instead, Queen Bey emblazoned herself in front of the LED backdrop "FEMINIST" and offered a selection from the 2013 visual album *Beyoncé*.

Much as Michael Jackson utilized the retrospective occasion of Motown's twenty-fifth anniversary to debut his iconic moonwalk, Beyoncé used the Vanguard performance to look forward, launching a more experimental sound and political posture. The climax of the Vanguard medley was "***Flawless," Beyoncé delivering the song's twin catchphrases "I woke up like this" and "bow down bitches" alongside a sample of Nigerian writer Chimamanda Ngozi Adichie's "We Should All Be Feminists" TEDx talk. Beyoncé's choice of "***Flawless" as the thematic and visual center of her Vanguard performance merits a reconsideration of how the song marked the pop icon's turn to more reflective material and a less commercial aesthetic.

Many now cite *Lemonade* (2016) as the debut of the politicized Beyoncé, when Queen Bey magically emerged in formation, turning haters to hive with Black feminist imagery, Black Panther homages, and tributes to slain victims of police brutality.[2] However, Beyoncé's engagement with racial and gender politics has been a much longer journey. The beginning sounds of this political shift emerged on "***Flawless," when she used a mixed media format to explore a relationship with the label "feminist." This essay will explore how "***Flawless" marked Beyoncé's move away from flat evocations of girl power into more complex mediations on womanhood and identity: through a disavowal of pageant imagery, disruption of the pop song formula, sampling of feminist theory, and eschewing of respectability politics.[3]

Even before the release of "***Flawless" or the Vanguard performance, the Beyoncé-feminist debate already contained many chapters. After identifying as a feminist in a 2013 interview with British *Vogue*, she ignited a maelstrom of academic, media, and fan responses to her use of this word.[4] Every musical and cultural act she then performed was judged by how it did or did not fit into the already complex and contested contemporary concept of feminism. The same month as the *Vogue* interview, Beyoncé announced a summer world tour called the Mrs. Carter Show, sparking outrage from critics, who began labeling her an antifeminist, an abandoner of girl power. Aisha Harris of *Slate* wrote one of many reactionary responses under the headline "Who Run the World? Husbands?"[5]

The Beyoncé-feminist debate gained a musical dimension later in 2013, when Beyoncé released the SoundCloud riff "Bow Down/I Been On." The snippet, not even a formal single, contained the phrase "bow down, bitches" to widespread disapproval from many music scholars and fans for employing a derogatory term associated with misogyny.[6] Rae Alexandra of *San Francisco Weekly* argued "Bow Down/I Been On" was a giant faux pas for an artist who has championed girl power since her days as ringleader of the girl group Destiny's Child with songs like "Independent Women Part I" and "Survivor." Alexandra wrote, "'Bow Down,' lyrically, goes against everything that her last 20-plus years in the spotlight have emphasized—and, oh boy, it rubs us the wrong way."[7] Alexandra's comments communicated more than a mere policing of language, rather that Beyoncé was intentionally violating the politics of Black respectability that have long guided behavioral expectations for powerful Black women.[8]

Critics unanimously policed this track, but few engaged with how "Bow Down" was later expanded and remixed into the feminist anthem "***Flawless," itself released on the visual album, *Beyoncé* in December 2013. "***Flawless" has since become the sonic center of Beyoncé's feminist capital, for the song samples feminist Nigerian writer Chimamanda Ngozi Adichie and spawned another catchphrase, "I woke up like this," an affirmational nod to one's own beauty that has become a popular social media hashtag. Perhaps oddest, few critics have engaged the video aspect of this mixed-media album. Emily Lordi suggests taking a closer look at how various identity politics emerge in the "texture and richness" of *Beyoncé* that abstract terms like feminism can often obscure.[9] Taking Lordi's cue, perhaps our discussion of Beyoncé's feminism should shift to a more nuanced, mixed-media approach.[10]

Analysis of the sonic, structural, and visual dimensions of "***Flawless" allows a more expansive understanding of Beyoncé's feminist turn and our own analytic systems for evaluating women artists who put sexuality at the center of their sound. "***Flawless" has many complexities and contradictions beyond the lyrical refrains of "bow down" or "woke up like this," in which it is much like feminism today. Beyoncé's feminism can be theorized sonically and visually and also allows for deeper cultural work outside an academic gatekeeping of feminist ideology and who can use the word.[11] Beyoncé's feminism can be usefully understood through Aisha Durham, Brittney Cooper, and Susana Morris's term "hip hop feminism," a perhaps contradictory, yet still politically sustainable, means of theorizing Black women's cultural production beyond the ivory tower.[12] They argue that women hip hop artists of the 1990s developed a more elastic rendering of feminist ideology that moved away from respectability politics and united Black feminist consciousness with the social project of hip hop.[13] Keeping with these cornerstones of consciousness and contradiction, Beyoncé's iteration of hip hop feminism in "***Flawless," can productively be read as a quest, a series of trials and obstacles, rather than a puzzle piece that does or does not fit the board.

"***Flawless" ponders feminism as a mixed-media, lived experience not unlike a literary quest. Writing of Zora Neale Hurston's *Their Eyes Were Watching God*, Missy Kubitschek defines a distinctly "female quest" created by the novel's narrative style and protagonist, Janie. *Their Eyes Were Watching God* tells the story of a Black woman in the segregated South seeking personal and romantic fulfillment after a failed teenage marriage to an older man. Janie's journey takes her through three communities and romantic partners in a journey to self-understanding. Kubitschek names the stages of Janie's female quest: answering a call to change, crossing the threshold to adventure, facing trials, and returning to the community.[14] These narrative stages are also present in "***Flawless" in the way the video traces Beyoncé's girlhood disappointment, trials in marriage and self-image, and interaction with new ideas and communities.[15] Beyoncé also bears a resemblance to Hurston's Janie, as a Southern-born, light-skinned Black woman trying to determine her place in the world, "to the horizon and back."[16]

"***Flawless" also presents its own quest to the horizon: for Beyoncé to break from the identity binary she created for herself on earlier projects, namely the 2008 double album *I Am ... Sasha Fierce*. The project contrasted good-girl Beyoncé who sang ballads with the ass-shaking, sexualized alter ego Sasha Fierce.[17] Although interpreted in music criticism as a sort of sonic Jekyll and Hyde, the Beyoncé–Sasha Fierce dichotomy is also a problematic replication of the madonna-whore construction, as demure Beyoncé sings ballads like "Ave Maria" and the Sasha Fierce persona emerges for tracks like "Sweet Dreams" and "Single Ladies."[18] Yet, on "***Flawless," Beyoncé strives for a breakdown of the dichotomy of sexuality and sainthood, as well as the related dichotomies of independence and marriage and creativity and commercialization.

Beyoncé's mixed-media approach to the lived quest of feminism emerges across the prelude, three unique verses, and outro of "***Flawless." Critically, there is no traditional chorus that links them, allowing her to frame a personal journey that is disjointed and nonlinear. Aligned with this unorthodox sonic structure, the lyrics and visual narrative of "Flawless" allow Beyoncé to move beyond a flat name-dropping of feminism. This essay will consider these sonic, visual, and lyrical dimensions in conversation. The discussion will analyze how "***Flawless" progresses in five narrative stages of Beyoncé exploring the quest of contemporary womanhood: first as a girlhood competition in the video prelude, then as a video game of trials in the first verse, a sampling of a famous feminist in the second verse, her own personal proclamation in the final verse, and paradoxical foreclosure of feminist possibility in the outro.

THE VIDEO PRELUDE: STAGING BLACK GIRLHOOD

"***Flawless" begins with an introductory visual prelude, a clip of Beyoncé's own childhood performance on the popular talent competition *Star Search*. The video clip underscores Beyoncé's history of performing femininity as a young child in talent competitions and later feminism for the world, using the stage as a metaphor to frame her continuously public relationship to this ideology. By opening with this real footage, "***Flawless" constructs a narrative of Beyoncé's journey from child pageant star to feminist icon. The first sound is that of applause, as a television set flickers on, showing a clip from Beyoncé's 1993 appearance on the popular talent competition. *Star Search* host Ed McMahon, iconic US comedian and game-show announcer, appears in a tuxedo against a colorful background introducing Beyoncé and her childhood singing group, Girl's Tyme, the precursor to Destiny's Child.

McMahon's short introduction, "Welcome Beyoncé, Latavia, Nina, Nicki, Kelly, and Ashley," full of butchered pronunciations, also indicates the tenuous place of Black girlhood on the national stage. The struggle for self-articulation thus becomes the thematic framing of "***Flawless," via McMahon's own gaze as a white man mediating the performance of six Black girls from Houston. Perhaps the competition is not even between singing groups, but rather the embattled perception of Black girlhood to the outside world. There is a flickering frame of the girls taking the stage, with the words "Challenger Girl's Tyme" at the bottom, but then the television set dissolves without further explanation.

It is tempting to read this video prelude as a flashback. Susannah Radstone has noted how the flashback traditionally serves as a form of cinematic memory, constructing "dissolves between a film narrative's present and its past."[19] In this case, however, viewers must consider whose memory is being constructed, what Radstone calls the video's "spectator position."[20] Is this Beyoncé's personal girlhood recollection of a *Star Search* attempt or a reminder of our own role in her making? Indeed, the clip is not a fictionalized restaging of her childhood or even a private home video. Rather, Beyoncé embeds real footage that aired on national television. By using such a clip, "***Flawless" merges Beyoncé's own narrative interiority with cultural memory. Thus, the video clip is closer to what Jaimie Baron terms "a found audiovisual document" placed inside a larger film that appropriates and mobilizes it for new contexts.[21] By staging this ambiguity of perspective and memory, Beyoncé has placed "***Flawless" within her own complex history of gendered performance politics and our own history of watching them. This tension between interiority and performance continues throughout the song.

The *Star Search* clip, while not part of the radio single version of "***Flawless," should not be dismissed as ornamental or another nod to her girl-group roots. In fact, it proves that reducing a mixed media offering such as "***Flawless" to a three-and-a-half minute audio clip limits its aesthetic impact. The introductory visual prelude remains critical in framing the rest of "***Flawless," as Girl's Tyme is battling against an all-white male group named Skeleton Crew. By starting "***Flawless" with a competition and her own girlhood, Beyoncé postulates performance, competition, and the male gaze as dangerous shapers of women's identity making. A drastic visual shift follows the colorful *Star Search*, as it dissipates into black-and-white footage of the now adult Beyoncé posed against a graffiti-covered wall. The change in cinematography signals a darker, more contemplative mood. Beyoncé is adorned in a plaid shirt and jean cutoff shorts rather than the glamorous pageant pristine outfit of *Star Search*, as the bass line of "***Flawless" begins.

THE SOUND: BEYOND THE POP SONG AND RESPECTABILITY

Beyoncé's foremost aesthetic break with her previous musical efforts comes in the structure of "***Flawless." Throughout her canon of memorable singles, Beyoncé has reliably adhered to a predictable verse-chorus format. From the pulsating wails of "got me so crazy in love" to the bouncy, didactic "if you liked it then you should have put a ring on it," Beyoncé's songs have lyrically and sonically been structured around a catchy, message-oriented chorus; in the case of the former two, messages that reinforced heteronormativity and traditional gender roles. On "***Flawless" she departs from the familiar pop-song formula. The structure of "***Flawless" can be mapped as follows:

Intro: *Star Search* clip 1
Verse 1: Beyoncé, "Bow Down"
Verse 2: Chimamanda Adichie sample
Verse 3: Beyoncé, "Flawless"
Outro: *Star Search* clip 2

Critically, there is no chorus that links these verses, allowing her to suggest a personal journey full of twists and turns. Just as the song does not follow the typical format for a pop song, neither does the narrative tell an easy story of feminist awakening. There are girlhood recollections of pageant gowns, grown-up marital frustrations, and a dialogue with a feminist theorist, melded with lingering attachments to materialism and capitalist frameworks. The lyrical musings often lack cohesion and structure, reinforced by the song's refusal to follow the verse-chorus musical format listeners are trained to expect. This disruption of pop-song structure is one that continues on the rest of the *Beyoncé* (2013) visual project and emerges again on *Lemonade* (2016) in tracks like "Formation." Yet "***Flawless" is the only song in her existing repertoire where the chorus is missing entirely.

The sonic disorienting goes beyond the song's structure: on the first verse, she dismantles both the familiar sounds of a pop song and the respectability politics that often marred her earlier work. Odd, electronic trap sounds precede the first verse of "***Flawless." Some critics have likened it to the background music in a 1990s Nintendo video game like *Donkey Kong*.[22] An autotuned backing vocal and the video-game-like bass line provide what Emily Lordi terms "parodied masculine swagger."[23] The autotuned backing vocalist gives a shout-out to Beyoncé's hometown of Houston: "I'm out that H-town / coming coming down I'm coming down / drippin' candy on the ground." Regina Bradley suggests the video game allusion refers to the "game" of hip hop and popular music but possibly also implicitly alludes to Houston rapper Lil' Flip's first single, "Game Over."[24] Bradley also insists that the intimation of Houston hip hop is a digression from Beyoncé's usual references to private airplanes and limousines and sends her back to her southern roots.[25] This sonic home-going mirrors the *Star Search* clip's construction of memory; both provide examples of understanding childhood experiences from inside her identity as a married adult woman.[26]

The first verse also addresses gender roles and the public perception of Beyoncé as a complacent wife:

> I took some time to live my life
> But don't think I'm just his little wife
> Don't get it twisted, get it twisted
> This my shit, bow down bitches
> Bow down bitches, bow bow down bitches
> Bow down bitches, bow bow down bitches

Here, she refers to her mogul husband Jay-Z, the perpetual elephant in the room whenever critics debate her "fit" with feminism.[27] She assures listeners she took time to be her own person before the marriage and remains that way inside it. Indeed, when placed in context with this comment on gender roles, "bow down, bitches," becomes more complicated than it might at first appear. Perhaps Beyoncé is expressing anger at the gendered stereotypes imposed on her and dispensing with expectations of the feminine, "polite" language is her way of breaking outside them. The most problematic part of "bow down, bitches" is not the cursing but the reinforcing of competition *between* women implied in the line, which directly contradicts the *Star Search* clip of girl power. Whereas *Lemonade* would later forcefully evoke Black women's collective power, Beyoncé seems, on this verse of "***Flawless," to distrust those around her—demonstrated by this lyric and her lack of interaction with other women at the party sequence in the video.

In December 2013, after "***Flawless" was released, Beyoncé finally clarified the first verse's "bow down bitches" refrain in an interview with iTunes Radio: "The reason I put out 'Bow Down' is because I woke up, I went into the studio, I had a chant in my head, it was aggressive, it was angry, it wasn't the Beyoncé that wakes up every morning. It was the Beyoncé that was angry. It was the Beyoncé that felt the need to defend herself. . . . But I feel strong. And anyone that says, 'Oh that is disrespectful,' just imagine the person that hates you. Imagine a person that doesn't believe in you."[28] The project of reclaiming a word associated with misogyny is certainly not Beyoncé's invention but a standard of the hip hop feminist tradition. Durham, Cooper, and Morris write of how respectability politics has long been utilized as a means of racial control, "surveillance, control, and repression—largely directed toward black women . . . and [they] ultimately succeed in reinscribing dominant systems of power."[29] By producing sounds and language outside respectability, Beyoncé momentarily steps outside these systems of power. She sounds Black women's anger in a catchphrase adorned with the same swagger male rappers often utilize without any kind of policing. Just recall husband Jay-Z's famous deployment of the same word in 2004's "99 Problems" ("but a bitch ain't one") or Kanye West's usage in 2013's "Famous" about Taylor Swift ("I made that bitch famous"). By demanding that her audience "bow down, bitches," she frees herself from these gendered codes of expression while also manipulating them to signify the power and respect she commands as a global superstar.

Yet Beyoncé's smooth, pristine vocals in the first verse seem to contradict the lyrical pushbacks against respectability and the jaunty otherness of the video-game bass line. The video-game bass line continues as Beyoncé sings in the first verse, "I know when you were little girls / You dreamt of being in my world / Don't forget it, don't forget it / Respect that, bow down bitches." There is a tension between the legato phrasing of her vocals and the grit of the lyrics and staccato interruption of the bass line. On the words "bow down," she flirts with what has been defined as a gravel timbre in gospel music, but it never reaches the same consistency; here it never persists for more than a word.³⁰ Beyoncé's otherwise simple vocal delivery leaves something to be desired, as she wraps the harshness of the lyrics and strangeness of the backing motif in a presentation as smooth and neat as one of her pageant gowns. For Beyoncé, even patriarchal entrapment is glamorous, a contradiction that remains throughout "***Flawless" and undermines the possibility of radical transformation.

Visually, this section of "***Flawless" also does little to disrupt patriarchal expectations, merely shifting the gaze from Ed McMahon to spectators at a dance party. In both the *Star Search* clip and this opening verse, Beyoncé has presented herself as an object, first of the pageant-competition gaze and then as merely a mogul's wife, much as Janie feels forced to think of herself as "the bell cow" in Hurston's text as the wife of rich Joe Starks.³¹ Cinematically, Beyoncé remains an object, not (yet) a subject, as she moves from the pageant girl to the mogul's wife. As Beyoncé recites this initial verse, we see her dancing at a party, running her hands all over her body as other crowd members stare. This can be interpreted as both a claim over her own body and also a paradoxical acceptance of the gaze around it.

The rest of "***Flawless," lyrically, sonically, and visually becomes a quest to break outside these respectable constructions of the pageant girl and the mogul's little wife. Emily Lordi suggests that this perhaps imperfect self-actualizing is Beyoncé "claiming the right to her own rich, complex imaginative landscape, one that can be just as dark and twisted and fantastic as any male artist's, in addition to being fun and self-critical and maternal and sad."³² By allowing the video-game bass line to continue throughout this verse, "***Flawless," suggests Beyoncé's quest of feminist identity formation is full of further trials, tasks, and errors.

THE SAMPLE: FEMINIST INVOCATIONS

In various iterations of the literary quest narrative, the seeker often encounters a sage figure who offers wisdom for the journey—from wise old men such as Tiresias in Homer's *Odyssey* to spiritual guides like Baby Suggs in Toni Morrison's *Beloved* or sexual mentor Shug Avery in Alice Walker's *The Color Purple*. In "***Flawless" a similar figure emerges inside the song, Nigerian feminist writer Chimamanda Ngozi Adichie. The second verse of "***Flawless" samples clips from Adichie's 2013 TEDx talk "We Should All

Be Feminists."³³ The choice of someone like Adichie is more radical than an iconic US feminist like Gloria Steinem or even Beyoncé's friend, Michelle Obama.³⁴ Adichie is Black, non-American, and deeply invested in intersectional politics.³⁵ In *Black Noise*, Tricia Rose defined sampling as "an invocation" of another's voice to help musicians express what they want to say, but perhaps what they alone cannot.³⁶ In "***Flawless" Adichie functions as that voice, a sort of feminist guide for Beyoncé. Janell Hobson has noted that Beyoncé's association with feminism, no matter how disputed or controversial, is positive, because it might lead young girls to more radical feminism outside commercial boundaries.³⁷ Indeed, Beyoncé allows Adichie an entire verse, and the TEDx speech provides the feminist backbone of "***Flawless."

The sudden appearance of Chimamanda Ngozi Adichie is both Beyoncé's interaction with a sage figure more versed in feminist thought and another sonic disruption. Typically, in a pop song, listeners would be expecting another Beyoncé verse, especially if they believe "bow down bitches" will return as the chorus. Suddenly, the motion of the party dancers slows down, and another voice enters the track. Adichie does not appear on screen, but her TEDx talk "We Should All Be Feminists" plays in the background of the party, forming the second verse of "***Flawless":

> We teach girls to shrink themselves. To make themselves smaller. We say to girls, "You can have ambition, but not too much." You should aim to be successful, but not too successful, otherwise you will threaten the man. Because I am female, I am expected to aspire to marriage. I am expected to make my life choices always keeping in mind that marriage is the most important. Now marriage can be a source of joy and love and mutual support. But why do we teach girls to aspire to marriage and we don't teach boys the same? We raise girls to see each other as competitors. Not for jobs or for accomplishments, which I think can be a good thing, but for the attention of men. We teach girls that they cannot be sexual beings in the way that boys are. Feminist: the person who believes in the social, political, and economic equality of the sexes.

This sample is also, itself, remixed: a one-minute splicing of clips from Adichie's nearly thirty-minute TEDx talk. In *The Archive Effect*, Jaimie Baron writes of how indexical images and archived sound recordings are "seductive in their seeming transparent textuality."³⁸ Beyoncé, in her reproduction of Adichie, exposes her listeners to an unreal and incomplete Adichie that is of Beyoncé's own manipulation. Her condensing of Adichie is also a reframing with several ideas: (1) the limitations of traditional gender roles, (2) the simultaneous benefits and entrapments of marriage, (3) a support of economic competition between girls, and (4) the definition of feminism as equality. The choice of these clips parallels Beyoncé's earlier allusion to competition in the *Star Search* prelude. Adichie's statements that girls cannot be sexual beings—at least not "in the way that boys are"—also mirrors Beyoncé's pushbacks on respectability throughout "****Flawless" and the *Beyoncé* visual project more broadly (and arguably even more viscerally in "Rocket" and "Partition").

These clips also divest Adichie's talk, and feminism, of its radical possibilities. Several fundamental and foundational aspects of Adichie's talk are silenced by this construction of the sample. Despite Adichie stating at the outset of the TEDx talk that she wanted to focus on why gender matters in Nigeria, that diasporic framework disappears in the more general fragments Beyoncé chooses.[39] Elsewhere in "We Should All Be Feminists," Adichie also highlights the longstanding dangers for women who claim feminism outside America: "a Nigerian woman told me that feminism was not our culture, that feminism wasn't Africa ... that word 'feminist' is so heavy with baggage, negative baggage. You hate men, you hate bras, you hate African culture."[40] Adichie then cites several examples of how identifying as a feminist can produce profound professional, personal, and even physical danger for women. Meanwhile, throughout "***Flawless," Beyoncé transmutes feminism into her own brand of affirmation without acknowledging the dangers or the incomplete work of feminist activism. To use Adichie's words, "gender as it functions today is a grave injustice. We should all be angry."[41] Finally, Adichie's complete speech also discusses constructions of masculinity in tandem with feminism, statements that do not appear in the "****Flawless" sample. Beyoncé's omission leaves a missing link between ideology and global power structures, the inextricable relationship between feminism and any dismantling of patriarchy. By curating such a simplistic sample of feminism, Beyoncé also avoids addressing how Adichie's words relate to her own life as a Black woman. The lack of explicit intersectionality distances Beyoncé in "***Flawless" from both the real world of gender inequality and the possibility of true interiority.

Indeed, performance seems to triumph over interiority when looking across media between the audio of Adichie and the sensual visuals of

Beyoncé. There is no diegetic relationship between Adichie speaking and Beyoncé at the party. Adichie is physically absent; the sample of the TEDx talk is muddled and distorted, like a voice over a loudspeaker. The video remains focused on Beyoncé at the dance party, still in the cutoffs dancing against an exposed brick backdrop. The motion of the bodies has slowed down, however, producing a series of suspended, contemplative shots. Beyoncé is also faintly singing in the background, but this voice does not emanate from the Beyoncé on screen, instead floating in the background. The bass line also never disappears and is just as high in the mix as Adichie's voice. This crowding of sounds and lack of cohesion across media obscures how Beyoncé herself relates to Adichie's proclamations, how she will be changed by this lecture in feminist thought.

THE LABEL: FLAWLESS, NOT FEMINIST

Critically, Beyoncé never speaks the word *feminist* in "***Flawless" but rather finds her own label of affirmation in the song's titular word. The third verse of "***Flawless" superficially presents Beyoncé transformed by Adichie, a newfound grown woman. After Adichie finishes speaking, Beyoncé takes back the vocal lead and the camera refocuses on her body at the party as a diegetic relationship between sound and video returns:

> You wake up, flawless
> Post up, flawless
> Ridin' round in it, flawless
> Flossin' on that, flawless
> This diamond, flawless
> My diamond, flawless
> This rock, flawless
> My rock, flawless
> I woke up like this
> I woke up like this
> We flawless, ladies tell 'em.

The vocals in this section have lost their pristine quality and are notably rougher and grittier, eschewing the pretty legato phrasing of the first verse. The short, abrupt phrases are half spoken, with a lot more bite. The use of "ladies" and "we" in this verse indicates a renewed faith in the collective power of women, as supporters rather than competitors. This lyrical section also contains "I woke up like this," a refrain that appears to champion the beauty of women in their natural state.[42] After the release of "***Flawless," "I woke up like this" overtook "bow down bitches" as the song's most memorable catchphrase, perhaps owing to its ambiguity. Although perhaps literally an homage to natural beauty, "I woke up like this" is also a sarcastic jab at the amount of time and money that modern beauty standards require. "***Flawless" surely presents a less glamorous Beyoncé, but her cutoffs, plaid shirt, chopped hair, and perfectly etched eyeliner are no less curated than the pageantry of *Star Search*.

Some critics have suggested Beyoncé infused the word *flawless* (traditionally meaning "without blemishes") with a dose of feminism. Parul Sehgal wrote in the *New York Times* that Beyoncé transformed *flawless* into a feminist declaration of "proud, almost swaggering femininity."[43] Segal continues: "It's perhaps our first untroubled word for human beauty, free of the whiff of sexism that clings to many others. It doesn't denote marriageability (like 'nubile') or beauty born of fragility ('comely'). Unlike its close relations 'fair,' 'perfect' and 'immaculate,' it carries no overt religious connotations. . . . It recasts beauty as something that can be *done*, pulled off—not just possessed."[44] In the years following the song's release, *flawless* worked its way into the US cultural vernacular, capacious enough to anoint the perfect drag brow on Instagram and intellectual feats such as Michelle Obama's speech at the 2016 Democratic National Convention. Yet an emphasis on achievements of the body and mind still does little to illuminate gendered power structures.

Beyoncé's flawless feminism is also linked to materialism. The references to "diamond" and "rock" indicate opulent wealth as an ingredient of her confidence on this final verse. "Rock" perhaps also doubles for "Roc Nation," the media empire belonging to husband Jay-Z. Writing of Beyoncé, bell hooks cautions us against this mercantile feminism: "Her vision of feminism does not call for an end to patriarchal domination. . . . In [her] world of fantasy feminism, there are no class, sex, and race hierarchies that breakdown simplified categories of women and men."[45] Beyoncé's flawless feminism may also be at odds with the feminism of Adichie. When asked about her appearance in "***Flawless," Adichie appreciated the exposure, but insisted that, "still, her type of feminism is not mine . . . as it is the kind that, at the same time, gives quite a lot of space to the necessity of men . . . did he hurt me, do I forgive him, did he put a ring on my finger?"[46] In the final few frames of "***Flawless," a confident, cursing Beyoncé in a fervent dance sequence shakes her ring finger at the camera, permanently binding her transformation inside a capitalist framework.

The last section of the verse further defines flawless through a disavowal of respectability: "Say I look so good tonight / God damn, God damn." In addition to these lyrical slides outside respectability, Beyoncé's voice also cracks on the last "goddamn," again breaking outside standards of the respectable, pretty pageant vocals of the early part of "***Flawless." The cursing, coupled with rougher vocals and confidant gyrating in this closing section, allows Beyoncé to assume the hypermasculine swagger of male rappers who use the same linguistic and visual gestures to signify their own power. In this final verse of "***Flawless," Beyoncé has moved beyond the roles of pageant girl and wife, but her grown womanhood and feminism remain dependent, even in their parody, on traditional notions of masculinity.

The outro of "***Flawless" is another clip from *Star Search*. The video returns to *Star Search* in full pageant color and the voice of Ed McMahon announcing the all-white male group Skeleton receiving four stars and Girl's Tyme receiving only three. The last sound is of *Star Search*'s own fading music, ushering Beyoncé and the girls offstage. With this outro, does Beyoncé end "***Flawless" foreclosing feminist possibilities? Or is she perhaps giving her audience a reality check, that no matter one's own internal feminist journey, white male patriarchy is still present? The last shot of the video is the flicker of a television set turning off. Significantly, it is a traditional cathode-ray tube television with a dramatic dissolving of the screen rather than a modern device. This choice of technology emphasizes the screen as a manufactured and performative space, raising the question of whether something so consumable as "***Flawless" could represent any authentic personal transformation.

THE AESTHETIC: BEYONCÉ'S FORMAL QUEST

The contradictory ending of "***Flawless" provides a way of reading Beyoncé's feminism at large as a diverse set of overlapping and at times paradoxical practices, a journey, not a label. Yet it is her ambiguous relationship to that word *feminist*, to literally stand before it without clarification, that forces us to draw the borders tighter around an ideology she will not explicitly define.

Regardless, the musical and visual dimensions of "***Flawless" allow a more careful reading of these contradictions and how they are embedded in her sonic and performance practices, not merely her lyrical references.

Beyoncé leaves viewers with ambiguities in not only feminist theory, but the outcome and purpose of her quest. The endpoint of the quest narrative is often the protagonist's return to the community, such as Janie's arrival back in Eatonville to serve as a "provocative storyteller" for the community.[47] At the end of "***Flawless," Beyoncé's chosen community is unclear. By avoiding intersectional language, Beyoncé misses an opportunity to create the Black feminist sisterhood that emerges so powerfully on *Lemonade*. One might argue her community is women of all races who look to her as a source of inspiration and empowerment. Yet "***Flawless" ends without any notion of women's collective power—instead, defaulting to the triumph of men.

The most striking quest in "***Flawless" is not intellectual or personal, but aesthetic. Most important, "***Flawless" was a means for Beyoncé to disentangle herself from the commercial pop single and chart a new artistic identity distinct from that of her forebears. On previous albums, live performances, and even her film roles, Beyoncé proved a careful student of previous Black women performers. From her fiery turn as Etta James in *Cadillac Records* and performance of the glamorous lead *Dreamgirl* to her 2008 Grammy tribute to Tina Turner, Beyoncé has always sought artistic inspiration in the biography and aesthetic of other iconic Black women.

Many draw a lineage from Turner to Beyoncé, but Beyoncé's legs do not tremble with quite the same ecstasy. Others have likened her militaristic dance practice to Janet Jackson's, yet her idea of control has always seemed more contained, first through her father's management of her career and then inside her marriage to Jay-Z. Another parallel is Diana Ross, the original girl-group lead, but Beyoncé alternates Ross's high glamour with Houston hip hop. Her vocals often imitate Whitney Houston, but they never quite reach Houston's register-scaling majesty. Considering these Black female performance lineages, Beyoncé can be understood as millennial pop pastiche: a recapitulation of other iconic Black women performers. There is a feminist practice in how she recycles and reiterates Black women's musical legacies, no matter how successfully she does it. As demonstrated through "***Flawless" and later on *Lemonade*, Beyoncé also understands sampling as a powerful form of quotation, a way to engage with other Black feminist thinkers and artists. Finding her place among this constellation of greats has always been the larger project of her career.

In the 2012 documentary *Life Is But a Dream*, Beyoncé herself claimed a rather different ancestor figure: civil-rights icon Nina Simone. Beyoncé noted she admired the way Simone was known for "the voice and the art."[48] This statement, at the time, seemed puzzling. In addition to sounding nothing like Simone's jagged contralto, Beyoncé naively placed Simone in a simpler moment for the music industry. She continues in the documentary: "But you didn't get brainwashed by her [Simone's] day-to-day life and what her child is wearing and who she's dating and, you know, all the things that really—it's not your business, you know? And it shouldn't influence the way you listen."[49] Simone did not live in Beyoncé's TMZ era of social media surveillance, but her activism inside the civil-rights movement undoubtedly affected her opportunities as a recording artist and how people responded to her music. Indeed, Simone's unapologetically radical music forced her to flee the United States and live in exile in Europe for the last three decades of her life.

Nevertheless, Nina Simone became a fitting muse for the way in which Beyoncé politicized and transformed her art on *Beyoncé* (2013) and *Lemonade* (2016). Simone, known for her searing protest anthems like "Mississippi Goddamn," once told a reporter that "An artist's duty, as far as I'm concerned, is to reflect the times. I think that is true of painters, sculptors, poets, musicians. . . . We will shape and mold this country or it will not be molded and shaped at all anymore. So I don't think you have a choice. How can you be an artist and not reflect the times? That to me is the definition of an artist."[50] Beyoncé's choice on "***Flawless" to engage with gender inequality—albeit through the conduit of Adichie—is the first step of moving toward Simone's artistic ideal, a quest that continues and expands on *Lemonade*. Nina Simone's influence also lingers over Beyoncé's visual albums in another significant way. Simone was known for her genre-defying musical mosaic that inserted classical fugues into soulful protest anthems, pioneering a type of collage Beyoncé emulated by fusing media in addition to genres. For both Beyoncé and Nina Simone, the collage was celebratory and angry, personal and political, local and global.

Through the use of mixed media, Beyoncé finally conjures her own aesthetic and artistic identity distinctive from her various foremothers.

Lemonade arguably presents a more cohesive integration of the visual, sonic, and political through its lush Louisiana setting, gothic antebellum imagery, and homages to Julie Dash's *Daughters of the Dust*. The album's political references are more deliberate and militant through the haunting appearance of Sybrina Fulton, Lezley McSpadden, and Gwen Carr, mothers of Trayvon Martin, Eric Garner, and Michael Brown, respectively. *Lemonade* also features an explicit engagement with Black feminist consciousness through another diasporic feminist writer, Warsan Shire. These visual and political dimensions are purposely integrated with the Black, Southern sounds she provides on "Formation" and "Daddy Lessons." But the 2013 visual album *Beyoncé*, particularly "***Flawless," formed the beginning of Queen Bey's mixed-media experiment and political realignment.

"***Flawless" also signaled that music critics must construct the dialectic between pop music and feminism in new ways to account for both the rise of these mixed-media formats and the unique visual economy of Black feminism. Through its dramatic shifts from ball gowns to cutoffs, from parties to the stage, from Ed McMahon to Chimamanda Adichie, "***Flawless" visually inhabits and then dispenses with the white male gaze while detailing the ways respectability politics can interfere with Black women's individuality, creativity, and self-confidence. Contemporary criticism must find a way to engage Black women's varied cultural production as a language through which feminism not merely is reflected but also can be created, debated, sounded, and staged. Regardless, the question of Beyoncé and feminism goes far beyond "bow down bitches."

JULIA COX is a doctoral student in the Department of English at the University of Pennsylvania.

NOTES

1. The MTV Video Vanguard Award, also known as the Michael Jackson Video Vanguard Award, is the lifetime achievement award at the annual MTV Video Music Awards. The award recognizes career-long contributions to the music video form. Past recipients include David Bowie, Michael Jackson, Janet Jackson, U2, and Britney Spears.

2. Beyoncé's 2016 Super Bowl performance, the first live performance of "Formation," featured all Black women dancers in dress and hairstyles inspired by the Black Panthers. Later that spring, the video footage that accompanied "Forward" on the *Lemonade* (2016) visual album included appearances by Sybrina Fulton, Lezley McSpadden, and Gwen Carr, mothers of Trayvon Martin, Eric Garner, and Michael Brown, respectively.

3. See, for example, the lyric of Destiny's Child's "Independent Women Part I" (2001), which postulates self-reliance and links independence to material accumulation: "If I wanted the watch you're wearin' / I'll buy it / The house I live in / I've bought it / The car I'm driving / I've bought it / I depend on me."

4. Beyoncé explained to *Vogue*: "But I guess I am a modern-day feminist. I do believe in equality, and that we have a ways to go and it's something that's pushed aside and something that we have been conditioned to accept. But I'm happily married. I love my husband." For more, see Jo Ellison, "Mrs. Carter UnCut," *Vogue*, April 4, 2013, http://www.vogue.co.uk/article/beyonce-interview-may-vogue.

5. Aisha Harris, "Who Run the World? Husbands?," *Slate*, February 2, 2014, https://slate.com/culture/2013/02/beyonces-mrs-carter-show-world-tour-why-use-her-married-name.html.

6. The media responses miss how Black women rappers like Lil' Kim and Missy Elliot had been reclaiming the term *bitch* from its misogynistic usage since the mid-1990s on tracks such as "Checkin' for You" and "She's a Bitch." Beyoncé's use of the term in "Bow Down" participates in this reclaiming and reversing of traditional power dynamics.

7. Rae Alexandra, "Beyoncé's 'Bow Down': How Did She Go So Wrong?," *San Francisco Weekly*, March 22, 2013, https://www.sfweekly.com/shookdown/2013/03/22/Beyonces-bow-down-how-did-she-go-so-wrong.

8. The term "politics of respectability" originated in Higginbotham's *Righteous Discontent*. Higginbotham argued that morality was a tool of self-determination for Black women in the early twentieth century and has continued to guide Black cultural politics. Incidentally, the apolitical pop artist Britney Spears released a hit single titled "Work Bitch" in 2013 that seemed to escape such scrutiny.

9. Emily Lordi, "Beyoncé's Boundaries," *NewBlackMan*, December 18, 2013, https://www.newblackmaninexile.net/2013/12/beyonces-boundaries-by-emily-j-lordi.html.

10. When I say "mixed media" I mean that the visual component of "***Flawless" is not merely an addendum or promotional tool as in the traditional music video but an integral part of the song's message and aesthetic posture. Beyoncé's choice to make her entire album a visual one further stages the visual and sonic in a deliberate call-and-response. In a 2013 interview with iTunes Radio, Beyoncé noted the video element "reflects the picture in my mind when I recorded the songs . . . a story or a fantasy." For more, see Beyoncé Knowles, interview with iTunes Radio, *iTunes*, December 16, 2013.

11. Durham et al., "The Stage Hip-Hop Feminism Built," 726.
12. Ibid., 723.
13. Ibid., 724.
14. Kubitschek, "Tuh the Horizon."
15. Ibid., 110.
16. Hurston, *Their Eyes Were Watching God*, 229.
17. Maya Francis, "From Janet to Beyoncé: Why It Matters When Black Women Sing about Sexuality," *XOJane*. Accessed January 13, 2014, but no longer available.
18. Ibid.
19. Radstone, "Cinema and Memory," 326.
20. Ibid.
21. Baron, *Archive Effect*, 7–8.
22. Regina Bradley, "I Been On (Ratchet): Conceptualizing a Sonic Ratchet Aesthetic in Beyoncé's 'Bow Down,'" *Red Clay Scholar*, March 19, 2013, http://redclayscholar.blogspot.com/2013/03/i-been-on-ratchet-conceptualizing-sonic.html.
23. Lordi, "Beyoncé's Boundaries."
24. Bradley, "I Been On (Ratchet)."
25. Ibid.
26. Beyoncé's fascination with Southern sounds continues on *Lemonade* in the county rock anthem "Daddy Lessons."
27. In their reviews of *Beyoncé*, music critics have been quick to contextualize the album's statements on sexuality inside her marriage. See Lily Rothman, "A Sobering Look at Beyoncé and Jay Z's Sexy Song 'Drunk in Love,'" *Time*, January 30, 2014, http://time.com/3090/drunk-in-love-controversy/.
28. Beyoncé Knowles, interview with iTunes Radio, *iTunes*, December 16, 2013.
29. Durham et al., "The Stage Hip-Hop Feminism Built," 725.
30. Legg, "Taxonomy of Musical Gesture."
31. Hurston, *Their Eyes Were Watching God*, 51.
32. Lordi, "Beyoncé's Boundaries."
33. Chimamanda Ngozi Adichie, "We Should All Be Feminists," talk presented at TEDxEuston, London, December 1, 2012, https://www.ted.com/talks/chimamanda_ngozi_adichie_we_should_all_be_feminists.
34. For a longer analysis of the relationship between Beyoncé and Michelle Obama, see Griffin, "At Last?" Griffin argues the entertainment mogul and First Lady paradoxically represent both the progress of race relations in the United States and lingering inequality.
35. At the time of the December 2013 release of "***Flawless," Adichie had not yet expressed her controversial views on trans women. In a March 2017 interview with Britain's Channel 4, Adichie came under fire for saying the experiences of trans women and cis women could not be equated. For more, see Noah Michelson, "Author Chimamanda Ngozi Adichie under Fire for Comments about Trans

Women," March 11, 2017, http://www.huffingtonpost.com/entry/chimamanda-ngozi-adichie-transgender-women-feminism_us_58c40324e4b0d1078ca7180b.

36. Rose, *Black Noise*, 79.

37. Janell Hobson, "Policing Feminism: Regulating the Bodies of Women of Color," *Ms. Magazine*, June 30, 2013, http://msmagazine.com/blog/2013/06/10/policing-feminism-regulating-the-bodies-of-women-of-color/.

38. Baron, *Archive Effect*, 3.

39. Adichie, "We Should All Be Feminists."

40. Ibid.

41. Ibid.

42. "#IWokeuplikethis," was named one of the most popular hashtags on social media in 2014, most frequently as a caption of self-affirmation on Instagram and Twitter photos. Yet, the lyric has also received a backlash from some feminist writers, who claim it puts too much emphasis on women's physical appearance. For more, see Alyx Gorman, "'I Woke Up Like This' Is the Biggest Beauty Myth of All," *Elle*, May 12, 2014, http://www.elle.com/beauty/makeup-skin-care/tips/a12718/wokeuplikethis-biggest-beauty-myth/.

43. Parul Sehgal, "How 'Flawless' Became a Feminist Declaration," *New York Times*, March 24, 2015, https://www.nytimes.com/2015/03/29/magazine/how-flawless-became-a-feminist-declaration.html?_r=0.

44. Sehgal, "How 'Flawless' Became a Feminist Declaration."

45. bell hooks, "Moving Beyond Pain," May 9, 2016, http://www.bellhooksinstitute.com/blog/2016/5/9/moving-beyond-pain.

46. Aimée Kiene, "Ngozi Adichie: Beyoncé's Feminism Isn't My Feminism," *Volkskrant*, October 7, 2016, http://www.volkskrant.nl/boeken/ngozi-adichie-beyonce-s-feminism-isn-t-my-feminism~a4390684/.

47. Kubitschek, "Tuh the Horizon," 113.

48. *Beyoncé: Life Is But a Dream*, dir. Ed Burke, Ilan Y. Benatar, and Beyoncé Knowles (HBO and Parkwood Entertainment, 2013).

49. Ibid.

50. Nina Simone, quoted in *What Happened, Miss Simone?*, dir. Liz Garbus (Netflix, 2015).

BIBLIOGRAPHY

Baron, Jaimie. *The Archive Effect: Found Footage and the Audiovisual Experience of History*. New York: Routledge, 2014.

Durham, Aisha, Brittney C. Cooper, and Susana M. Morris. "The Stage Hip-Hop Feminism Built: A New Directions Essay." *Signs* 38, no. 3 (2013): 721–37.

Griffin, Farah Jasmine. "At Last . . .?: Michelle Obama, Beyoncé, Race & History." *Daedalus* 140, no. 1 (2011): 131–41.

Higginbotham, Evelyn Brooks. *Righteous Discontent: The Women's Movement in the Black Baptist Church, 1880–1920.* Cambridge, MA: Harvard University Press, 1993.

Hurston, Zora Neale. *Their Eyes Were Watching God.* New York: Harper Perennial Modern Classics, 2006.

Kubitschek, Missy. "Tuh the Horizon and Back: The Female Quest." *Black American Literature Forum* 17, no. 3 (1983): 109–15.

Legg, Andrew. "A Taxonomy of Musical Gesture in African American Gospel Music." *Popular Music* 29 (2010): 103–29.

Radstone, Susannah. "Cinema and Memory." In *Memory: Histories, Theories, Debates.* Edited by Susannah Radstone and Bill Schwartz, 325–42. New York: Fordham University Press, 2010.

Rose, Tricia. *Black Noise: Rap Music and Black Culture in Contemporary America.* Hanover, NH: Wesleyan University Press, 1994.

FIVE

"At Last a Dream That I Can Call My Own"

Beyoncé and the Performance of Stardom in Dreamgirls *and* Cadillac Records

JAAP KOOIJMAN

In the 2013 HBO television documentary *Beyoncé: Life Is But a Dream*, credited as "A Film by Beyoncé Knowles," Beyoncé discusses the difficulties of being a celebrity whose actions are continuously scrutinized by the tabloid press and social media. She refers to soul singer Nina Simone to argue that the current emphasis on the private lives of celebrities overshadows their artistic accomplishments: "When Nina Simone put out music, you loved her voice. That's what she wanted you to love, that was her instrument. But you didn't get brainwashed by her day-to-day life, and what her child is wearing, and who she is dating, and you know all the things, they're really—it's not your business, you know. And it shouldn't influence the way you listen to the voice and the art, but it does."[1] As Beyoncé speaks the words "the voice and the art," her own singing voice is heard in the background, implying a connection between the legendary singer and herself. The scene suggests that, like Nina Simone, Beyoncé wants to be recognized for her vocal artistry, but also that, unlike Simone, she cannot escape the reality of being a celebrity. Even her own documentary, as HBO promises, "provides raw, unprecedented access to the private entertainment icon," including Beyoncé's revelation that she has suffered a miscarriage and her eventual joy in becoming a mother, in addition to presenting her as an accomplished artist and celebrated superstar.[2]

By comparing herself to Nina Simone (rather than to more obvious predecessors like Diana Ross, Janet Jackson, or Madonna), Beyoncé highlights the distinction between the pop star as commodity and the "authentic" artist, a common trope in debates on pop music and specifically in discussions of African American female superstardom.[3] Referring to Beyoncé's performance of "At Last" at President Barack Obama's first inauguration in 2009 (which will be discussed in more detail later in this chapter), Olusanya Osha places Beyoncé in juxtaposition with Etta James, whose 1960 soulful rendition of "At Last" is often considered the song's decisive version. In Osha's words, James is "an artist in the old fashioned sense of the word" whose "true grit" made her a "warrior of blood and fire," whereas Beyoncé is an "industrial commodity," "a manufactured mannequin of a record industry that churned out stars like assembly line products," concluding that "when an industry-manufactured pop star tries to understand [Etta James's] depth, it seems not only superficial but perhaps also somewhat insulting."[4] Such a rigid dichotomy between the glamorous yet "superficial" superstar and the "authentic" struggling soul singer is reminiscent of the criticism that Diana Ross received three decades earlier when she starred as Billie Holiday in the biopic *Lady Sings the Blues*,[5] when critics argued that a "superficial" pop singer like Ross could never fully embody the "depth" and "tragedy" of a legendary jazz and blues singer like Holiday.[6]

In the films *Dreamgirls* and *Cadillac Records*,[7] Beyoncé embodies both sides of this dichotomy, starring respectively as the "industrial commodity" Deena Jones, a fictional character based on the real-life Diana Ross, and as the "warrior of blood and fire," Etta James. Taken together, the two roles can be perceived as part of Beyoncé's "total star text" (Richard Dyer's concept) or "metanarrative of stardom" (Andrew Goodwin's concept), meaning that her on-screen performances in these films are not just contained within the diegetic film world, but are also part of Beyoncé's off-screen star image; in other words, her performances as Deena Jones and Etta James also inform our perception of the "real" Beyoncé as star.[8] One could argue that her music videos are far more relevant to the discussion of Beyoncé's star image than the feature films in which she starred. For example, none of the essays in *The Beyoncé Effect*, an academic essay collection entirely devoted to Beyoncé, discusses her relatively extensive set of seven Hollywood films.[9] Beyoncé's Hollywood films, however, and in particular *Dreamgirls* and *Cadillac Records* (released respectively three and five years after the launch of her solo career), established and reaffirmed Beyoncé as a major star beyond just being a recording artist, like her predecessors Diana Ross with *Lady Sings the Blues* and *Mahogany*, Whitney Houston with *The Bodyguard* and *Waiting to Exhale*, and Janet Jackson with *Poetic Justice*.[10]

This chapter focuses explicitly on the period from *Dreamgirls* of 2006 to *Beyoncé: Life Is But a Dream* of 2013, thus before the release of the single "Formation" and the visual album *Lemonade* in 2016. As Inna Arzumanova has argued, Beyoncé's recent work "refuses to be open-source," meaning that for white audiences its specific Black content is more difficult to access, and thus less easily appropriated, in contrast to her earlier work that fits the logic of the white-dominated culture industry, in which Black female artists need "to invoke an otherness, and to then—urgently—make that otherness palatable, legible, and, of course, commercially portable."[11] This need to cater for white audiences is perhaps especially true of Hollywood, an industry that historically has provided few opportunities for African American actresses and often—at least until recently—relied on pop music stars for Black female leads.[12] By now, Beyoncé has become a multifaceted superstar who combines her global commercial success with potentially progressive political messages about racial and gender equality. This chapter focuses on specific moments in Beyoncé's metanarrative of stardom to explore how the connection to the star images of some of her predecessors—Diana Ross and Etta James in particular—has enabled the solidification of Beyoncé as a superstar and the incorporation of different traditions of Black female stardom within her star image. In addition, I will discuss how Beyoncé's performances have positioned her predecessors in the past, for example, through her appropriation of James's signature song "At Last" that she has used on various occasions, both as a call for racial and gender equality and as a reaffirmation of her own stardom. Unlike her Black female predecessors, Beyoncé has been able to merge the glamour of Diana Ross, the soulful authenticity of Etta James, and—eventually—the politics of Nina Simone into one commercially successful yet empowering image of a Black female star.

BEYONCÉ AS DEENA JONES/DIANA ROSS

In her essay on Diana Ross, Nicole Fleetwood discusses how, with her performances, Ross has recognized and paid tribute to the "many black female entertainers who came before her [and] paved her way to stardom," including

Billie Holiday and Josephine Baker.[13] Beyoncé has done the same, paying tribute to Tina Turner and Janet Jackson and, like Ross, to Josephine Baker on stage and to Etta James on screen. Her role as Deena Jones in *Dreamgirls* explicitly connected Beyoncé to the star image of Ross. In interviews, Beyoncé has told that, during the filming, she felt that she "was channeling Diana Ross," that she had watched Ross's films *Lady Sings the Blues* and *Mahogany* "over and over again," and that she had a "shrine" of Ross photographs in her trailer during the shooting.[14] These homages to their famous predecessors enabled both Diana Ross and Beyoncé to claim their own place within the tradition of Black female superstardom.

Although without explicitly referring to the original Motown girl group, *Dreamgirls* obviously was based on the story of Diana Ross and the Supremes, as was widely recognized by the press when the musical premiered in 1981.[15] The 2006 film version made the connection even more obvious by mimicking the style of the Supremes through close copies of their album covers and television performances. *Dreamgirls* presents the story of how the 1960s African American girl group the Dreams/the Supremes become a success after the original lead singer Effie White/Florence Ballard was replaced by the less talented but more commercially appealing Deena Jones/Diana Ross, all based on the business decision of their manager Curtis Taylor Jr./Berry Gordy Jr., founder and president of the record company Rainbow Records/Motown. While in real life Florence Ballard died from cardiac arrest at the age of thirty-two, eight years after she had left the Supremes, in the musical Effie rejoins Deena and the Dreams for one grand final performance. The musical's main premise is that "authentic" Black culture, as embodied by Effie, is betrayed for commercial reasons, with the aim to be attractive to a mainstream white audience. However, as I have discussed in more detail elsewhere, the betrayal of Effie—and thus of "authentic" Black culture that is sold out—functions merely as a melodramatic backstory to the excessive spectacle that the musical presents. Conforming to musical genre conventions, *Dreamgirls* ends up celebrating the glitter and glamour of Deena and the Dreams instead.[16]

Almost immediately after its successful premiere on Broadway in 1981, gossip about a possible film adaptation arose, focusing on the question of who would play Deena. During the late 1980s, the tabloid press reported that Whitney Houston was considering the role, much to the chagrin of

Diana Ross who, as a *Vanity Fair* cover story claimed, was "obsessed" with Houston's recent success and "snapped" when confronted with the rumor: "I heard that isn't true! I heard Whitney *wasn't* doing the movie!"[17] Eventually Houston would star with Kevin Costner in *The Bodyguard*, which, tellingly, was initially conceived in the late 1970s as a star vehicle for Ross with first Steve McQueen, then Ryan O'Neal.[18] Two decades later, Beyoncé as Deena seemed an obvious choice, for her star image already had been connected to Ross's. When still with Destiny's Child, Beyoncé was rumored to "do a Diana Ross" and leave her group for a solo career, which she eventually did in 2003. The cover of *Vibe* magazine (February 2001) features Destiny's Child mimicking a 1968 publicity photograph of the Supremes with Beyoncé pictured as Ross. The article inside the magazine discusses how Destiny's Child is merely a "vehicle designed to promote Beyoncé's inevitable solo career," thereby foreshadowing the trajectory Beyoncé would follow.[19] The fictional story of Deena Jones and the Dreams not only resembled that of Diana Ross and the Supremes but also the one of Beyoncé and Destiny's Child to such an extent that Beyoncé publicly wondered whether "audiences would think [*Dreamgirls*] is my life story."[20] Beyoncé's candidacy as the obvious choice for the role of Deena, like Whitney Houston before her, reconfirmed Beyoncé's status as the next Black female superstar.

In the unauthorized biography *Becoming Beyoncé: The Untold Story*, J. Randy Taraborrelli suggests that Beyoncé should have followed Whitney Houston's example by not accepting the role of Deena. The musical's two showstoppers—the torch songs "And I'm Telling You I'm Not Going" and "I'm Changing"—are both sung by Effie, not Deena, making her the star of the show. Although the film version included an additional torch song, "Listen," as a solo performance for Deena, showcasing that Beyoncé has the same vocal prowess as Jennifer Hudson (who plays Effie), Taraborrelli concludes that Beyoncé was deemed to be outshone by her costar.[21] Whether Beyoncé made a smart career move by starring in *Dreamgirls* is open to debate and hardly relevant for the present study. Far more significant, what is missing in Taraborrelli's assessment is that the film adaptation of *Dreamgirls*, even more than the original stage musical, emphasizes the glamorous spectacle of the Dreams with excessive performances and costumes, presenting Deena—and thus in extension Beyoncé—as the celebrated superstar. Mirroring the real-life metanarratives of stardom of both Diana Ross and Beyoncé, *Dreamgirls* shows how Deena launches her solo career by leaving the Dreams to star in a Hollywood movie. As Kimberly Springer has pointed out, her portrayal of Deena connects Beyoncé explicitly to the diva status of Diana Ross: "It is hard to separate legend from fact, but with her ascension from group singer to lead singer in the Supremes and the larger than life aspects of her film roles it is nearly impossible to tell the difference between Diana and the Diva."[22] *Dreamgirls* is significant for solidifying Beyoncé's status as a glamorous Black female superstar in the tradition of Ross, in which Diana, Deena, Beyoncé, and "the Diva" indeed are indistinguishable. Not without irony, Taraborrelli ends up implying the same by using "Dreamgirl" as title for the sixth part of his *Becoming Beyoncé* biography, which covers Beyoncé's career from the 2005 filming of *Dreamgirls* to the 2013 documentary *Beyoncé: Life Is But a Dream*.[23]

In the promotion of *Dreamgirls*, Beyoncé was presented as the film's most important female star. "Eddie Murphy, Jamie Foxx, and Beyoncé star in *Dreamgirls*, the year's most spectacular movie musical!" the cover of *Vanity Fair* magazine (January 2007) reads, featuring a photo of the three stars; unmentioned by name, Jennifer Hudson is pictured on the other, not immediately visible, half of the foldout cover. Although Hudson is included in the special episode of *The Oprah Winfrey Show* (November 20, 2006) devoted to *Dreamgirls*, the show's highlight is Beyoncé's live performance of "Listen." Perhaps most telling is the annual BET (Black Entertainment Television) Awards show, broadcast on June 26, 2007. The show opens with Hudson singing the signature song of *Dreamgirls*, "And I'm Telling You I'm Not Going," and halfway through she is joined by Jennifer Holliday, who played Effie in the original 1981 Broadway musical. At the end of their performance, the camera singles out two applauding audience members in close-up: Diana Ross and Beyoncé. Later on in the show, Beyoncé performs her latest single, "Get Me Bodied," emphasizing that she has moved beyond *Dreamgirls* as a solo superstar. That night, Hudson wins the awards for Best Actress and Best Newcomer, Beyoncé for Best Female R&B/Pop Artist, and Diana Ross the Lifetime Achievement Award. Yet, just as *Dreamgirls* uses Effie as a melodramatic backstory to its glamorous spectacle, the television show reduced both Effies—Jennifer Holliday and Jennifer Hudson—to their signature fictional roles while celebrating Beyoncé and Diana Ross as, respectively, the "new" and "old" Black female superstar who embodies the success and fame of the "Dream" beyond the fictional world of *Dreamgirls*.

BEYONCÉ AS ETTA JAMES

On November 14, 2008, one month before *Cadillac Records* premiered, the *New York Times* published a short interview with Beyoncé, aptly titled "Pop Music's Dreamgirl Awakens Her Earthy Side." Recognizing Beyoncé's performance in *Dreamgirls* as her "most significant previous role," interviewer Alan Light highlights the convincing way the "wholesome, good-girl" Beyoncé portrays Etta James, the latter described as "the heroin-addicted daughter of a prostitute, whose powerhouse sound conveyed a lifetime of heartbreak and defiance in songs like 'At Last' and 'Tell Mama,' incorporating a blues attitude into a wide range of pop genres."[24] This move of "pop music's Dreamgirl" appropriating not only the songbook of the "authentic" Black performer, but also her troubled "real" life—and through that move "awakens [Beyoncé's] earthy side"—mirrors the trajectory traveled by the "original Dreamgirl," Diana Ross, three decades earlier. As Donald Bogle has argued about Ross starring as Billie Holiday in the 1972 biopic *Lady Sings the Blues*: "Diana, the princess of ghetto chic, a girl-woman known as *plastic*, goes through Billie's horrors and humiliations. By doing so, she acquires a certain depth and relevance."[25] Although seemingly challenging the rigid distinction between the manufactured superstar and the authentic blues singer, the "depth and relevance" that enables a triumphant performance by Ross also reduces Billie Holiday to a one-dimensional figure of tragedy, which becomes blatantly apparent in the movie's final scene. While Ross as Holiday performs "God Bless The Child" at New York's Carnegie Hall, newspaper headlines announcing Holiday's drug-ridden downfall and subsequent death are superimposed on the screen, an irony recognized by James Baldwin: "The film fades out with a triumphant Billie who is already, however, unluckily, dead, singing on-stage before a delirious audience."[26] The triumph of new-movie-star Diana Ross is at the cost of Billie Holiday's tragedy, or, as the *New York Times* tellingly titled its short interview with Ross about her successful film debut: "Diana Ross: Lady *Doesn't* Sing the Blues."[27]

Beyoncé's portrayal of Etta James seems to function in a similar way, though to a lesser extent. Whereas *Lady Sings the Blues* is a biopic about Billie Holiday, making Diana Ross the film's main attraction, Beyoncé merely plays a supporting role in the story about the 1950s record company Chess. Moreover, Holiday is a legendary performer, whereas Etta James—quite undeservedly—remains relatively unknown (although Beyoncé's portrayal did renew interest in James's career). In his pivotal book *Brown Sugar: Over One Hundred Years of America's Black Female Superstars*, Donald Bogle discusses Billie Holiday at length but mentions Etta James just once as one of those young Black female singers of the early 1960s who had "individual style and presence" and "were getting their records played on radio and going on tour" yet often "lacked drive" or "became disillusioned after having been exploited by record companies and shifty promoters"—only to be followed by a full chapter on the success of Motown's Diana Ross and the Supremes.[28] In their respective books *She Bop* and *Just My Soul Responding*, both Lucy O'Brien and Brian Ward merely mention "blues belter" Etta James (twice) in passing, whereas Billie Holiday (in O'Brien's book) and Diana Ross and the Supremes (in both books) are featured quite extensively.[29]

It is intriguing that, to Diana Ross, not Billie Holiday but Etta James was "the One, my original inspiration," her teenage idol whom she had mimicked by singing along to her records in front of the mirror. As Ross, just six years younger than James, recalls in her autobiography: "The shock of hearing a voice so powerful and so deep made me marvel that one young woman could claim such power and passion!"[30] In 1987, Ross invited Etta James as guest on her television special *Red Hot Rhythm & Blues*,[31] in addition to Little Richard and rapper LL Cool J. Intended to trace the roots of African American music, the show ended up instead, as the *New York Times* critically noted, celebrating Ross as "a superstar, solidly established, still vibrant and glamorous, ... who is capable of reducing Etta James and Little Richard to fuzzy supporting acts."[32] James recognized that she was expected to perform as an authentic yet stereotypical blues singer and felt uncomfortable in the role she was assigned. As she reported, Diana Ross "had me doing some red-hot blues number like I was a red-hot mama from the twenties. I was wearing this ridiculous heavy gown, singing while walking down a flight of stairs, feeling like a fool. I had to do the damn song over four dozen times, and finally I flat refused. Diana wasn't happy. But I didn't budge. Don't get me wrong; I appreciate Miss Ross holding me in high regard. I admire her. But I hate all that phony-baloney Hollywood crap and would rather stay home eating popcorn."[33] Although that "some red-hot blues number" was actually her signature song "At Last," James correctly pointed out how the television special used her as a relic from the past that was placed in juxtaposition with the glamorous superstar. Yet James's account also repeats the depiction of herself as a (no less stereotypical) down-to-earth blues singer who—literally—is not at home in the superficial "phony-baloney" world of superstardom.

Dreamgirls and *Cadillac Records* are similar in recounting the story of an independent record label from the 1950s and 1960 that aims to sell African American music to a larger mainstream audience. Whereas *Dreamgirls* depicts the Black-owned Rainbow Records (read Motown) as a company that betrays Black pop culture for white commercial success, *Cadillac Records* represents Chess and its white owner Leonard Chess (Adrien Brody) as enabling the success of African American artists such as Muddy Waters (Jeffrey Wright), Chuck Berry (Mos Def), and Etta James (Beyoncé).[34] In stark contrast to Deena Jones, who embodies the artificial whitewashed pop music sold to mainstream audiences, the film portrays Etta James as a performer of authentic Black culture that is preserved and given a public platform though the help of a white man. All three of the Etta James songs that Beyoncé performs in full version—"At Last," "All I Could Do Is Cry," and "I'd Rather Go Blind"—are used to comment on her relationship with Leonard Chess, who is shown closely watching all these performances. "At Last" and "All I Could Do Is Cry" highlight their romantic yet complicated relationship, suggesting that Etta is expressing her own personal joy and heartache through her songs. One James song performed by Beyoncé—"Trust in Me"—is not part of the film's diegesis but is heard during the scene in which Leonard finds and saves Etta after her heroin overdose. Like *Lady Sings the Blues*, which features a similar drug scene, the film not only emphasizes the tormented life of the authentic soul singer (Etta/Billie) but also showcases the dramatic acting quality of its performing star (Beyoncé/Diana Ross). The end of *Cadillac Records* has Leonard telling Etta that he is leaving her and the company because his work is done: "You know, back when I started this, nobody let a Black man do what I got done. Doors weren't open. Now they are." As Leonard is leaving, Etta sings "I'd Rather Go Blind." In this way, their personal relationship is used to represent the film's main premise of a white record company (as embodied by Leonard) discovering and preserving "authentic" Black culture (as embodied by Etta) without critically questioning such a white-savior narrative.

Although merely a supporting role, the portrayal of Etta James enabled Beyoncé to incorporate the authenticity that James embodied within her own star image and metanarrative of stardom, both through the dramatic performance of James's troubled life and through the appropriation of her songbook of soul classics, "At Last" in particular. Moreover, in a maneuver reminiscent of the promotion of *Dreamgirls*, Beyoncé was presented as the film's biggest star: she was its most important female character as well as one of its coproducers. Her performance of "At Last" makes up a large part of the film's trailer and was released as the first single of the sound track, with the film segment used as the single's music video. By starring as Etta James, Beyoncé—like Diana Ross starring as Billie Holiday in *Lady Sings the Blues*—"acquire[d] a certain depth and relevance," as her performance connected her to the struggles of Black female performers in a white-dominated entertainment industry and to the authenticity of a musical tradition rooted in soul and rhythm and blues, in stark contrast to her own glamorous celebrity. In addition, and again like Diana Ross, this reconnection to "authentic" African American culture as well as her demonstration of dramatic acting solidified Beyoncé's status as a serious actress and celebrated superstar.

I AM . . . ETTA JAMES/BEYONCÉ

Although most people will surely associate "At Last" with Etta James, who recorded her version in 1960, the original version of the song was performed two decades earlier by the Glenn Miller Orchestra in the Hollywood musical *Orchestra Wives*, sung as a romantic ballad by the white couple John Payne and Lynn Bari.[35] Whereas now, in retrospect, Etta James's version of "At Last" tends to be considered authentic soul, back in the 1960s, soul was still seen as a crossover genre, a commercial adaptation of jazz and rhythm and blues. James's manager Leonard Chess was thrilled by the success of "At Last," as James remembered: "He went up and down the halls of Chess announcing, 'Etta's crossed over! Etta's crossed over!' I still didn't know exactly what that meant, except that maybe more white people were listening to me."[36] Not until later did the song become part of the sound track of the civil-rights movement. Recorded before Dr. Martin Luther King Jr.'s famous "I Have a Dream" speech of 1963, the song's title and lyrics—"I found a dream that I could speak to, a dream that I can call my own"—evoke Dr. King's message: "Free at last! Free at last! Thank God Almighty, we are free at last." From that association, Etta James's "At Last" has moved from a love song celebrating individual romance to an anthem expressing the promise of collective progress that racial equality can be accomplished.

The first time Beyoncé performed "At Last" on television was at the fifth annual Fashion Rocks concert, produced by publisher Condé Nast and CBS television, on September 5, 2008. Taped live at New York's Radio City Music Hall, the performance was introduced by actress Charlize Theron: "In music, as in fashion, there are passing fads and timeless classics. The next song is an enduring standard that has been performed by everyone from Glenn Miller to Stevie Wonder, but no one ever did it quite like one of the most soulful singers of all time, the eternally great Etta James. In the upcoming film *Cadillac Records*, the remarkable woman about to take the stage plays the role of Etta James and sings her songs with soul and style. Here to salute this everlasting legend, Beyoncé." After the introduction, the screen features black-and-white publicity photographs of James from the late 1950s shown consecutively. While the instrumental opening of "At Last" plays, Beyoncé's spoken voiceover can be heard: "Miss Etta James. A force of nature. Music's original bad girl, with your platinum hair, wild cat eyes, your Felliniesque sexuality and dangerous voice. A voice that could be raspy with hardness of pain and turn into silk on the drop of a dime. The master of jazz, blues, R&B, and rock 'n' roll, we celebrate your unapologetic boldness, your genius and innovation. Thank you, Etta James."

I quote these introductions at full length because they not only establish the stature of Etta James as the "eternally great [and] everlasting legend" with an audience that is most likely more familiar with the song than with the singer but also show how James is presented as the stereotypical authentic soul singer, the "original bad girl." As Emily Lordi has argued, "African Americans have historically been represented as 'naturally' gifted singers and dancers [and] female representation has been marked as a matter of the (sexualized) body rather than the reasoning mind."[37] James is literally described in terms of nature and the bodily, as "a force of nature" that is animalistic sexual and uncontrolled ("wild cat eyes" and "dangerous"), tormented ("raspy with hardness of pain"), and overall "unapologetic."

After Beyoncé's spoken tribute, the last black-and-white photograph of Etta James's face dissolves into a live color close-up of Beyoncé's face, dressed up as James in a 1950s-style yellow dress and wearing a platinum blonde, short-cropped wig. Throughout her performance of "At Last," the camera remains focused on Beyoncé, with the exception of one long shot of the violinists on stage, emphasizing the song's status as a classic. Unbeknownst (yet) to the viewers, the real Etta James is in the audience, sitting on the front row. At the end of the song, Beyoncé walks over to her and says, "If it wasn't for you, Etta James, artists like me would not have this opportunity. God bless you. Everyone give it up for Etta James. I love you." James's presence legitimizes Beyoncé's impersonation by not only giving it a stamp of approval but also enabling the promotion of the film to be presented as a tribute to a legendary singer who finally receives the recognition that she deserves. Whereas James's endorsement provides Beyoncé with authenticity as a soul singer, Beyoncé's performance reconfirms James's status as a soul legend to the larger mainstream audience.

Three months later, on December 8, 2008, Beyoncé performed "At Last" live on *The Ellen DeGeneres Show*. Broadcast three days after the premiere of *Cadillac Records*, the performance obviously is intended to tie in with the film. This time, however, Etta James is not mentioned at all. When host Ellen announces "one of the greatest performers in the world is back to sing a song from her new film *Cadillac Records*; please welcome the one and only Beyoncé," she is standing in front of two large photographs of Beyoncé's face taken from the photo shoot of her then latest solo compact disc *I Am . . . Sasha Fierce*, which was released one month earlier and does not include "At Last." Ellen is also holding the disc in her hands. Instead of impersonating Etta James in dress, Beyoncé wears an elegant olive-green evening gown and has her hair pulled back, befitting the song's classic style without explicitly referencing the 1950s. Although also promoting the film, the performance is above all a promotion of Beyoncé as "one of the greatest performers in the world" who successfully combines her recording career with being a movie star. Here "Etta" merges with "Deena," as the authentic soul singer and the manufactured pop star come together to form a diva superstar, much as Beyoncé's new album incorporated her sexually more provocative alter ego Sasha Fierce within her overall wholesome star image.[38] Etta James no longer needs to be mentioned; "At Last"—and all its possible connotations—has become part of Beyoncé's own songbook that does not require a reference to its past performer to be relevant.

SINGING THE DREAM

In their respective essays on Beyoncé, both Ellis Cashmore and Farah Jasmin Griffin start with Beyoncé's televised live performance of "At Last" at the Neighborhood Ball, part of the celebration of President Barack Obama's first inauguration on January 20, 2009. Cashmore uses the performance to emphasize his argument that Beyoncé is most of all a commodity that transcends race, viewing the song as an "ideological validation" of her commercial success: "The power of Beyoncé was in her living of the Dream, not just singing about it."[39] Farah Jasmin Griffin, in contrast, perceives Beyoncé's performance as an allegedly "post-racial" celebration of the collective promise and accomplishments that both Beyoncé and Obama—the African American superstar and the first Black president of the United States—embody, arguing that "the song signified the triumphant culmination of what had long been a rather one-sided romance between black Americans and their nation."[40] Although these two interpretations may seem contradictory, they are not mutually exclusive, for Beyoncé's star image includes both the notion of the Black female star as a commodity to be sold to a mainstream audience and a political symbol of African American achievement.

Broadcast live by ABC, Beyoncé's performance of "At Last" at the Neighborhood Ball had a double function. On the one hand, the performance was the romantic highlight of the inaugural festivities, harking back to the song's initial status as love song celebrating individual romance. Dressed in an elegant lavender satin evening gown, Beyoncé serenades the slow-waltzing presidential couple as they perform the opening dance. Intercut with shots of Beyoncé singing, the camera slowly circles around Barack and Michelle Obama, enhancing the sense of romantic intimacy. On the other hand, the performance expresses the promise that the collective ideal of racial equality could be achieved, recalling the song's acquired status as part of the civil-rights movement's sound track. Four decades after Dr. Martin Luther King Jr.'s "I Have a Dream" speech, the first Black presidential couple of the United States are dancing underneath the presidential seal to a song performed by America's biggest Black female pop star, singing, "At last a dream that I can call my own." Together, Beyoncé and the Obamas embody the possibility that "the dream" can be fulfilled, that racial discrimination and inequality can be overcome.

As mentioned in the introduction to this chapter, Beyoncé's performance of "At Last" received some criticism for appropriating a song that was so explicitly connected to Etta James. Even James herself allegedly said, "I'm gonna whup Beyoncé's ass," which was widely and eagerly quoted in the press, as her vernacular reconfirmed the preconceived reputation of her "unapologetic boldness" that Beyoncé had praised just three months earlier.[41] After also raising the question "why was Etta James not singing her own song that night?" Emily Lordi finds the answer in the "symbolic shift from the older to the younger guard," with Aretha Franklin's performance of "America (My Country, 'Tis of Thee)" during the day representing the 1960s civil-rights movement and Beyoncé's performance of "At Last" in the evening representing the fulfillment of its promise. If "At Last" had been sung by Etta James, the song could not have functioned in the same way: "The political valence Beyoncé brought to 'At Last'—what may best be termed black political *relief*—was safer than the meaning the song might have acquired if sung by the famously hard-living survivor of the sixties and seventies."[42] Etta James could be perceived as belonging to the past, whereas Beyoncé symbolized not only what had been accomplished but also the promise of a postracial future.

During her 2009–10 *I Am . . . World Tour*, Beyoncé performed both "At Last" and "Listen" in a segment devoted to her movie career, wearing a silver sequined evening dress that emphasized the segment's glamorous Hollywood theme, in contrast with the more revealing costumes she wears throughout the concert. When Beyoncé sings "At Last," the screen behind her shows black-and-white archival news footage from the civil-rights movement, including the 1963 March on Washington when Dr. Martin Luther King Jr. gave his "I Have a Dream" speech, intercut with images from *Cadillac Records*, also in black-and-white, of her singing "At Last." Almost at the end of the song, when Beyoncé sings the lines "you smile, you smile," a close-up—in full color—of President Obama at the inauguration ceremony is shown, intercut with images, also in full color, of Beyoncé's Neighborhood Ball performance and the slow-waltzing Obamas. This movement from black-and-white to full color highlights the historical significance of Obama's election, with both Obama and Beyoncé embodying the collective achievement of the civil-rights movement. "At Last," however, also celebrates Beyoncé's success as Black female superstar by emphasizing her connection to the Obama presidency and her Hollywood movie career as well.

"At Last" acquired an additional layer of meaning when Beyoncé performed the song at the Sound of Change benefit concert in London on June 1, 2013, produced by Chime for Change, "a global campaign" founded by the fashion company Gucci to "raise funds and awareness for girls' and women's empowerment."[43] This time dressed in her one of her typical stage costumes rather than an evening dress, Beyoncé first sings Sam Cooke's "A Change Is Gonna Come"—which, like "At Last," often is perceived as part of the civil-rights movement's sound track—yet without any visuals on the large video screen behind her. When Beyoncé starts singing "At Last," the screen opens with the quotation "no" from Rosa Parks, the famous civil-rights activist of the 1950s. Subsequently, the screen features a wide range of women who have been recognized for their historical significance, such as Amelia Earhart, Princess Diana, Mother Theresa, Aesha Mohammadzai, Hillary Clinton, Gloria Steinem, Barbra Streisand, and Marilyn Monroe, ending with a quotation from Oprah Winfrey: "You get in life what you have courage to ask for." Although Billie Holiday and Aretha Franklin are included, Etta James (and Diana Ross for that matter) remains unmentioned, emphasizing that "At Last" has become a signature Beyoncé song, which can combine the struggle of the civil-rights movement with a feminist movement for equal rights—simultaneously reinforcing Beyoncé's stardom.

On February 7, 2016, Beyoncé performed her new single, "Formation," during the Super Bowl halftime show, which was widely perceived as unapologetically Black because of its lyrics and its visual references to the Black Panthers and Malcolm X. The Super Bowl performance was similar to Beyoncé's inaugural performance of "At Last" in that both were done in front of a large national television audience and both referred to the 1960s civil-rights movement. Although "At Last" evoked Dr. Martin Luther King Jr.'s "I Have a Dream" speech, thereby celebrating the progress and promise that both President Obama and Beyoncé embodied, the references to the Black Panthers and Malcolm X in the performance of "Formation" emphasized that the end of racial discrimination and inequality had not been achieved and that Black militancy was still needed. And, when she performed "Formation" at a rally for Hillary Clinton four days before the 2016 presidential elections, Beyoncé explicitly connected the song to the promise of change:

"Eight years ago, I was so inspired to know that my nephew, a young Black child, could grow up knowing his dreams could be realized by witnessing a Black president in office. And now we have the opportunity to create more change. I want my daughter to grow up seeing a woman lead our country and know that her possibilities are limitless."[44] As in her performance of "At Last" at the Sound of Change benefit concert, Beyoncé connected the civil-rights movement to the feminist movement, presenting racial and gender equality as shared goals of progress. Moreover, by performing "Formation" at the Clinton rally, Beyoncé suggested that, in addition to its original protest against racial discrimination and inequality, "Formation" could be used in a way similar to "At Last"—as an affirmative political message of progress and change. One could easily argue that the Clinton-Beyoncé connection in 2016 did not embody the same progressive promise as the Obama-Beyoncé connection did in 2009, but that in fact it was just another celebrity endorsement (as Republican candidate Donald Trump claimed when calling Beyoncé's support of Clinton a form of cheating).[45] More relevant is how adaptable both "At Last" and "Formation" are in connecting the Beyoncé star performance to explicitly political causes, using the spectacle of her stardom to highlight the importance of racial and gender equality, while simultaneously celebrating her success, the dream that Beyoncé personifies.

AT LAST . . . LIFE IS BUT A DREAM

Beyoncé's Hollywood movie career is completely ignored in the 2013 HBO autobiographical documentary *Beyoncé: Life Is But a Dream*. The only implicit reference is an early scene, called "Independence" on the DVD edition, in which Beyoncé is singing "Listen" to herself in the limousine on the way to *The Oprah Winfrey Show* (to tape the *Dreamgirls* promotion episode of November 20, 2006). The song is used to explain Beyoncé's firing of her father-manager Mathew Knowles as a declaration of independence, much as her fictional character Deena in *Dreamgirls* stands up against the patriarchal control of her manager Curtis. Beyoncé's desire for professional and artistic independence is the film's main theme, which, as several reviewers have noted, seems more like an infomercial promoting the brand Beyoncé than like a documentary. Instead of "stripping away the veneer of stardom," as HBO had promised, the documentary combines private footage and personal testimonies with stage performances to strengthen Beyoncé's star image as creative artist and hardworking entertainer, as well as loving wife and mother, celebrating her superstardom.[46]

Also unmentioned, at least explicitly, is race. In his review of the documentary, Jody Rosen describes Beyoncé as "by far the 'blackest'—musically and aesthetically—of all the post-Madonna pop divas," concluding that "the privilege to ignore race altogether is a sign of Beyoncé's queenly status."[47] None of her Black diva predecessors (even Diana Ross and Etta James) are mentioned as important influences or inspirations, with the exception of the previously quoted reference to Nina Simone, yet Beyoncé emphasizes Simone's vocal artistry rather than her role in the Black Power movement of the late 1960s. In retrospect, after the release of the unapologetically Black single "Formation" and the visual album *Lemonade* in 2016, the reference to Simone makes much more sense. While in the documentary Beyoncé refers to Simone's artistry rather than her political activism, Nina Simone is significant because her unapologetic Blackness meant that her career in mainstream culture was over.[48] Beyoncé's predecessors—Diana Ross, Etta James, Tina Turner, Whitney Houston, Janet Jackson, and even Aretha Franklin—could not have made such a political move as Beyoncé did in 2016 without dire consequences, as the fate of Nina Simone shows.

Here it is relevant to note that both *Dreamgirls* and *Cadillac Records* are set in the past and that both comment on the workings of the culture industry of its time. Deena in *Dreamgirls* is under Black patriarchal control and can achieve commercial success only by betraying her Black culture. Not without irony, the film suggests that white Hollywood can offer Deena independence. In *Cadillac Records*, it is the white manager Leonard Chess who makes the commercial success of Etta James possible, reinforcing the Hollywood white-savior narrative. In both cases, the Black female singer has to balance being a commercial commodity (Deena) with remaining authentic (Etta). By performing as both Diana Ross and Etta James, Beyoncé not only paid tribute to her predecessors but also solved this Deena-versus-Etta dichotomy within her own star image. The recent "unapologetic Black" turn in Beyoncé's metanarrative of stardom shows that Beyoncé has successfully challenged the *Dreamgirls* narrative that African American female superstardom comes at the cost of betraying one's authentic Blackness, as well as the notion that authenticity is just to be found in the stereotypes of Black female tragedy as embodied by Billie Holiday or Etta James. Beyoncé's superstardom is built on the star images of her predecessors—the larger-than-life glamour of Diana Ross and the nitty-gritty soul of Etta James—making it possible to be political like Nina Simone without sacrificing her commercial success.

JAAP KOOIJMAN is Associate Professor of Media Studies and American Studies at the University of Amsterdam. He is author of *Fabricating the Absolute Fake: America in Contemporary Pop Culture* and editor, with Patricia Pisters and Wanda Strauven, of *Mind the Screen: Media Concepts according to Thomas Elsaesser*.

NOTES

1. Perhaps surprisingly, Beyoncé refers only to Nina Simone's role as a creative artist, thereby ignoring her role as political activist during the civil-rights movement of the 1960s (Feldstein, "I Don't Trust You Anymore").
2. "Beyoncé Documentary to Premiere in February," *Rolling Stone*, November 26, 2012, https://www.rollingstone.com/music/music-news/beyonce-documentary-to-premiere-in-february-247795/.
3. Brooks, "Let's Talk about Diana Ross"; Kooijman, "True Voice"; Lordi, *Black Resonance*, 8–9.
4. Osha, "Chess Queen," 213.
5. *Lady Sings the Blues*, dir. Sidney Furie (Paramount, 1972, 144 minutes).
6. Bogle, *Brown Sugar*, 181; Griffin, *If You Can't Be Free*, 59.
7. *Dreamgirls*, dir. Bill Condon (DreamWorks/Paramount, 2006, 130 minutes); *Cadillac Records*, dir. Darnell Martin (TriStar, 2008, 109 minutes).
8. Dyer, "A Star Is Born"; Goodwin, *Dancing*, 98–130.
9. Trier-Bieniek, *Beyoncé Effect*. In addition to *Dreamgirls* and *Cadillac Records*, Beyoncé has starred in the musical films *Carmen: A Hip Hopera*, dir. Robert Townsend (MTV, 2001, 88 minutes) and *The Fighting Temptations*, dir. Jonathan Lynn (MTV/Paramount, 2003, 123 minutes), the comedies *Austin Powers in Goldmember*, dir. Jay Roach (New Line, 2002, 95 minutes) and *The Pink Panther*, dir. Shawn Levy (Metro-Goldwyn-Mayer/Columbia, 2006, 93 minutes), and the thriller *Obsessed*, dir. Steve Shill (Screen Gems, 2009, 108 minutes).
10. *Mahogany*, dir. Berry Gordy (Paramount, 1975, 109 minutes); *The Bodyguard*, dir. Mick Jackson (Warner Brothers, 1992, 129 minutes); *Waiting to Exhale*, dir. Forest Whittaker (20th Century Fox, 1995, 124 minutes); *Poetic Justice*, dir. John Singleton (Columbia, 1993, 109 minutes).
11. Arzumanova, "Culture Industry," 423.

12. Alexander, "Fatal Beauties"; hooks, *Reel to Real*, 138; Kooijman, "Triumphant Black Pop Divas."

13. Fleetwood, *On Racial Icons*, 72–73.

14. James Ulmer, "After Conquering 'Chicago,' It's On to Motown," *New York Times*, September 10, 2006, http://www.nytimes.com/2006/09/10/movies/moviesspecial/10ulme.html; Beyoncé on *The Late Show with David Letterman*, aired December 19, 2006.

15. See, for example, Peter Bailey, "Dreams Come True on Broadway for Young Stars in Dreamgirls," *Ebony*, May 1982, 90–96; Gerri Hirshey, "Did the Dream (Girls) Come True?" *Esquire*, May 1984, 163–68; Frank Rich, "*Dreamgirls*, Michael Bennett's New Musical, Opens," *New York Times*, December 21, 1981, http://www.nytimes.com/1981/12/21/theater/stage-dreamgirls-michael-bennet-s-new-musical-opens.html.

16. Kooijman, "Whitewashing the Dreamgirls."

17. Lynn Hirschberg, "Diana Ross: The Re-Happening," *Vanity Fair*, March 1989, 140–45, 202–203, quotation on 144 (emphasis in original).

18. Kooijman, "True Voice," 310.

19. Angela Arambula, "Divas Live!" *Vibe*, February 2001, 74–81, quotation on 78.

20. Ulmer, "After Conquering 'Chicago.'"

21. Taraborrelli, *Becoming Beyoncé*, 349–56.

22. Springer, "Divas," 256.

23. Taraborrelli, *Becoming Beyoncé*, 347–421.

24. Alan Light, "Pop Music's Dreamgirl Awakens Her Earthy Side," *New York Times*, November 14, 2008, http://www.nytimes.com/2008/11/16/arts/music/16ligh.html.

25. Bogle, *Brown Sugar*, 181 (emphasis in original).

26. Baldwin, *Devil Finds Work*, 104. Although he was very critical of the film, Baldwin was impressed by the acting qualities of its star: "Diana Ross, clearly, respected Billie too much to try to imitate her. She picks up on Billie's beat, and, for the rest, uses herself, with a moving humility and candor, to create a portrait of a woman overwhelmed by the circumstances of her life."

27. Aljean Harmetz, "Diana Ross: Lady *Doesn't* Sing the Blues," *New York Times*, December 24, 1972, http://www.nytimes.com/1972/12/24/archives/diana-ross-lady-doesnt-sing-the-blues-diana-ross-lady-doesnt-sing.html, emphasis in original.

28. Bogle, *Brown Sugar*, 166.

29. O'Brien, *She Bop*, 83, 235; Ward, *Just My Soul*, 46, 167.

30. Ross, *Secrets*, 90.

31. Originally broadcast on ABC, May 20, 1987, 57 minutes.

32. John J. O'Connor, "'Diana Ross' on ABC," *New York Times*, May 20, 1987, http://www.nytimes.com/1987/05/20/arts/diana-ross-on-abc.html.

33. James and Ritz, *Rage to Survive*, 234.

34. In his discussion of *Dreamgirls*, Timothy Laurie convincingly shows how the film presents the Black entrepreneur as villain within a white entertainment industry (Laurie, "Come Get These Memories").

35. *Orchestra Wives*, dir. Archie Mayo (20th Century Fox, 1942, 98 minutes). The performance was initially intended for the Hollywood musical *Sun Valley Serenade*, dir. H. Bruce Humberstone (20th Century Fox, 1941, 86 minutes), which ended up featuring merely an instrumental version of the song. The vocals of Lynn Bari were dubbed by ghost singer Pat Friday.

36. James and Ritz, *Rage to Survive*, 103.

37. Lordi, *Black Resonance*, 9.

38. On Beyoncé's alter ego Sasha Fierce, see Avdeeff, "Beyoncé"; Cashmore, "Buying Beyoncé"; Durham, "Check On It."

39. Cashmore, "Buying Beyoncé," 136.

40. Griffin, "At Last?," 132.

41. Sean Michaels, "Etta James: I'm Gonna Whup Beyoncé's Ass," *Guardian*, February 6, 2009, https://www.theguardian.com/music/2009/feb/06/beyonce-etta-james-barack-obama.

42. Lordi, *Black Resonance*, 212–13 (emphasis in original).

43. See the Chime for Change press release, https://www.unicefusa.org/press/releases/gucci-launches-new-global-campaign-girls'-and-women's-empowerment/8212.

44. Daniel Kreps, "See Beyonce's Powerful Speech at Jay Z's Hillary Clinton Rally," *Rolling Stone*, November 4, 2016, http://www.rollingstone.com/music/news/see-beyonces-powerful-speech-at-jay-zs-clinton-rally-w448773.

45. Emma Stefansky, "Trump Says Clinton's Beyoncé and Jay Z Concert Is 'Almost Like Cheating,'" *Vanity Fair*, November 6, 2016, https://www.vanityfair.com/news/2016/11/trump-beyonce-jay-z-cheating.

46. HBO promotional website.

47. Jody Rosen, "Her Highness," *New Yorker*, February 20, 2013, http://www.newyorker.com/culture/culture-desk/her-highness.

48. Feldstein, "I Don't Trust You Anymore." See also the Netflix documentary *What Happened, Miss Simone?*, dir. Liz Garbus (Netflix, 2015, 101 minutes).

BIBLIOGRAPHY

Alexander, Karen. "Fatal Beauties: Black Women in Hollywood." In *Stardom*. Edited by Christine Gledhill, 45–54. New York: Routledge, 1991.

Arzumanova, Inna. "The Culture Industry and Beyoncé's Proprietary Blackness." *Celebrity Studies* 7, no. 3 (2016): 421–24.

Avdeeff, Melissa. "Beyoncé and Social Media: Authenticity and the Presentation of Self." In *The Beyoncé Effect: Essays on Sexuality, Race and Feminism*. Edited by Adrienne Trier-Bieniek, 109–23. Jefferson, NC: McFarland, 2016.

Baldwin, James. *The Devil Finds Work: An Essay.* New York: Dial, 1976.
Bogle, Donald. *Brown Sugar: Over One Hundred Years of America's Black Female Superstars.* 2nd ed. New York: Continuum, 2007.
Brooks, Daphne A. "Let's Talk about Diana Ross." In *Let's Talk about Love.* Edited by Carl Wilson, 205–20. New York: Bloomsbury, 2014.
Cashmore, Ellis. "Buying Beyoncé." *Celebrity Studies* 1, no. 2 (2010): 135–50.
Durham, Aisha S. "Check On It: Beyoncé, Southern Booty, and Black Feminism in Music Video." *Feminist Media Studies* 12, no. 1 (2012): 35–49.
Dyer, Richard. "A Star Is Born and the Construction of Authenticity." In *Stardom: Industry of Desire.* Edited by Christine Gledhill, 132–40. New York: Routledge, 1991.
Feldstein, Ruth. "'I Don't Trust You Anymore': Nina Simone, Culture, and Black Activism in the 1960s." *Journal of American History* 91, no. 4 (2005): 1349–79.
Fleetwood, Nicole R. *On Racial Icons: Blackness and the Public Imagination.* New Brunswick, NJ: Rutgers University Press, 2015.
Goodwin, Andrew. *Dancing in the Distraction Factory: Music Television and Popular Culture.* Minneapolis: University of Minnesota Press, 1992.
Griffin, Farah Jasmine. "At Last . . . ?: Michelle Obama, Beyoncé, Race & History." *Daedalus* 140, no. 1 (2011): 131–41.
———. *If You Can't Be Free, Be a Mystery: In Search of Billie Holiday.* New York: Ballantine, 2001.
hooks, bell. *Reel to Real: Race, Class and Sex at the Movies.* New York: Routledge, 2009.
James, Etta, and David Ritz. *Rage to Survive: The Etta James Story.* New ed. New York: Da Capo, 2003.
Kooijman, Jaap. "Triumphant Black Pop Divas on the Wide Screen: *Lady Sings the Blues* and *Tina: What's Love Got to Do with It.*" In *Popular Music and Film.* Edited by Ian Inglis, 178–92. London: Wallflower, 2003.
———. "The True Voice of Whitney Houston: Commodification, Authenticity, and African American Superstardom." *Celebrity Studies* 5, no. 3 (2014): 305–20.
———. "Whitewashing the Dreamgirls: Beyoncé, Diana Ross and the Commodification of Blackness." In *Revisiting Star Studies: Cultures, Themes and Methods.* Edited by Sabrina Yu and Guy Austin, 105–24. Edinburgh: Edinburgh University Press, 2017.
Laurie, Timothy. "Come Get These Memories: Gender, History and Racial Uplift in Bill Condon's *Dreamgirls.*" *Social Identities* 18, no. 5 (2012): 537–53.
Lordi, Emily J. *Black Resonance: Iconic Women Singers and African American Literature.* New Brunswick, NJ: Rutgers University Press, 2013.
O'Brien, Lucy. *She Bop: The Definitive History of Women in Rock, Pop and Soul.* New York: Penguin, 1995.
Osha, Olusanya. "Chess Queen Etta James (1938–2012)." *Journal of International Women's Studies* 13, no. 3 (2012): 211–14.

Ross, Diana. *Secrets of a Sparrow: Memoirs.* New York: Villard, 1993.
Springer, Kimberly. "Divas, Evil Black Bitches, and Bitter Black Women: African American Women in Postfeminist and Post-Civil-Rights Popular Culture." In *Interrogating Postfeminism: Gender and the Politics of Culture.* Edited by Yvonne Tasker and Diane Negra, 249–76. Durham, NC: Duke University Press, 2007.
Taraborrelli, J. Randy. *Becoming Beyoncé: The Untold Story.* New York: Grand Central, 2015.
Trier-Bieniek, Adrienne, ed. *The Beyoncé Effect: Essays on Sexuality, Race and Feminism.* Jefferson, NC: McFarland, 2016.
Ward, Brian. *Just My Soul Responding: Rhythm and Blues, Black Consciousness, and Race Relations.* Berkeley: University of California Press, 1998.

SIX

For the Texas Bama Femme

A Black Queer Femme-inist Reading of Beyoncé's "Sorry"

OMISE'EKE NATASHA TINSLEY

For Black Southern women, Beyoncé's *Lemonade* serves up a special deliciousness: homegrown, hip-switching, cornrowed celebration of flawless Southern femininities. "Beyoncé is country as cornbread. As bamafied as okra and stewed tomatoes, watermelon with salt, grits, and gravy. She is sweet as honeysuckle nectar, as hot as the chow-chow that goes on your greens. Numberless debates after the release of her hotly anticipated visual album *Lemonade*, one thing is strikingly, abundantly clear: Beyoncé is black, and Southern, down to her very core," Terryn Hall says in praise.[1] In a year when news about Black women in Texas—Beyoncé's home state, where I currently reside—included Sandra Bland's death in police custody, a Black girl's beating by a police officer at a pool party, and a report documenting Black women's disproportionate maternal mortality, *Lemonade*'s images of the South as somewhere Black women survive, resist, remember, and slay reminded us of our power. "When black women see that, we see ourselves," Hall continues. "When we see her on porches that look like those of our grandmothers, we rejoice."[2]

Now, for those of us who are queer Black women living in the South, *Lemonade* offers another kind of celebration. Sydney Gore hails *Lemonade* as "A Love Letter from Beyoncé to Black Women," and Hall tellingly compares it to Alice Walker's story of Black women's queer Southern love, *The Color Purple*.[3] "The love between Celie and the women in her life is the same thick love that Beyoncé shows to her tribe of women in this film," she writes.[4] Unlike *The Color Purple*, *Lemonade* has no explicit lesbian plot—but its story of fierce, not-sorry, no-men-allowed love between Black Southern women is queer in another way, "queer in the sense of... loving your own kind when your kind was supposed to cease to exist."[5] Composing a Black women's love story in iconography that privileges images of Black Southern womanness over the white, urban, assigned-male-at-birth imagery that signifies queerness in the dominant national imaginary, *Lemonade* visualizes what Gayatri Gopinath calls the *queer region*. She explains: "Shifting our critical lens away from the gay male public cultures of the global city, such as Mumbai, Delhi, London, or New York, to nonmetropolitan locations that are just as saturated by global processes although they may appear 'purely local,' allows us to foreground those spaces and bodies that are elided within dominant narratives of global gayness."[6]

Whereas dominant scripts privilege gender-nonconforming folk as queer representatives, queer regionalism opens space to highlight the gender and sexual complexity not only of women but of *femmes*—that is, those of us who perform a "lesbian or queer gender marked by a highly stylized and aestheticized" femininity, in the words of blogger Sublimefemme.[7] Gopinath adds, "These 'other' sexual cultures may not be readily intelligible as either 'public' or 'gay': they may well be enacted by female subjects and take place not in the bar or the club but rather the confines of the home, the beauty parlor, the women's hostel."[8] Or, in *Lemonade*, Black femmes can act out their love in the Storyville brothel, on the front porch, or at the women's revival meeting. The fact that most folks (even Black folks) don't go looking for queerness often enough in spaces like these—that we imagine Black femmes in northern cities rather than Southern down-homes, in the company of butches rather than other femmes—relates to the abjectness ascribed to both rurality and fem(me)ininity. In "Hood Femmes and Ratchet Feminism," Ashleigh Shackelford calls out the narrowness of dominant representations of Black femmes by asking, "What about the bisexual trap queens, the queer hood femmes, or the sexually fluid thotties?"[9] In the same spirit, *Lemonade* pushes me to ask, what about the Texas bama femme?

These next pages indulge in a Black queer femme-inist reading of *Lemonade*'s "Sorry," which showcases Beyoncé enjoying a twerking cameo by tennis player Serena Williams. My reading is one femme's answer to Sydney Fonteyn Lewis's call for a Black femme-inist criticism: that is, a set of critical reading practices that "investigate the ways that black women's cultural productions critique white heteropatriarchal construction of black women's race, gender, and sexuality."[10] Lewis's understanding of Black femme-ness began with her rapturous engagement with popular culture images: "My particular articulation of femme resulted from my interaction with pop culture and the black femme images, which I found in the lithe frame of Josephine Baker, the climatic whispers of Donna Summer, the uncontrollable curls of Diana Ross, the rasp of Billie Holiday, and the poetics of Toni Morrison, Nella Larsen, and Zora Neale Hurston. These images provided sustenance for my culturally malnourished queer of color spirit."[11] When she entered graduate school to theorize *something* about Black femme-ness, Lewis faced a glaring gap in Black feminist and queer studies. Although Black butches and transmen were beginning to theorize transmasculinities, Black femme scholars rarely centered our own queer genders in our work. "The key to deciphering this 'something' was not to be found in mainstream feminist or queer theory: in fact, the black femme remains largely invisible in both domains," she rightly observes. "I turn, then, to culture as a site from which to launch a black femme-inist critique."[12] In homage to Barbara Smith's classic essay "Toward a Black Feminist Criticism," Lewis turns to Toni Morrison's *Sula* as the cultural object through which she theorizes Black femme-ness. Thinking Black femme-ness through *Lemonade*, I engage a decidedly uncanonical cultural object—but arguably the most widely accessible text produced by a Black feminist at the present moment.[13]

My Black femme-inist reading is also a reparative reading, in the sense explored by Eve Sedgwick in "Paranoid Reading and Reparative Reading."[14] I write this in a moment of hyper-broadcast Black death, when, as Austin YouTube vlogger Evelyn Ngugi puts it, "every reblog, retweet, repost of citizen video footage that ultimately will never see the light of a courtroom, every Vine you watch of someone you know from Twitter getting pepper sprayed, and every link to a racist GoFundMe page . . . takes a toll" on Texas's Black women viewers.[15] The paucity of images of Black Southern women's lives in popular media could easily inspire what Sedgwick calls paranoid academic readings: critiques that register resistance to dominant media images by following "academic protocols like maintaining critical distance, outsmarting (and other forms of one-upmanship), refusing to be surprised (or if you are, not letting on), believing the hierarchy, becoming boss," as Heather Love glosses paranoid reading.[16] A *reparative* reading practice, in contrast, fights to extract sustenance from a popular culture largely uninterested in the survival of marginalized—including Black and queer—communities. Though so often dismissed as "sappy, aestheticizing, defensive, anti-intellectual or reactionary that it's no wonder few critics are willing to describe their acquaintance with such motives," the reparative reading, Sedgwick argues, is "no less acute than a paranoid position, no less realistic, no less attached to a project of survival, and neither less nor more delusional nor fantasmatic."[17] A paranoid reading of "Sorry" would catalog limitations to Beyoncé's vision of Black femme-ininity even as it bemoaned violence toward real-life Black cis- and transfemmes eclipsed by the video. But my reparative reading intends to piece together fragmented images of Black femme power in "Sorry" to create images of Black/queer/women's wholeness from whatever (admittedly flawed) cultural objects I have available. Like Lewis watching Donna Summer and Diana Ross, I reflect on how *Lemonade* offers public space—the music video—that visualizes possibilities for performing race, gender, sexuality, and region *Black femme-ly*, in ways other mainstream representations currently don't. And when Beyoncé sings *Ladies*, I invite us to also hear: *Femmes, now, let's get in formation*.

RIDING WITH THE RATCHET FEMME

Opening on an abstract, black-and-white close-up of light glancing off metal, "Sorry" begins with Beyoncé's voiceover: "What will you say about me now that you've killed me?" As Beyoncé recites Warsan Shire's poetry accompanied by a jewelry-box rendition of *Swan Lake*, the camera pans to what we now recognize as the floor of a moving bus, revealing the planted and dangling feet of Black women in power shoes ranging from stiletto combat boots to Adidas Superstars. The shot moves to the women's upper bodies to focus on deep brown faces crowned by artistic braids and arms, chests, and faces decorated in white-painted "Afromysterics" designs by Nigerian artist Laolu Senbanjo.[18] The seated dancers sway left and right, bend at the waist and circle forward, alternating body rolls before the camera finally finds Beyoncé's face among them and her voiceover intones: "My heaven will be a love without betrayal." The "Boy Bye" bus (as its destination sign reads) opens the video as the vehicle ferrying a figuratively murdered Beyoncé to heaven *and* as the heaven she imagines: an afterlife found in the love of Black women, who circle, move with, and protect her in ways (her lyrics suggest) her side-chick-collecting husband has not.

Throughout *Lemonade*, Chris Kelly notes, "there are no clear demarcations between reality and surreality"—earth or heaven—"or past and present."[19] And although cars and buildings outside bus windows look decidedly twenty-first century (like New Orleans streets in other videos), the Boy Bye bus has the movable windows, manual destination sign, metal poles, riveted ceiling, and exterior lines of mid-twentieth-century buses. In other words, the Boy Bye bus recalls vehicles that were part of Southern Black women's quotidian and history-making experiences in the era of civil-rights bus boycotts. Boycotts in Baton Rouge (1953) and Montgomery (1955–56) were initiated and spearheaded by working-class Black women who formed the vast majority of riders on public transportation, and the deuce-flashing dancers on the Boy Bye bus perform a fantasy of boycotted buses reclaimed by the women for whom they were once sites of "private misery" and public protest.[20] Building on "her own heritage," as Melissa Harris-Perry puts it, Beyoncé creates a Southern past that never existed but should have; she engages the past not for historical realism but "for sustenance, guidance, and finally, flight."[21] Playful eroticism circulates like hips in *this* bus as Beyoncé lifts her legs opened wide to laugh and sing, "suck on my balls, pause," and women in movement clap for sister riders as they dance on the center pole, exuberantly arch off window frames, and roll shoulders to lean in toward one other.

Now, the gender performance of these body-painted, artistically coiffed dancers could certainly fit Sublimefemme's description of *high femme*: a feminine-of-center queer gender that "uses exaggeration, artifice, and/or theatricality to denaturalize femininity."[22] But I'd call the distinctly Southern, unapologetically Black, open-leggedly sexual nature of femme-ininity on the Boy Bye bus ratchet femme. A Black Southern cousin of *high*—as in *ratcheted up*—the adjective *ratchet* comes out of the Cedar Grove neighborhood in Shreveport, Louisiana, and circulates in Dirty South rap and hip hop as "a derogatory term leveled mostly at women, but especially black women . . . that are unintelligent, loud, classless, tacky, and hypersexual, among other things," in Heidi Lewis's words.[23] But the word has also been reclaimed by proponents of ratchet feminism like Brittney Cooper, who, according to John Ortved, "sees women embracing 'ratchet . . . as an attempt to de-pathologize it' and to celebrate both its edginess and its roots in the southern working class. A man or woman can be ratchet in a way that emphasizes their authenticity, their realness, or their fierceness."[24] Where Cooper watches *Love and Hip Hop Atlanta* and sees ratchet feminism in action as "'ghetto,' 'hood rich' or struggling" sisters "call[ing] out sexism and challeng[ing] its operation in their lives," I watch "Sorry" and see ratchet femme-inism ferrying Beyoncé to a heaven of Black woman-centered pleasure: a heaven of "love without betrayal" by ride-or-die heterocentricity, white-acting self-effacement, or siddity respectability politics.[25]

Beyoncé's ratchet twist on high femme manifests in the unapologetic blackness of her dancers'—and her own—self-aestheticizing on the Boy Bye bus. Not opening any space to paint Texas bama femme as a darker-skinned version of white queer, "Sorry" aestheticizes fierce Southern femme-ininity that's *so Black* its African roots show. Ratchetness is often imputed to recognizably African elements of Black women's self-styling, like Senegalese box braids and large hoop earrings, and of all *Lemonade*'s videos, "Sorry" features the most distinctly African costumes and makeup. They include the Ankara-print jumpsuit Beyoncé wears when she spreads her legs and invites dancers to suck on her balls, the Masai necklaces she layers as she dances in front of the Boy Bye bus, and—most dramatically—the Afromysterics body art that decorates Beyoncé and her dancers. Resembling chalk drawings, this white body paint looks *cool*: as in the Black Atlantic *aesthetic of cool* Robert Farris Thompson identifies traveling between West Africa, the US South, and the Caribbean, "often linked to the sacred usage of water and chalk (and other substances drenched with associations of coolness and cleanliness) as powers that purify men and women by returning to freshness, to immaculate concentration of mind, to the artistic shaping of matter and societal happening."[26] Coolness—remaining unruffled, collected, on fleek in the face of challenges like sleepless nights, side chicks, and husbandly disrespect—is an Afrocentric aesthetic Boy Bye dancers share not only with Nigerian sisters but with bus-boycotting Southern foremothers. These maids, nannies, and seamstresses insisted on dressing flawlessly during months of walking several miles to work daily—wearing sharply pleated dresses, starched white shirts, neatly waved hair, and well-placed accessories as they told white bus drivers *boy, bye*.

But the Boy Bye femmes depart from the self-styling of bus boycotters, too. Male movement leaders enjoined women in the Montgomery boycott to publicly exhibit "many of the accepted ideals of respectable female behavior—even in the midst of their bold insurgency . . . to appear more 'lady-like' than many of their white segregationist opponents," Marisa Chappell, Jenny Hutchinson, and Brian Ward find.[27] Nine months before Rosa Parks's arrest, fifteen-year-old Claudette Colvin was arrested for similarly refusing to give her seat to a white patron; but because she failed to conform to codes of respectability—police claimed she was dragged off the bus "kicking and clawing" and the press reported she was unmarried and pregnant—civil-rights leaders deemed her "an inappropriate figure around whom to organize a mass movement."[28] Ratchet fem(me)inism, on the other hand, would bow down for any pregnant teen with balls enough to fight police while a bus full of folks watch. Bradley celebrates ratchetness as an "oppositional parallel" for Black Southern women who resist the "aesthetic of respectability" represented by the Southern belle,[29] and Cooper declares, "We have to think about how the embrace of ratchetness is simultaneously a dismissal of respectability, a kind of intuitive understanding of all the ways that respectability as a political project has failed Black women and continues to disallow the access that we have been taught to think it will give."[30] And in true ratchet fashion, instead of accepting betrayal with quiet dignity and hoping for moral victory, the antibelles of the Boy Bye bus take (queer) pleasure in reacting like angry Black women and fine-ass thotties.

Starting with the second chorus and verse, "Sorry" cuts to shots of the Boy Bye bus parked on a dark rural road—having traveled "from civilization to an open field," Kamaria Roberts and Kenya Downs believe—with Beyoncé and riders dancing angrily and sexily in front of the bus in wide-open public space.[31] From the waist up, their choreography publicizes anger by flashing hand movements, raising middle fingers, waving palms in talk-to-the-hand circles, and, the lyric tells us, "chunking my deuces": a Houston expression for waving peace fingers as a sign of dismissal—*peace out, boy*.[32] At the same time, powerful leg movements broadcast unapologetic sexuality from the waist down as bodysuit-clad dancers bounce down-and-up with knees dropped low to the ground in the foreground, bare-legged sisters circle their hips in the midground, and Beyoncé opens and closes her thighs while popping her ass on the bus's hood. In front of the bus, she sings, "Now you gotta see me wilding. . . . And I don't feel bad about it." A (now deleted) note on Lyrics Genius wondered: "While she's wilding, is she out with her girlfriends or getting frisky on the dance floor with some other dude?"[33] But the video suggests she might be out with her girlfriends getting frisky with *them*. "Headed to the club... me and my ladies sip my D'usse cup": yes, like Belly in "Might Not (Remix)"—who takes out a date who "say she ain't gay but she curious" and buys her "a shot of the D'usse and a shot for her ass"—these unapologetically Black, unapologetically (t)hot dancers share Beyoncé's cunnic cup to power the Boy Bye bus toward heaven. And Beyoncé ratchetly declares: "I ain't sorry... hell nah."

BALLING WITH THE AGGRESSIVE FEMME

Still dancing between past and present, historical reality and Black femme fantasy, the next location for "Sorry" is the moss-draped, lemon-flowered, white-columned Greek Revival mansion at Madewood Plantation. This mansion is a real place, a former sugarcane plantation and National Historic Landmark on Bayou Lafourche near Napoleonville, Louisiana; director Khalil Joseph transforms it into a fantasy space, an opulent estate dedicated to Black women's pleasure and power rather than forced labor. The first interior shot follows Serena Williams as she descends a flying staircase clad in a black bodysuit, stiletto ankle boots, powerful bare legs, and switching hips, her long-nailed left hand trailing the bannister. The camera follows her as she walks backward through the hall and turns with hair swinging, and then it finally stops in front of Beyoncé as the singer lounges jauntily in a thronelike chair with her bare left leg slung over its ornate arm. Beyoncé's pose flashes an intertext with "Déjà Vu" (2006), shot at Louisiana's Oak Alley Plantation and featuring Jay-Z sprawled in the great house in a similar high-backed chair, his left leg flung over the chair's arm as Beyoncé literally bends over backward dancing for him (a scene some viewers saw as stylized fellatio). But in "Sorry" Beyoncé sits still as Serena twerks for *her*, fulfilling the singer's request that the generous-thighed tennis legend "just be really free and just dance like nobody's looking and go all out."[34]

Posed like Jay-Z but styled in a bodysuit and stilettos like Serena, Beyoncé shows up at Madewood sporting an aggressive femme persona. Discussing aggressive femme presentation in Beyoncé's earlier videos, Anne Mitchell explains that "The aggressive femme identity is multiplicitous, but can be characterized as a gender identity or presentation that takes charge, tops, actively initiates and participates in sexual intercourse. She takes no shit, appreciates the female body, and wants to please it."[35] Or, as one Black aggressive femme describes her gender, these are "femmes who 'got they own'": own house, own throne, own dancers, own strap-on, own *whatever they need*.[36] "Aggressive"—which refers to female masculinity as a noun, but signifies female (often sexual) dominance as an adjective—came to queer lexicons from New York's ballroom scene, reaching national audiences in Daniel Peddle's documentary (2005) about Black aggressive subculture in New York.[37] Far away from that urban East Coast life as she sits spread-legged in a plantation foyer and watches Serena grind on the bannister, Beyoncé keeps aggressive femme's Blackness but gives it a Southern twist: "Sorry" moves queer femme-ininity out of the ballroom scene into the quadroon ball, away from voguing toward twerking.

Like *Lemonade*'s Madewood, quadroon balls hover somewhere between historical reality and sexual fantasy. "There is a common myth told about 19th-century New Orleans," Laine Kaplan-Levenson reflects. "It goes something like this: Imagine you're in an elegant dance hall in New Orleans in the early 1800s. Looking around, you see a large group of white men and free women of color, who were at the time called quadroons. . . . Mothers play matchmakers, and introduce their daughters to these white men, who then ask their hand in a dance. The ballroom is fancy, and the invited guests look the part."[38] Quadroon balls—where white men paid entrance fees to dance and negotiate sexual relationships with women of color—loom large in New Orleans lore (despite historians' claims they were rare). Films like *The Courage to Love* (2000) and *The Feast of All Saints* (2001) romanticize quadroon balls into the twenty-first century, lending filmic clichés to the Madewood shots in "Sorry": Greek Revival columns, chandeliers, candelabras, flying staircase, and Black women dancers—yes, the Boy Bye dancers—seated in chairs against the wall.[39] Only color-struck male suitors are missing from Beyoncé and Serena's ball: this party is femme-on-femme only. Now, despite their mythic part in Old South interracial heterosexual economies, quadroon balls always fostered homosocial space. A nineteenth-century writer scoffed they were "mere places of rendezvous for all the gay females in town,"[40] and recent representations like *The Feast of All Saints* imagine ballrooms as glorified brothels where quadroons lived together upstairs. Nineteenth-century prostitutes who roomed together, Graham Robb suggests, partnered in "brothel marriages,"[41] and Leonard Le'Doux's historical romance *The Belles of Chateau Vidal* (2016) imagines "quadroon marriages" between women of color who spent time between balls in lip-biting, pussy-fingering sex.[42] So why shouldn't Beyoncé and Serena cut men out of the quadroon fantasy, since there's always been enough femme sex to go around without them?

But Beyoncé's aggressive femme twists the quadroon fantasy harder. White voyeurs eroticized the quadroon's feminine passivity in contrast to lovers' forceful, manly dominance. Rixford Lincoln sighs in "The Quadroon Ballroom" (1911): "The half-white woman was a creature strange / A petted, fawning thing, of love and sin. / Her beauty was a dream surpassing rare, / Whose charms their masters oft' in fight did win. / And proud, these girls were petted darlings fair."[43] Beyoncé may look the part of a fair-skinned, long-haired quadroon, as Kimberly Chandler remarks,[44] but, instead of fawning as a petted, passive object of desire, she sits tall as the femme top Serena dances for, showing she "appreciates [Serena's] body, and wants to please it" by pointing admiringly to the body-rolling athlete as she commands her addressee to "stop interrupting my grinding" and then raises her arms and dances in her chair as Serena twerks.[45] Serena—whose father is from Louisiana—spectacularly refuses to perform the passive quadroon either. Media responses to dark-skinned, powerfully muscled, Afrocentrically coiffed Serena recycle the gendered colorism that made quadroons prized sexual objects while darker women were excluded from balls. Most notorious is Russian tennis official Shamil Tarpischev's 2014 reference to Serena and sister Venus as "the Williams brothers," a comment Serena called out as "insensitive and extremely sexist as well as racist at the same time."[46] Resonating with the song's message—"I am not sorry about anything. I really connected with those lyrics and felt good about that"—Serena rules as belle of the ball, and Beyoncé's light-skinned aggressive femme celebrates the athlete's beauty without reducing her power.[47] When invited for this cameo, Beyoncé's team told Serena "Sorry" was "about strength and it's about courage and that's what we see you as"—and that's what she looks like, too.[48] The youngest Williams gets a shot posing by herself in the power chair, visualizing Beyoncé and Serena's Black femme play as power exchange rather than unilateral dominance.

This brings me to the dance Serena expertly works for her aggressive femme: twerking. Like the adjective *ratchet*, the verb *twerk* comes out of

Louisiana's Black music scene. Twerking, Kyra Gaunt explains, is "a kind of kinetic orality that began as a black social dance in New Orleans over 20 years ago that involves bouncing your booty to the rhythmic changes and lyrical bars of a popular rap or twerk song."[49] What differentiates twerking from other African-derived booty dances, she says, "is in part due of the fact that this rap-based style of song and dance emanates out of the Dirty South as opposed to the dominant realms of East and West coast commercial rap and hip hop."[50] Linked with ratchetness and unapologetic Black feminine sexuality, twerking isn't often (enough) imagined as an expression of Black women loving themselves and other women. Annie Lennox famously dismissed Beyoncé's claim to feminism with the quip "twerking is not feminism,"[51] and academic feminists like Margaret Hunter complain twerking hypersexualizes Black women by its "focus on buttocks and vaginas and 'getting low' to the floor where these orifices would be more exposed to a viewer. . . . [Twerking is] done exclusively by women for a male audience, much like dancing in the strip club."[52] No one denies twerking's association with New Orleans queerness, its most famous performers remaining hard-hitting transfeminine artists like Katey Red, Big Freedia, and Sissy Nobby.[53] But no one talks much about the Black *lesbian* erotics of twerking, either. Slipping into this Black (w)hole,[54] "Sorry" opens space to revel in the sex-positive, thigh-loving, booty-celebrating Black fem(me)inism of one high femme twerking for another—in the woman-centered eroticism of the world's most famous black women celebrating their unapologetically Black, undeniably skilled asses with no white feminists or Black men interrupting their grinding.

As Serena twerks by her chair, Beyoncé tells the song's male addressee: "I ain't thinking 'bout you." And why would she? Challenging mainstream media's inability to appreciate Serena's ample ass, Janell Hobson claps back with Black feminist affirmation of the woman-centered erotics of booties bouncing on tennis courts, dance floors, or anywhere else. Remember, she intones, Black girls learn to *shake what our mama gave us* not for boys but for *other Black girls*: in "female-centered space for affirmation and pleasure in their bodies" offered by childhood games like "Little Sally Walker," "Brown Girl in the Ring," or "Lemonade."[55] (This last hand-clapping song ends with girls dancing to the chant "turn around, touch the ground / kick your boyfriend out of town"—another version of the "boy, bye" of "Sorry."[56]) Hobson concludes, "We may need to recreate that circle of women—first enacted in childhood—who reaffirm that our bodies are fine, normal, capable, and beautiful.... Only then will we be able to follow the lead of Serena Williams, proudly displaying our behinds while continuing our winning streak."[57] Serena's twerking at Madewood looks like a winning streak, too—a sexual winning streak for her and her aggressive femme. One fantasy about twerking is it brings dancers to orgasm,[58] and one way (I like) to read the multiple shots of Serena twerking is as Beyoncé encouraging, demanding, and manipulating multiple orgasms for her dancer—the consummate "win" for an aggressive femme. "Let's have a toast to the good life," she sings just after Serena rolls on the floor in front of her throne. Oh yes, Serena and Queen Beyoncé enjoying this twerking (un)quadroon ball together looks like a sweet taste of that *good* life.

WORSHIPPING THE STONE FEMME

"Sorry" glides out with a minute-long outro that shifts musically—into a minor chord recalling the minor key of the intro's music box—at the same time it shifts visually, cutting a third scene between Madewood and the Boy Bye bus. These are the Nefertiti shots: gold-painted Beyoncé seated on the floor of a bare room haloed in light, knees bent with one foot on the floor, breasts weaponized in a Zana Bayne bullet bra and hair braided into a sculpture stylist Kim Kimble designed to resemble the Egyptian queen's crown.[59] The singer's kohl-rimmed eyes, pronounced eyebrows, and crown of braids style her in the image of the famous Berlin limestone bust of the Great Royal Wife of Egyptian pharaoh Akhenaten. At this point in the video, viewers can imagine Beyoncé singing to us from Nefertiti's home in Amarna, Egypt, or from Egypt, Louisiana, a town in once plantation-rich Natchitoches Parish not far from Madewood. Cut between other recognizable Louisiana locations on a visual album set entirely in the US South, the Nefertiti shots in "Sorry" to me read as somewhere in the South, but somewhere deliberately unlocatable: an interior space accessible only through the Black fem(me) inine imagination, somewhere the protagonist is as invulnerable as limestone to betrayal, hurt, and unappreciation.

Unlocatable and unaccompanied, Beyoncé's Nefertiti also looks untouchable—a figurative representation of *stoneness*, the sexual expression of someone who, in Francesca Royster's words, draws sexual boundaries so she "is not touched or penetrated by a lover, but to be stone can include a spectrum of control and a variety of acts."[60] *Stone* as an intensifier comes out of early twentieth-century African American English and, from midcentury on, was paired with *butch* to mean a masculine lesbian who enjoys sex without being touched genitally or emotionally. But butches aren't the only ones who enjoy being stone. Stone femme, Sasha of Card Carrying Lesbian explains, is a "femme lesbian that may appear to be an ultra femme in her appearance but expresses butch attributes in bed and may not allow her lovers to fuck her at all." She continues, "She's figured out a way to expose her body and hide her heart in her nudity. Her sexuality has become a weapon, not a weakness. She understands that when they're looking at her body they're not really looking at *her* at all. So she's able to hide in plain sight, to hide in full view, naked and aroused but untouched where it really counts."[61] Closing off the open-legged pose of the Boy Bye bus, Beyoncé's Nefertiti is also untouchable where she wants to be: you can't grab her spiked breasts without getting hurt, can't fit a hand between her yogicly crossed legs. Unreachable from her first line ("I left a note in the hallway / By the time you read it I'll be far away"), Bey Nefertiti returns to punctuate: *"But I ain't fuckin' with nobody."* As she does, she draws her top knee closer to her chest and contracts her breasts to demonstrate unfuckability. As Royster writes of stoneness, these lyrical and physical poses "convey a physical and emotional armor to the public—an armor that is nonetheless erotically and emotionally charged."[62]

Beyoncé's metallic Nefertiti reminds me of Black femme colleague Jennifer Brody's description of another queerly reimagined Egyptian queen: Cleopatra Jones, the silver made-up, (sometimes) lingerie-clad heroine played by Tamara Dobson in *Cleopatra Jones* (1973) and *Cleopatra Jones and the Casino of Gold* (1975). By the second film, Cleopatra has become her own kind of stone femme—arrayed in a sexy armor of rapidly changing costumes like a bejeweled bodysuit, "sequined lingerie-inspired gown and matching sheer boudoir-cape," but closed to sexual contact with male and female admirers alike.[63] Yet the fabulousness Brody highlights in Cleo's stone femme style isn't only or primarily how it "disrupts the fantasy that *all* [women of color] are sexually available."[64] It's how "Cleo's outrageous outfits and her surreal, silvery eye shadow serve to illustrate her awareness of self-construction as a source of power," a feminine sexual power that has nothing to do with penetrability and *everything* to do with controlling her own body.[65]

Brody's phrase "self-construction as a source of power" resonates as a description for Beyoncé's project in *Lemonade*. Released as an MTV special in April 2016, *Lemonade* was Beyoncé's second consecutive visual album to drop with no announcement, a power move Salamishah Tillet calls "Beyoncé pulling a Beyoncé."[66] News outlets exploded, reeling from the singer's unexpected release not merely of a visual album but of a short film—one whose theme is a husband's serial infidelity, subject matter many viewers took as autobiographical. "On Saturday, Beyoncé flipped a middle finger at your going-out plans AND her husband with *Lemonade*," Amy Zimmerman declared. "*Lemonade* isn't the first time Beyoncé has changed the game, exhibiting a level of control, artistic autonomy, and pop culture prowess unheard of in the digital era."[67] Beyoncé's unprecedented control of her message styles her as the stone femme of popular music: not only because of her industry dominance, but because of her closely controlled artistic project of exposing herself while hiding in plain view. "*Lemonade* is being lauded for its intimacy, the bold and painfully candid admissions with which Beyoncé cuts herself open, offering the organs and heart of her marriage as material for her creative process and sustenance for her fans," Zimmerman continues. "However, it's important not to confuse this performance of intimacy with total honesty, or the surrender of any degree of control. Beyoncé is pre-packaging the story of her husband's infidelity, manufacturing it as an art piece that then feeds directly into her pocket."[68] Far from leaving her royally fucked, Beyoncé's story of infidelity in *Lemonade* styles her as royal and unfuckable. "Houston's own Beyoncé has proven once again that she is the queen of all media," Black anchor Mia Gradney summed it up on Houston's CBS affiliate KHOU after the album's release.[69]

And hard-glittering queen Bey Nefertiti is the femme who closes out "Sorry." Looking directly at the camera and raising and lowering her head for punctuation, she delivers the song's most-discussed line: "You better call Becky with the good hair." Much speculation has swirled around this line, but for me—assuming "Becky" is slang for a white woman—part of its meaning is, simply: *you can't fuck me and you better not fuck (with) any other Black woman or femme, either.* The final shot returns to Bey Nefertiti, her bottom leg now uncrossed as she leans slightly to the left and the camera pans backward, recording her complete silence and immobility from an ever-increasing distance. "Sorry" tells, dances, and costumes a lot about Blackness, womanness, Southernness, histories, futures, desires, pleasures, pains: but there's a whole world this composition keeps unlocatable, untouchable, and unspoken, and we end with Bey Nefertiti's gaze regally marking this limit. The video offers us visions of a Black-woman-powered South—but it also creates this unmappable room of Beyoncé's own where she rules as inaccessible queen. And the choreography embodies downhome Black femmeness in motion—but keeps the ratchet, aggressive, and stone femme body out of easy reach, making sure there's no opening for "femmes getting the short end of the dick" (as Hadassah Hill puts it).[70] Sorry, Beyoncé's black femme will *never* be sorry.

OUTRO: FOR THE FUTURE OF BLACK FEMME-INIST STUDIES

Thank you for reading along as I traveled with the Boy Bye bus toward a Black femme-inist criticism. Because Black femmes—and *all* femmes—have so few chances to see our complexities reflected in popular culture or academic texts, I wanted this to be an enjoyable ride. But my embrace of pleasure takes nothing away from the seriousness of queer regionalism as a project that affects the conditions of possibility for *all* Black lives. In her groundbreaking study of Black Southern regionalism, Riché Richardson explains her choice to focus on cis hetero masculinities as stemming from the predominance given to Black manhood in dominant discourses. She quotes Brian Philip Harper's observation that "all debates and claims to 'authentic' African-American identity are largely animated by a profound anxiety about the status of black *masculinity*,"[71] meaning straight cisgender masculinity. But this privileged status could just as easily point to the importance of focusing Black Southern regionalism around cis hetero manhood's "opposite," Black queer femme-ininity. Because as Richardson is keenly aware, the full recognition of African American humanity cannot be achieved by valorizing Black straight men above their queer femme sisters. When media overexposure of Black heteromasculinity is countered by bringing the Black femme into the spotlight from time to time, maybe more Black women *and* men can "succeed in extracting sustenance from the objects of a culture—even of a culture whose avowed desire has been not to sustain them," as Sedgwick wishes for reparative reading.[72]

Most of all, though, I wanted my trajectory here to serve as an invitation to other scholars to offer other roadmaps toward Black femme-inist cultural studies. High femme, low femme, tomboy femme, sporty femme, bi-femme, stemme, classic femme, strong femme, extreme femme, lipstick femme, wallflower femme, hood femme, trap queen femme: the array of Black femme genders whose resistance to white heteropatriarchy deserve to be explored is ever-expanding. Neither is there a shortage of popular culture texts set in the US South that lend themselves to Black femme-inist readings: *Love and Hip Hop Atlanta, True Blood, American Horror Story: Season 5,* Hurray for the Riff Raff's "The Body Electric," TT the Artist's "Fly Girl," Solange's "Cranes in the Sky." Most important, I wrote this into a celebration because I live in a political climate where often feel I *must* find something to celebrate or die; but Black femme-inist criticism also needs to come in other moods and modes. Not all Black femme-inist readings can, or should be, reparative, just as not objects of dominant culture can, or should be, repurposed. Anger at Black women and femmes' vulnerability to male violence; trenchant criticism of femme invisibility as femmephobia; concern for Black femmes' mental and relationship health; mourning for partners and friends targeted by state violence; shady deconstructions of Eurocentric beauty standards; big-laughing humor at our bawdy burlesque: we need all these and more to understand how misogynoir and queerphobia interact—and can be resisted—in the current political moment of escalating Black death, rape culture, and trans- and cisfem(me)icide.

OMISE'EKE NATASHA TINSLEY is Professor of Black Studies at the University of California at Santa Barbara. She is author of *Thiefing Sugar: Eroticism between Women in Caribbean Literature, Ezili's Mirrors: Imagining Black Queer Genders,* and *Beyoncé in Formation: Remixing Black Feminism.*

NOTES

1. Terryn Hall, "Southern Girl: Beyoncé, Badu, and Southern Black Womanhood," *Rumpus,* June 2, 2016, http://therumpus.net/2016/06/southern-girl-beyonce-badu-and-southern-black-womanhood/.
2. Ibid.

3. Sydney Gore, "'Lemonade' Is a Love Letter from Beyoncé to Black Women," April 25, 2016, https://www.nylon.com/articles/beyonce-lemonade-review.
4. Hall, "Southern Girl."
5. Tinsley, "Black Atlantic," 199.
6. Gopinath, "Queer Regions," 344.
7. Sublimefemme, "Rethinking High Femme, Part 1," October 27, 2008, https://sublimefemme.wordpress.com/2008/10/27/rethinking-high-femme-part-1/.
8. Gopinath, "Queer Regions."
9. Ashleigh Shakelford, "Hood Femmes and Ratchet Feminism: On Amandla Stenberg, Representation, and #BlackGirlMagic," For Harriet, January 28, 2016, www.forharriet.com/2016/01/hood-femmes-ratchet-feminism-on-amandla.html.
10. Lewis, "Everything I Know," 118.
11. Ibid., 101.
12. Ibid.
13. Beyoncé's claim to the label "feminist" has, of course, been contested. I strongly believe that anyone who self-identifies as a Black feminist should be recognized as such. Black feminism is not monolithic, and although some Black feminists may disagree with Beyoncé's political and artistic stances, policing her right to identify as a feminist seems deeply problematic. For a more extensive consideration on the debates around Beyoncé's feminism. see Janell Hobson's "Feminists Debate Beyoncé."
14. Sedgwick, "Paranoid Reading."
15. Evelyn Ngugi, "Call in Black," July 20, 2015, https://www.youtube.com/watch?v=cpVeUVcFMAU.
16. Love, "Truth and Consequences," 235.
17. Sedgwick, "Paranoid Reading," 150.
18. On Laolu's "Afromysterics," see Tamara Best, "An Artist Who Uses the Skin As His Canvas," New York Times, November 30, 2016, https://www.nytimes.com/2016/11/30/arts/design/a-nigerian-artist-who-uses-the-skin-as-his-canvas.html?_r=1.
19. Chris Kelly, "Lemonade: The Hidden Meanings Buried in Beyoncé's Filmic Journey through Grief," April 27, 2016, http://www.factmag.com/2016/04/27/lemonade-beyonce-meaning-visual-album/.
20. Frystak, Our Minds, 67.
21. Melissa Harris-Perry, "Beyoncé Evokes New Orleans in New Video," MSNBC, February 7, 2016, http://www.msnbc.com/melissa-harris-perry/watch/beyonce-evokes-new-orleans-in-new-video-618221635632; Lewis, "Everything I Know," 118.
22. Sublimefemme, "Rethinking High Femme."
23. Heidi R. Lewis, "Exhuming the Ratchet before It's Buried," Feminist Wire, January 7, 2013, http://www.thefeministwire.com/2013/01/exhuming-the-ratchet-before-its-buried/.

24. John Ortved, "Ratchet: The Rap Insult That Became a Compliment," *New York*, April 11, 2013, https://www.thecut.com/2013/04/ratchet-the-rap-insult-that-became-a-compliment.html.
25. Brittney Cooper, "Ratchet Feminism," *Crunk Feminist Collective*, August 14, 2012, https://crunkfeministcollective.wordpress.com/2012/08/14/ratchet-feminism/.
26. Thompson, "Aesthetic," 41.
27. Chappell et al., "'Dress Modestly,'" 70.
28. Ibid., 85.
29. Regina Bradley, "I Been On (Ratchet): Conceptualizing a Sonic Ratchet Aesthetic in Beyoncé's 'Bow Down,'" *Red Clay Scholar*, March 19, 2013, http://redclayscholar.blogspot.com/2013/03/i-been-on-ratchet-conceptualizing-sonic.html.
30. Brittney Cooper, "(Un)Clutching My Mother's Pearls, or Ratchetness and the Residue of Respectability," *Crunk Feminist Collective*, December 31, 2012, http://www.crunkfeministcollective.com/2012/12/31/unclutching-my-mothers-pearls-or-ratchetness-and-the-residue-of-respectability/.
31. Kamaria Roberts and Kenya Downs, "What Beyoncé Teaches Us about the African Diaspora in 'Lemonade,'" *PBS NewsHour* "Art Beat," April 29, 2016, http://www.pbs.org/newshour/art/what-beyonce-teaches-us-about-the-african-diaspora-in-lemonade/.
32. See definitions of "chunk the deuce," *Urban Dictionary*, June 10, 2006, http://www.urbandictionary.com/define.php?term=chunk%20a%20deuce.
33. The comment was previously available at http://genius.com/Beyoncé-sorry-lyrics, accessed December 6, 2016.
34. Serena Williams quoted in Cindy Boren, "Serena Williams Explains How She Ended Up Twerking in Beyoncé's 'Lemonade,'" May 9, 2016, https://www.washingtonpost.com/news/early-lead/wp/2016/05/09/serena-williams-explains-how-she-ended-up-twerking-in-beyonces-lemonade.
35. Mitchell, "Beyoncé," 42.
36. See Justa Notha (June 11, 2011), comment on Sasha, "Aggressive Femme," *Card Carrying Lesbian*, June 11, 2011, http://www.cardcarryinglesbian.com/aggressive-femmes.
37. *The Aggressives*, dir. Daniel Peddle (Seventh Art, 2005, 75 minutes).
38. Laine Kaplan-Levenson, "TriPod Mythbusters: Quadroon Balls and Plaçage," *WWNO*, September 22, 2016, http://wwno.org/post/tripod-mythbusters-quadroon-balls-and-pla-age.
39. *The Courage to Love*, dir. Kari Skogland (Lifetime, 2000, 95 minutes), and *The Feast of All Saints*, dir. Peter Medak (Showtime, 2001, 140 minutes).
40. Louis Tasistro, quoted in Clark, *Strange History*, 178.
41. Robb, *Strangers*, 157.
42. Le'Doux, *Belles*, 44.

43. Quoted in Voltz, "Black Female Agency," vii.
44. See Chandler, "Creole Queen."
45. Mitchell, "Beyoncé."
46. Shamil Tarpischev and Serena Williams, quoted in Nolan Feeney, "Serena Williams Blasts Official's 'Sexist' and 'Racist' Remarks," *Time*, October 19, 2014, http://time.com/3522553/serena-williams-sexist-racist-shamil-tarpischev/.
47. Serena Williams quoted in Hannah Flint, "Serena Williams: 'I'm Not Sorry for Anything,'" *Grazia*, July 11, 2016, http://lifestyle.one/grazia/celebrity/news/serena-williams-wimbledon-Beyonce-lemonade/.
48. Serena Williams quoted in Tory Barron, "Serena Williams Explains Why Beyoncé Wanted Her in 'Lemonade' Video," *ESPN*, May 10, 2016, http://www.espn.com/espnw/culture/the-buzz/article/15499708/serena-williams-explains-why-beyonce-wanted-lemonade-video.
49. Gaunt, "YouTube," 247.
50. Ibid., 253.
51. Annie Lennox quoted by Laura Stampler, "Annie Lennox: 'Twerking Is Not Feminism,'" *Time*, October 21, 2014, http://time.com/3529403/annie-lennox-twerking-feminism/.
52. Hunter, "Shake It, Baby," 27.
53. Gaunt, "YouTube," 256–58.
54. I use this phrase in homage to Hammond's watershed essay "Black (W)holes."
55. Hobson, "'Batty' Politic," 102.
56. Thanks to my daughter, Baia Tinsley, for teaching me this rhyme and game.
57. Hobson, "'Batty' Politic," 103.
58. See, for example, the category "Twerking Orgasm" videos on pornhub.com.
59. Kim Kimble quoted in Patrice Grell Yursik, "A Complete Breakdown of Beyoncé's Hair Looks from *Lemonade*," *Elle*, April 28, 2016, http://www.elle.com/beauty/hair/news/g28184/beyonce-lemonade-hair/.
60. Royster, *Becoming Cleopatra*, 179.
61. Sasha, "High Femme vs. Stone Femme: One Interpretation," *Card Carrying Lesbian*, June 23, 2008, https://www.cardcarryinglesbian.com/interracial-lesbian-dating-and-race-in-the-lgbtq#comment-758246.
62. Royster, *Becoming Cleopatra*, 185.
63. Brody, "Returns of 'Cleopatra Jones,'" 113.
64. Ibid., 107.
65. Ibid., 106.
66. Salamishah Tillet, in Jeffrey Brown and Salamishah Tillet, "With 'Lemonade,' Beyoncé Shows She's an Artist in Control," *PBS NewsHour*, April 25, 2016, http://www.pbs.org/newshour/bb/with-lemonade-Beyonce-shows-shes-an-artist-in-control/.

67. Amy Zimmerman, "How Beyoncé Manipulates the Media: From Elevatorgate to 'Lemonade,'" *Daily Beast*, April 27, 2016, updated April 13, 2017, http://www.thedailybeast.com/how-beyonce-manipulates-the-media-from-elevatorgate-to-lemonade.
68. Ibid.
69. Mia Gradney in "Beyoncé Rules the World with 'Lemonade' Release," *KHOU*, April 25, 2016, http://www.khou.com/entertainment/music/beyonce-rules-the-world-with-lemonade-release/152993007.
70. Hill, "Femme Fuck Revolution," 63.
71. Richardson, *Black Masculinity*, 8.
72. Sedgwick, "Paranoid Reading," 150–51.

BIBLIOGRAPHY

Brody, Jennifer DeVere. "The Returns of 'Cleopatra Jones.'" *Signs* 25, no. 1 (1999): 91–121.
Chandler, Kimberly. "Creole Queen: Beyoncé and Performing Plaçage in the New Millennium." In *The Beyoncé Effect: Essays on Sexuality, Race, and Feminism*. Edited by Adrienne Trier-Bieniek, 193–202. Jefferson, NC: McFarland, 2016.
Chappell, Marisa, Jenny Hutchinson, and Brian Ward. "'Dress Modestly, Neatly . . . As If You Were Going to Church': Respectability, Class, and Gender in the Montgomery Bus Boycott and the Early Civil Rights Movement." In *Gender in the Civil Rights Movement*. Edited by Peter Ling and Sharon Monteith, 69–100. New York: Garland, 1999.
Clark, Emily. *The Strange History of the American Quadroon: Free Women of Color in the Revolutionary Atlantic World*. Chapel Hill: University of North Carolina Press, 2013.
Frystak, Shannon. *Our Minds on Freedom: Women and the Struggle for Black Equality in Louisiana, 1924–1967*. Baton Rouge: Louisiana State University Press, 2009.
Gaunt, Kyra. "YouTube, Twerking and You: Collapse and the Handheld Co-presence of Black Girls and Miley Cyrus." *Journal of Popular Music Studies* 27, no. 3 (2015): 244–73.
Gopinath, Gayatri. "Queer Regions: Locating Lesbians in Sancharram." In *The Blackwell Companion to Lesbian, Gay, Bisexual, Transgender, and Queer Studies*. Edited by George Haggerty and Molly McGarry, 341–54. Oxford: Blackwell, 2007.
Hammond, Evelynn. "Black (W)holes and the Geometry of Black Female Sexuality." *differences* 6, nos. 2–3 (1994): 127–45.
Hill, Hadassah. "Femme Fuck Revolution." In *Visible: A Femmethology*, vol. 1. Edited by Jennifer Clare Burke, 63–65. Ypsilanti, MI: Homofactus, 2009.

Hobson, Janell. "The 'Batty' Politic: Toward an Aesthetic of the Black Female Body." *Hypatia* 18, no. 4 (2003): 87–105.

———. "Feminists Debate Beyoncé." In *The Beyoncé Effect: Essays on Sexuality, Race, and Feminism*. Edited by Adrienne Trier-Bieniek, 11–26. Jefferson, NC: McFarland, 2016.

Hunter, Margaret. "Shake It, Baby, Shake It: Consumption and the New Gender Relation in Hip Hop." *Sociological Perspectives* 54, no. 1 (2011): 15–36.

Le'Doux, Leonard, Jr., *The Belles of Chateau Vidal*. Kansas City, MO: Midwest, 2016.

Lewis, Sydney Fonteyn. "'Everything I Know about Being Femme I Learned from *Sula*'; or, Towards a Black Femme-inist Criticism." *Trans-scripts* 2 (2012): 100–25.

Love, Heather. "Truth and Consequences: On Paranoid Reading and Reparative Reading." *Criticism* 52, no. 2 (2010): 235–41.

Mitchell, Anne. "Beyoncé as Aggressive Black Femme and Informed Black Female Subject." In *The Beyoncé Effect: Essays on Sexuality, Race, and Feminism*. Edited by Adrienne Trier-Bieniek, 40–54. Jefferson, NC: McFarland, 2016.

Richardson, Riché. *Black Masculinity and the U.S. South: From Uncle Tom to Gangsta*. Athens: University of Georgia Press, 2007.

Robb, Graham. *Strangers: Homosexual Love in the Nineteenth Century*. New York: Norton, 2003.

Royster, Francesca. *Becoming Cleopatra: The Shifting Image of an Icon*. New York: Palgrave Macmillan, 2003.

Sedgwick, Eve Kosofsky. "Paranoid Reading or Reparative Reading; or, You're So Paranoid You Probably Think This Essay Is about You." In *Touching Feeling: Affect, Pedagogy, Performativity*. Edited by Eve Kosofsky Sedgwick, 123–51. Durham, NC: Duke University Press, 2003.

Thompson, Robert Farris. "An Aesthetic of the Cool." *African Arts* 7, no. 1 (1973): 40–43, 60–67, 89–91.

Tinsley, Omise'eke Natasha. "Black Atlantic, Queer Atlantic: Queer Imaginings of the Middle Passage." *GLQ* 14, no. 2–3 (2009): 191–215.

Voltz, Noël. "Black Female Agency and Sexual Exploitation: Quadroon Balls and Plaçage Relationships." Senior Thesis, Ohio State University, 2008. https://kb.osu.edu/dspace/bitstream/handle/1811/32216/Quadroon_Balls1.pdf.

SEVEN

Gypsying Beyoncé
The Latin Crossover through Hispanic Stereotypes

EDUARDO VIÑUELA

Why would Beyoncé want to become a gypsy? And, if she did, how would she do it? These two key questions help to understand how Beyoncé enhanced her star persona by adding some gypsy touches in various periods of her solo career.[1] At the very early stages, even before leaving Destiny's Child, she starred in the film *Carmen: A Hip Hopera* (2001), where she played the role of Mérimée's famous gypsy female character. The success of this musical film persuaded Pepsi to make a commercial with Beyoncé performing the "Habanera" of Bizet's opera *Carmen* in 2002. This was her first spot for "The Joy of Pepsi" campaign and it served too to prepare the promotion of her first solo album in 2003. Later on, Beyoncé launched a disc in EP format of Spanish-language versions of several songs from her second album, *Irreemplazable* (2007), where the gypsy tinge is evident both in the flamenco style of the opening track, "Amor Gitano" ("Gypsy Love") and in the Romani background melodies of "Bello Embustero" ("Beautiful Liar").

Beyoncé has neither gypsy roots nor Latin ancestors; she does not speak Spanish. She was born in Houston, Texas, and she has articulated a strong African American identity throughout her career. At the same time, however, she expanded her personal narrative by incorporating gypsy topics within her star persona, enabling her to become (or to appear) more versatile and multifaceted. In this chapter, I will argue that her embodiment of gypsy characters, such as Carmen, and the presence of gypsy patterns in some of her songs are not circumstantial, but central to her strategy to become an international star. On the one hand, gypsy stereotypes (both Romani and flamenco) have been part of Latin identity since the early twentieth century and have played an important part in the definition of the Latin sound. Thus, the use of such stereotypes proved a successful strategy for artists to achieve crossover into the profitable Latin market, which has grown significantly since the late nineties. On the other hand, playing the role of a gypsy woman connects solo female artists with a world of connotations (freedom, determination, and passion, to name but a few) that have been circulating in popular culture in the last hundred years. The empowered female gypsy has become almost a cliché in all manner of cultural productions (cinema, music, literature), especially since the success of Bizet's *Carmen* in 1875. The strength of this character, embodied by Beyoncé at the beginning of her solo career, contributed to building her personality and individuality, as a part of the process of establishing her distance from Destiny's Child, positioning her as a strong, individual artist with agency.

The power of gypsy women has a counterpart, however: the price of their freedom and agency can be tragic (as in the story of *Carmen*) or at least socially condemned, and the character normally appears as an outsider. She is at the same time admired and avoided for her connection with tarot, magic, and illegal practices. Gypsy identity has been orientalized (borrowing Said's term) and, thus, placed in the margins of the hegemonic forces in Western societies as "its cultural contestant, and one of its deepest and most recurring images of the Other. In addition, the Orient has helped to define Europe (or the West) as its contrasting image, idea, personality, experience."[2] Said explains that the frontiers of the Orient are determined not by geography but by their cultural position; thus, the borders are blurred and, beyond the cultural pale of the West, everything enters, fits in, and is fitted into the undefined category of oriental. Under the tag of Latin music, one finds music traditions from various latitudes that have been commodified to conform to the patterns of Western mainstream music. This explains, for one instance, how straightforwardly Latin music seems to embrace features of gypsy music without distinguishing between Spanish flamenco and Romani music.

Gypsy identity is just another piece in the puzzle of this exotic and attractive Otherness, re-presented and reinscribed especially since the nineteenth century. Here, however, I will explore how Beyoncé uses the figure of the gypsy woman to create her own narrative on a different axis: first, through her vindication of empowered Black women (establishing a connection with the filmic Black character Carmen Jones), and, second, via her links to Latin culture as a manifestation of the exotic Other in the context of anglophone hegemonic culture in the United States. Performing a gypsy role helps Beyoncé to acquire a strong position in her performance of ethnicity, race, and gender, locating her star persona in the music market. The gypsy role, then, is a symbolic performance of her stardom.

CARMEN RAPS IN THE UNITED STATES: GYPSYNESS, AGENCY, AND THE VINDICATION OF BLACK FEMININITY

While still immersed in a successful career with the R&B girl group Destiny's Child, Beyoncé decided to take her own path by starring in the film *Carmen: A Hip Hopera* (2001), a new version of Bizet's opera that updated the Hollywood musical *Carmen Jones* (1954). Thus, Beyoncé claimed her individuality through embodying a gypsy character, a *femme fatale* positioned at the margins of society both for her belonging to a landless community and for not assuming a conventional female role in a patriarchy. The strategy may seem risky commercially for a mainstream star—recollecting Don José's comment in Prosper Mérimée's *Carmen*: "I spoke to Carmen of leaving Spain / And trying to live honestly in the New World. She laughed at me."—but her move was not in vain.[3] Gypsy female characters have a long tradition in popular culture, and their multiple representations in Western cultural productions serve to control, stereotype, and normalize their meanings. Thus, at the beginning of this century, performing a female gypsy character in a film was nothing but a stylized exercise with little threat and many opportunities to build a strong discourse for a star, especially in the tricky initial stages of her career.

The gypsy identity has been articulated since the nineteenth century according to the principles of the romantic stereotype, deploying multiple characteristics of an itinerant ethnic group that arrived in Europe in the twelfth century and spread all over the continent as a stateless population, suffering persecution across the European nation-states. Gypsies maintained their cultural structures and resisted assimilation as a nomadic community, which played an important role in their acquiring of an aura of authenticity that was so attractive in the romantic era. The first evidence of gypsies in Spain dates from 1425. They suffered under the unification politics of the

"Catholic Monarchs" in the late fifteenth century and, thereafter, they were constantly persecuted and rejected both by the Spanish authorities and the population at large. Gypsies appeared in Spanish literature, art, and popular culture as thieves and tricksters, as early as in *La gitanilla* (1613) by Cervantes and in Goya's tapestries. The gypsy was also used to represent natural life. Moreover, imagined as outsiders and rebels, they were celebrated by the Romantics. Travel literature in the nineteenth century was fascinated with gypsy life, and gypsies became part of the bohemian imaginary. As Colmeiro observes, "by fantasizing and symbolically transposing their desires onto an exotic outside, bohemian artists found in the Spanish Gypsy the instrument needed to safely reconcile their differences with bourgeois ideology."[4]

It was at this time when gypsies in Spain themselves started to perform an identity influenced by the expectations and imaginations of foreign tourists. One such traveler was Prosper Mérimée, author of the short story *Carmen* (1845). His piece contributed to the stereotype of gypsies and, by extension, the image of a picturesque Spain in Europe. Bizet's opera (1875) adapted the story of Carmen to great success and served to advance *gitanismo* through the outline of a recognizable narrative.[5] Before that, in the mid-nineteenth century, "Madrid became a transitory residence for artists who, poorly paid, sought economic well-being in foreign lands, on long tours that would take them to Europe's most cosmopolitan, and often faraway, cities."[6] Thus, the stereotyping of the gypsies was negotiated from the very beginning within both a Spanish and a spectacular context, and, moreover, it was rapidly spread all around the world. At the same time and as a part of this process of internationalization, "gypsies become symbolic token figures in the process of constructing a national identity. The mythical figure of the Gypsy is then reduced to a discursive trope, a convenient synecdoche for Spanishness."[7]

Carmen is not only a gypsy, but also a female character, a feminine icon that helped Spanish singers and dancers to articulate their identity and the narrative of their performance: it is my contention that an almost identical maneuver happens in the case of Beyoncé.[8] The character of Carmen is the perfect archetype to perform what Isabel Clúa identifies as the three core discourses for female artists to succeed in public performance: eccentricity, fatality, and exoticism,[9] in other words, a display of Otherness and *différance* that constantly resignifies the role of the rebel woman. Hence, *Carmen* has been regularly refigured in popular culture to assume new locations and cultural contexts, new features for its characters and updated forms of expression, though always maintaining its underlying narrative structure. In this process, the gypsy identity of Carmen has also been redefined and, consequently, the meanings of gypsyness have been transformed. Space does not allow for a detailed outline of the process here, but it may give a sense of its scale to note that in cinema alone there are more than seventy versions of the story. My concern here is, rather, with the capacity of this story to adopt new forms while maintaining the exoticism and orientalism of Carmen as a former gypsy character. Thus, the different versions of *Carmen* contribute to emphasize the meaning of gypsyness as an unstable identity that becomes an epitome of Otherness and simultaneously reimagines Carmen as a mutable—and mutable *because* marginal, minoritized, other, and unstable—feminine icon, aspects of whom can, thus, branch off and be redeployed in the building of a star persona, just as, I argue here, Beyoncé does.

In the United States, gypsy identity becomes inscribed in the margins of society with other minorities. Its inscription thus is quite evident in the context of performances since the late nineteenth century; as Meira Goldberg states, "in the illicit moral and aesthetic values of the tangos via which flamenco absorbed cake-walk, we find the interwoven images of the black Moor, the enslaved African, and the Gitano as minstrel figure."[10] In this context, the emergence of a Black Carmen was only a question of time. Kiko Mora recalls the activity of Susana Brown, "The Colored Carmencita," a minstrel actress in the United States during the 1890s.[11] Though there are other Black Carmens, I will treat the musical film *Carmen Jones* as a recognizable antecedent of Beyoncé's *Carmen: A Hip Hopera*.[12]

Carmen Jones updates the plot of Bizet's opera, situating the action in the south of the United States during World War II. Dorothy Dandridge introduces elements of the existing gypsy stereotypes of the Carmen persona to a character *also* figured as an attractive and outgoing Black woman who works in a military base: whether causal or not, Dandridge was the first African American nominated for the Best Actress (or, indeed, Actor) Academy Award for her role in *Carmen Jones*, cementing her already developing success.

In Preminger's film, Carmen seduces Joe, a young soldier who hopes to follow a career in the air force; he irremediably falls in love with Carmen and ruins his exemplary life when he does not succeed in establishing a conventional relationship with her. Apart from the significant modifications of the original plot (not least: location, period, occupation of the main characters), the major point here is the creation of new role for a Black female character in an American movie. Carmen Jones does not fit into the—self-evidently rather limited—filmic Black female stereotypes of the time; she is neither a shunned prostitute nor an old mammy. She is an independent young woman who decides how she wants to live her life: she gains this agency by performing the role of a character who evokes the stereotypes of a gypsy woman.

Dorothy Dandridge embodied new narratives for Black women as Carmen Jones, new possibilities of representation that challenged the status quo questioning not only race but also gender issues. David Schroeder states that, in this film, "Carmen represents a very different kind of black culture, one which many whites fear since it strikes them as hovering at the edge of crime, loose morals, and perhaps even primitivism."[13] Even if Schroeder seems close to collapsing Dandridge's performance into precisely that of the prostitute figure, if not one who is shunned, at the same time, she represents a model that (Black) patriarchy fears, as seen in the constant attempts of Joe to control Carmen. She enjoys her freedom and seems to live according to a carpe diem philosophy, defying the rules, the roles, and the conventions of romance, without any desire to settle down and form a family. Instead, Carmen Jones is sexually active: she uses her sensuality to seduce men, and that is what, repeating familiar patriarchal tropes, seems to prompt Joe to murder her.

Carmen Jones had a significant impact at the time and undoubtedly the individuality of the main character was a major factor in Dorothy Dandridge's Academy Award nomination. She was also the first Black woman to appear on the cover of *Life* magazine, in November 1954. It is significant that in the *Life* photograph she appears with a red rose in her hair and casting a defiant glance over her shoulder, while the text presents her as "Hollywood's fiery Carmen Jones." Once again, the connotations of the character are related to wildness, primitivism, and savagery, and all of them highlight both her singularity and her Otherness, an Otherness that stereotypical and racist constructions of both gypsyness and Blackness hold in common. As André stresses, "there is no room for a middle-class black Carmen Jones outside of the factory or domestic sphere for raising children.... As the marginalized

'Other' Carmen Jones still needs a narrative that is different than the acceptable feminized model allowed for white womanhood."[14]

Beyoncé plays the main character in *Carmen: A Hip Hopera*.[15] The film, directed by Robert Townsend and produced by MTV, follows the narrative structure of *Carmen Jones*, like its model updating the story to a contemporary context. The film is also a musical, but the music is not that of Bizet's opera (as it was in *Carmen Jones*), but a new score composed by Kip Collins. Musical numbers in the film are not sung but rather rapped and integrated into the narrative action. The film's events take place in Philadelphia and Los Angeles and, from the opening scene, the attempt to combine elements from opera and hip hop is evident: an ensemble of urban musicians playing orchestra instruments (violin and timpani) in the streets of a suburb, and rapper Da Brat introducing the story. The prologue evidences the literary nature of the story by using the figure of a narrator and, at the same time, it constitutes a sort of hip hoperatic overture that captures the mix of classical and popular musical tradition that also coexisted in Bizet's opera.[16]

I argue that this film is a more effective way for Beyoncé to show power and gain agency as a solo artist than any music video. It inscribes her star persona within the narrative of a character, which is to say Carmen, who is by one reading empowered and liberated, if by another always already terminally silenced. Moreover, as André stresses, "Even as the century drew to a close, the story was still presented in a segregated setting—an all-black cast where the action was focused in the urban centers of Philadelphia and Los Angeles."[17] Even if André is right, that "the movie did not significantly catapult anyone into the spotlight,"[18] at the same time, in the adaptation of the story to the context of contemporary hip hop culture, Beyoncé writes her *own* narrative as a star.[19] Carmen Brown is not a woman who simply lives for the moment: she has the dream of becoming an artist, a star. Carmen Jones convinces Joe to escape from the rural South to metropolitan Chicago, the city where many African Americans gained prosperity in the mid-twentieth century, and Carmen Brown convinces Derek to escape to Los Angeles, the city where the mainstream studios are located. This desire for success in life—or the yoking together of art and stardom—is not in the original story; it could hardly be, given its capitalism is at odds with the aspirations of Romanticism.[20] As André puts it, "While Carmen Jones does not present an alternative path, besides working in the factory and possibly marrying into wealth, ... Carmen Brown has aspirations and goals to 'make it big' and become a singer and actress," even if this must be set against André's simultaneously reminder that "despite the vast gains black people in America had made, Carmen Jones and Carmen Brown love and pursue segregated dreams, fifty years apart in the United States at midcentury and the dawn of the new millennium."[21]

Both *Carmen Jones* and *Carmen: A Hip Hopera* have been criticized for several reasons. Virginia Guarinos considers the latter a mere updating of the former,[22] while Susan McClary perceives no rebellion in any of these Carmens—"'bad girls' turn out to be only misguided good girls" she says—and stresses the loose and dubious treatment of the musical numbers in both films.[23] But it is the issue of race that attracts more criticism; both films present an all-Black cast, portraying a sort of utopia that avoids any consideration of racial tension. James Baldwin noted the explicit exclusion of white America in *Carmen Jones*, and *Carmen: A Hip Hopera* appears to be a celebratory narrative of Black community that emphasizes its *imaginarium*, its sense of bonding and brotherhood.[24] It is a utopian representation of an imagined community that encompasses elements associated with hip hop: suburbs, violence, slang, and, of course, rap.[25] Yet, as seen already, André reads both films as representing and reproducing "segregated dreams."[26]

Nevertheless, it is my contention that these films can hardly be criticized for those reasons, because they are, in fact, simply reproducing the stereotypes that have always characterized *any* version of *Carmen*. Indeed, as André notes, "While Carmen Jones is more domesticated from her original roots, the realities of the 1950s Hollywood film allies well with Mérimée and Bizet's story."[27] Both Mérimée's short story and Bizet's opera are situated in an "imaginary geography" (in Said's terms), in a picturesque Spain that never existed, through a love triangle of archetypal characters, while displaying all the possible contemporary topics on gender, ethnicity, race, and nation. Those seminal narratives did not reflect the context of Seville in the mid-nineteenth century, but they rather participated in the building of an imaginary Spain presenting and establishing links among a group of topics: gypsies, flamenco music, bullfighters, macho men, passion, and so on. It is not surprising that the translation of the story to other imaginary communities and geographies is quite direct and uncomplicated, which is what is found in both *Carmen Jones* and *Carmen: A Hip Hopera* in their respective treatments of Black identity. In the making of footage from the latter, actor Mos Def (Lieutenant Miller in the film) highlights how the film tries to "locate the Black people" (4:15), and stresses that the director, Robert Townsend, "is Black" (4:30), as a guarantor of his suitability to direct the film. This suggests that race is a part of the message of the film, which connects the exclusion that stigmatizes the history of the gypsy people to the "epic" of the Black community in the United States, implicitly linking the "outsiderness" and historical persecution of gypsy and Black communities.

Undoubtedly, Beyoncé profits from this updated version of Carmen. She cannot avoid the death of Carmen Brown, but as Susan McClary observes, "it isn't even Derek who murders his Carmen but rather the corrupt police officer."[28] This evil character (Lieutenant Miller) does not appear in the original story, nor in *Carmen Jones*, and takes on all culpability for the crimes in the plot. Thus, both main characters stay blameless and the story is reduced to a passionate and impossible love story with neither betrayal nor sin. Beyoncé embodies the role of an empowered female gypsy, but Carmen Brown is a composite of only the positive qualities of the original character: she is sensual, charming, powerful, passionate, and free but rejects other aspects of the original character that may be controversial: she is not unfaithful or an outlaw, nor is she unstable. Besides, she is inscribed in a scenario where all the topics of hip hop are displayed, gaining authenticity as a rapper, while taking no risks that involve problematic issues related to race and ethnicity.

The foregoing discussion provides the main reasons to consider *Carmen: A Hip Hopera* a significant step in the promotion of Beyoncé's solo career, a sort of rite of passage from a group to an individual identity. Through Carmen Brown, she evokes the gypsy female character from a safe distance, in dialogue with other Carmens, like Carmen Jones, figuring a Carmen still occupying this "gypsy" territory, but simultaneously elaborating the story of her own "Black Carmen." The external elements surrounding Beyoncé's Carmen produce a certain sort of agency in the same way and to the same degree that the sound track incorporates the flavor of the original opera, including the "Habanera." The association of Beyoncé with Carmen proved to be successful, since the next year Pepsi made use of the Carmen character to launch its first spot with Beyoncé. The commercial, directed by Spike Lee, is a one-minute scene of a Broadway-style musical with Beyoncé singing a version of the famous "Habanera," dressed in red and black, like Carmen

Jones, with the red rose in her hair. The result is a pastiche, an aesthetic commodification of the character who nonetheless reinscribes Beyoncé's relationship with this gypsy archetype even some time after the movie that had first explicitly made the link.

IRREEMPLAZABLE: BEYONCÉ'S LATIN SOUL AND THE CROSSOVER

Beyoncé started her solo career in a turbulent period for the music industry. Digital technologies and the development of online peer-to-peer practices caused a sharp decrease in record sales. In parallel with this, however, there was a niche in the music market that had been growing significantly since the 1990s: the Latin music market. In the late twentieth century what has been called "the Latin explosion" took place, a massive success of Latin artists in the United States (for example, Gloria Estefan, Maná, Ricky Martin) that demonstrated the significance of the Latin community for the cultural industries and, especially, for the music industry.[29] In 2002, there were 38.8 million Hispanics registered in the census of the United States (comprising 13.3% of the total population), which made them the largest minority in the country, with an average age of twenty-four years old. Their spending power had significantly increased since the 1980s and, of course, popular music was one of their main interests. But they were born in the United States and "they are the unique generation of immigrants that does not claim to be recognized as North Americans."[30] They assert their Latin identity, and popular culture (music, cinema, television) is a key medium through which to articulate it. Obviously, it is no coincidence that MTV Latino was launched in 1993, the same year that Gloria Estefan published her album *Mi Tierra* (the first number-one album on *Billboard*'s new Latin chart), and the Latin Grammy Awards started in 2000, the same year that *College Music Journal* established a section called "Ñ Alternative."

The career of Destiny's Child ran almost entirely in parallel with the Latin explosion on the axis of R&B; by the early 2000s, almost every mainstream artist had already performed at least a song in Spanish, Destiny's Child doing it in the Grammy Awards of 2002, singing "Quisiera ser" with Spanish songwriter Alejandro Sanz. Beyoncé has always referred to the public acceptance of this first experience as critical for her decision to record the

Spanish version of some of the songs from her second solo album on the EP *Irreemplazable* (2007). Nevertheless, the crossover to the Latin market is not simply a question of recording Spanish covers; it is not only about language, but a more complex process that involves many issues: nationality, race, and ethnicity, not least. In other words, the Latin crossover has to do with *performing* an identity and articulating a convincing discourse. I will explore how Beyoncé's Latin crossover contributed to her global success, especially with the release of her second solo album, but also in previous recordings and performances. I have already explained how embodying the character of Carmen situated her in proximity to the Spanish stereotypes, but the picture would be incomplete without examining this wider context.

But, how can Latin music be defined? It is a category that has been created in the United States. It refers not to the music of any particular country but rather embraces musical forms from various traditions. In this sense, it is connected to notions of Otherness and orientalism, because it has always been defined in opposition to the hegemonic anglophone repertoire. Returning to the late nineteenth century to track the category, the seminal traces in the repertory can be found in the Spanish artists who succeeded in the main cities of the United States, such as Carmencita and La Bella Otero. The latter, as well as Tórtola Valencia, invented their own genealogies to fit the stereotypes of *Carmen*, and they pretended to be from Andalusia and to have gypsy heritage.[31] As Colmeiro points out, "the conflation of orientalism with the exoticized and idealized images of Gypsies has also been intimately linked and confused with the modern construction of Spanishness."[32]

In parallel with this, in the early 1900s, Spain and its former American colonies strengthened their relationships to face the increasing power of the United States and the decay of the so-called Latin nations.[33] The diplomatic movement represented the political consolidation of so-called panhispanism, but many previous manifestations demonstrated a constant cultural interaction between Spain and the Americas, as in the case of the "Habanera," a musical form that made the round trip and emerged in the nineteenth century; it became very popular in France at the 1850s as a musical representation of Spanishness and succeeded in America by merging with flamenco sounds, contributing in turn to shaping the melting pot of panhispanic music. Of course, the popularity of Bizet's "Habanera" in *Carmen* was one of the determining factors in linking this form to gypsyness and, then, to the association between the form and notions of sensuality and exoticism. The syncopated pattern of the "Habanera" is noticeable in early jazz compositions (as in the music of Scott Joplin and William Handy), and Peter Manuel argues that the "Habanera" is a constituent part of the Creole musical tradition of New Orleans in the mid-nineteenth century.[34] But it is not only a matter of habaneras: gypsyness was displayed in other music genres in the mid-twentieth century, such as the popular "Gypsy Mambo" and "Gypsy Conga" by Spanish Cuban composer Xavier Cugat.

The examples outlined in this longish detour, before my return to Beyoncé, demonstrate the difficulties in tracing the origins and evolution of so-called Latin music, but, more important, they also confirm the existence of the category as a mélange in which many musical traditions collide. These are the roots of contemporary Latin pop, a label that, as Daniel Party stresses, "needs to be understood as the result of postnational modes of production that successfully hybridize Latin and North American elements."[35] He explores the "Miamization" of contemporary Latin culture "as a process of change including Americanization and the adoption of a particular Latino quality" that in music resulted in a more-or-less homogeneous style called the Miami sound.[36] Thus, Miami becomes the place where the Latin forms are negotiated and defined; known as "the Latin Hollywood," in this city are concentrated the main Latin popular culture infrastructures and productions (music, cinema, soap operas) consumed by the Latino community. This situation facilitates crossovers both for the Hispanic artists who aim at international success and for the anglophone stars who aim to reach the Latino community. I will focus on the latter strategy in order to explore the case of Beyoncé.

Ed Morales asserts that "the only things that hold together the concept of Latin music are the same things that unify Latinos—a language, Spanish; Spain's cultural traditions; and large helpings of African and indigenous traditions that vary by region."[37] These ingredients are surely too vague to explore the features of what is called Latin music nowadays; gypsyness, however, seems to be the perfect vehicle to navigate across such wide margins. Madonna's "La Isla Bonita" (1987) represents a precedent. The lyrics describe San Pedro (a utopian island), mixing tropical and Spanish topics, and referring to samba and an undefined Spanish lullaby. Madonna sings several verses in Spanish and the song combines flamenco guitar and castanets and

Cuban percussion (bongo drums, maracas). The music video represents the singer in a Latin nowhere, dancing in a red flamenco dress and praying in a Catholic chapel. Madonna had also displayed Latin topics in the video of "Like a Prayer," and more recently she included a thirty-minute "Latin-gypsy" medley in the tour for her 2015 album, *Rebel Heart*.

Other mainstream artists have followed the Latin-gypsy path. For instance, Jennifer Lopez embodied a Romani dancing flamenco in the music video of "Ain't It Funny" (2000). Like Madonna in "La Isla Bonita," Lopez starts whispering a verse in Spanish, and flamenco guitars and castanets are heard during the song. There is also flamenco clapping and the tune of a famous pasodoble played by a trumpet, but there is no musical signification relating to the Romani scenario of the video. For her part, Shakira plays constantly with these topics in her music. She has Romani ("Eyes like Yours") and flamenco songs ("La Tortura"), combining both traditions in the significantly titled "Gypsy." Madonna, Jennifer Lopez, and Shakira can easily articulate this Latin discourse in their star persona by pointing toward their Latin roots. Doing so was more difficult for Beyoncé, but she succeeded by appealing not so much to her origins as to her "Latin soul."

In January 2003, immediately after her Carmen film and Pepsi commercial, Beyoncé was invited to perform at the Super Bowl pregame with Carlos Santana. The match took place in San Diego and, at that time, Latin music was already a commercial success. Santana can be considered as a gatekeeper of the Latin crossover: he is the representative figure of Latin rock in the 1960s and, by the end of the century, he had released several successful albums featuring artists such as Maná, Rob Thomas, and Michelle Branch. In the show, Beyoncé performed with Santana an arrangement of Tito Puente's mambo "Oye Cómo Va?" She sings in English, and the piece results in a convincing encounter between mambo and soul traditions. In an interview prior to the show for ABC-TV, Santana presented the concert as an opportunity to "represent the ghetto, the shanty towns, the barrio, the hood ... all the people who a lot of times seem that they're invisible. So, I'm very grateful that they invited us and Beyoncé to keep the America rainbow thing happening.... We are really grateful to represent the multi-rainbow thing that America is."[38] Thus, Beyoncé gets close to the Latin music, featuring an authorized voice in one of the most watched television broadcasts.

Nevertheless, it is in her second solo album where she clearly aims to effect the Latin crossover, publishing the EP *Irreemplazable* (2007) with some Spanish covers from *B'Day* and a new duet with Mexican Alejandro Fernández. The album was produced by Cuban American Rudy Pérez, who already had succeeded in developing Latin crossovers with Christina Aguilera and Il Divo, among others. Beyoncé doesn't speak Spanish, and she apparently sang the lyrics phonetically, but the result is nevertheless quite convincing. The release of the album was carefully prepared, with interviews in which Beyoncé explains how she grew up in Houston surrounded by Latin culture and how she learned some Spanish at school and through listening to Selena.[39] She also alludes to her Creole heritage to emphasize her connection with the Latin culture. The promotion of the album was especially striking in *People en español* magazine, the top-selling Spanish-language magazine in the United States; an interview entitled "The Latin Soul of Beyoncé" was published in March, and in May she appeared on the cover of a special edition of "Los 50 más bellos" (50 most beautiful) Latins of the year. The editorial in this issue explains that, even if Beyoncé is not Latin, she appears as an "honorary Latin Beauty,"[40] and that she gained the honor because of her new album in Spanish.

Not by chance, Beyoncé appears in the cover with Alejandro Fernández, a former ranchera singer who undertook the Latin crossover to the Miami sound in the late nineties. The two sing the duet "Amor Gitano" ("Gypsy love"), the opening song of the album, which maps perfectly onto the Latin style. The introduction is clearly in a flamenco manner: a male *quejío* (groan chant) singing "gitana" is accompanied by a Spanish guitar and the sound of castanets. Then, Beyoncé and Fernández start to sing, and the song runs on in a flamenco pop style (like that of Alejandro Sanz). The chorus is a harmonic sequence of chords deploying the Andalusian cadence, the rhythmic pattern reinforced with flamenco clapping. In the final cadence of the song, right after the climax, Beyoncé inserts a hint of soul in a brief descending scale. The music is consonant with the (Spanish) lyric that describes the passionate love story of a gypsy couple, which is to say Beyoncé and Alejandro Fernández.

"Amor Gitano" served as the theme song for the Colombian soap opera *El Zorro, la espada y la rosa*, a new version of the stories of the masked crusader that was broadcast in Latin America and Europe. Zorro may be read as another Latin archetype: his adventures take place in Los Angeles, when the city was under the control of Mexico, and, in this retelling, the plot is packed with Latin-gypsy topics. Thus the song (and the singers by extension) absorbs all these connotations.

"Bello Embustero" ("Beautiful liar") appears in three versions on the album: one sung by Beyoncé alone, another in Spanglish featuring her alter ego Sasha Fierce, and the most popular one with Shakira. The song was also recorded in English for *B'Day*. It begins with a swaying guitar pattern that moves only a semitone, thus creating harmonic tension, a melody that recalls Romani music and a pasodoble flourish played by a trumpet create a further sense of expectation before Beyoncé and Shakira start to sing. All together, these elements figure a simultaneously exotic and erotic sound, reinforced by the repeated moaning of the two singers during the performance. The song also inserts flamenco clapping in the chorus and presents a brief passage (2:20) in an explicit Romani style.

The only modification in the title track, "Irreemplazable" ("Irreplaceable"), is the translation of the lyrics, as also happens in "Oye" ("Listen"). The album, however, includes a norteña remix of the song that connects it with north Mexican popular music. The structure is the same, but the sound of an accordion from the very beginning, the syncopated and offbeat rhythmic patterns and the Latin percussion (shaker, bongo drums) give a different air to the song. The final track is a remix of "Get Me Bodied" featuring Puerto Rican rapper Julio Voltio. This version combines music styles, but Voltio clearly drives the piece to the formal patterns of reggaetón.

Irreemplazable gathers together in eight tracks a wide variety of styles that fit Latin music—flamenco, norteña, romantic ballad, and reggaetón—and it has a male-female duet with Beyoncé, both Latin American artists who had already succeeded in the Latin market. The album contains, then, all the ingredients to appeal to a wide target from different Spanish-speaking countries, but especially to the Latino community in the United States. Even if Beyoncé did not specifically aim to consolidate her developing crossover into the Latin market, I argue that *Irreemplazable* was a must for an artist who was forging her career as a global star. The lack of convincing links to the Latin community (idiom, culture, lineage) forced Beyoncé to appeal to her "Latin soul," adopting roles and displaying topics associated with a Latin identity, a strategy in part *enabled* by the embodiment of Carmen she had earlier performed.

CONCLUSION

Approaching the star persona of an artist is not an easy task. It involves the consideration of many identity patterns that interact and collide, articulating complex discourses that in turn need to be studied from different perspectives. In this chapter, I analyzed Beyoncé's attempts to effect a Latin crossover; my intention was not to reveal her commercial strategies to succeed in this market, but rather to explore the way an African American female artist deeply entwined with the R&B musical tradition could develop Latin features. As I have demonstrated, it is not only a question of language; singing in Spanish is key for the Latin crossover, but a Latin identity too must be performed, and any move to highlight a particular cultural issue in the discourse of an artist has implications for her star persona. Thus, when Beyoncé played the title character in *Carmen: A Hip Hopera*, she was expressing a position on gender, race, ethnicity, and so on that affected (and surely was affected by) her subject position.

Of course, any performance establishes intertextual relations. I have focused on the gypsy archetype that Beyoncé displayed several times in her career and, to do so, I have had to consider the configuration and the evolution of gypsyness in Western music from the nineteenth into the twentieth century. Thus, in Carmen Brown we can observe some traces of Carmen Jones, but also a bit of Bonnie and of Maria; we see an empowered Black female rapper, but also the trace of the sensuality and exoticism of Bizet's and Mérimée's seminal characters. In the same way, a song like "Amor Gitano" is inscribed in a configuration of topics that, again, recall the nineteenth-century tradition and archetypes like El Zorro but also establish a dialogue with contemporary artists such as Madonna, Jennifer Lopez, and Shakira. I have explored these relations as part of the same discourse: the orientalism and the exotic Otherness that made it possible for Latin music to embrace gypsyness.

This analysis may be approached from a different point of view and paying attention to other issues. My intention was not to study a universal articulation of gypsyness in Latin music, but rather to analyze the discursive strategies deployed by Beyoncé to reach a relevant target in the contemporary music business. Undoubtedly, her positioning and her moves would have been very different in another context if, for example, the Latin explosion hadn't happened. But, as I argue above, the Latin strategy was essential for her to become a truly *global* hit, and it contributed to the articulation of a more complex and kaleidoscopic star persona. In other words, it enriched and consolidated her career.

EDUARDO VIÑUELA is Professor of Music and Director of Pop Rock Studies at the Universidad de Oviedo in Spain. He is author of *El videoclip en España (1980–1995): gesto audiovisual, discurso y mercado* and coeditor of *Rock around Spain: historia, industria, escenas y medios de comunicación*.

NOTES

1. I understand "star persona" in the terms outlined in Dyer, *Stars*, and Dyer, *Heavenly Bodies*.
2. Said, *Orientalism*, 2.
3. Don José in Mérimée, *Carmen*, 47.
4. Colmeiro, "Exorcising Exoticism," 132.
5. The term *gitanismo* encompasses not only the notion of gypsy customs, but also the cultural expression of the gypsies more broadly understood.
6. Mora, "Some Notes," 111.
7. Colmeiro, "Rehispanicizing Carmen," 92.
8. This point is central to the arguments of Colmeiro, "Exorcising Exoticism," and Mora, "Carmencita."
9. Clúa, *Cuerpos*, 10.
10. Goldberg, "Jaleo de Jerez," 136.
11. Mora, "Carmencita," 229. Carmencita, "The Pearl of Seville," was a Spanish-style dancer in pre-vaudeville US variety and music hall ballet.
12. *Carmen Jones*, dir. Otto Preminger (20th Century Fox, 1954, 105 minutes).
13. Schroeder, *Cinema's Illusions'*, 251.
14. André, *Black Opera*, 152.
15. *Carmen: A Hop Hopera*, dir. Robert Townsend (MTV, 2001, 88 minutes).
16. McClary, "Carmen," 207.
17. André, *Black Opera*, 157.
18. Ibid.
19. Derek is the only character who retains his original role, that of the policeman (or nearly: José was a soldier in Mérimée's short story); Escamillo is not a bullfighter as in the opera, nor a boxer as in *Carmen Jones*, but a successful rapper.
20. By contrast, when José tries to convince Carmen to leave Spain and start a new life in the New World, in America, she laughs at him.

21. André, *Black Opera*, 157.
22. Guarinos, "Carmen Jones," 189.
23. McClary, "Carmen," 213.
24. Baldwin, quoted in Furman, "Screen Politics," 125.
25. Anderson, *Imagined Communities*. See, too, Adam Krims, *Music and Urban Geography* (Abingdon, Routledge, 2007), 118.
26. André, *Black Opera*, 157.
27. Ibid., 152.
28. McClary, "Carmen," 213.
29. The expression "Latin explosion" appeared in many magazines, and it is the title of a recent music documentary produced by HBO.
30. Pereira, *Buscando el crossover*, 24.
31. Clúa, *Cuerpos*, 198.
32. Colmeiro quoted in Guarinos, "Carmen Jones," 179.
33. Alonso, "En el espejo," 97.
34. Manuel, "Introduction," 20.
35. Party, "Miamization," 76.
36. Ibid., 69.
37. Morales, *Latin Beat*, xi.
38. Carlos Santana on jorgebayarea YouTube post, "Carlos Santana Celine Dion Beyonce," November 13, 2012, https://www.youtube.com/watch?v=G9nYf2XEvOQ.
39. Selena was the best-selling Latin female singer of the 1990s in the United States and Mexico.
40. "¿Quiénes son los 50 más bellos?" *People en español*, April 30, 2007, http://peopleenespanol.com/article/quienes-son-los-50-mas-bellos/.

BIBLIOGRAPHY

Alonso, Celsa. "En el espejo de 'los otros': andalucismo, exotismo e hispanismo." In *Creación musical, cultura popular y construcción nacional en la España contemporánea*, 83–104. Madrid: Instituto Complutense de Ciencias Musicales, 2010.

Anderson, Benedict. *Imagined Communities: Reflections on the Origin and Spread of Nationalism*. Rev. ed. London: Verso, 2006.

André, Naomi. *Black Opera: History, Power, Engagement*. Urbana: University of Illinois Press, 2018.

Brewer, Roy. "The Use of Habanera Rhythm in Rockabilly Music." *American Music* 17, no. 3 (1999): 300–17.

Clúa, Isabel. *Cuerpos de escándalo: celebridad femenina en el "fin-de siècle."* Barcelona: Icara, 2016.

Colmeiro, José. "Exorcising Exoticism: 'Carmen' and the Construction of Oriental Spain." *Comparative Literature* 54, no. 2 (2002): 127–44.

———. "Rehispanicizing Carmen: Cultural Reappropriations in Spanish Cinema." In *Carmen: From Silent Film to MTV*. Edited by Chris Perriam and Ann Davies, 91–106. New York: Rodopi, 2005.

Dyer, Richard. *Heavenly Bodies: Film Stars and Society*. New York: St. Martin's Press, 1986.

———. *Stars*. London: British Film Institute, 1979.

Furman, Nelly. "Screen Politics: Otto Preminger's *Carmen Jones*." In *Carmen: From Silent Film to MTV*. Edited by Chris Perriam and Ann Davies, 121–33. New York: Rodopi, 2005.

Goldberg, K. Meira. "*Jaleo de Jerez* and *Tumulte Noir*: Primitivist Modernism and Cakewalk in Flamenco, 1902–1917." In *Flamenco on the Global Stage. Historical, Critical and Theoretical Perspectives*. Edited by K. Meira Goldberg, Ninotchka Devorah Bennahum, and Michelle Heffner Hayes, 124–42. Jefferson, NC: McFarland, 2015.

———. "The Latin Craze and the Gypsy Mask: Carmen Amaya and the Flamenco Aesthetic: 1913–1963." In *100 Years of Flamenco in New York City*. Edited by Ninotchka Bennahum and Goldberg, 68–99. New York: New York Public Library for the Performing Arts, 2013.

Guarinos, Virginia. "*Carmen Jones* ¿Una Carmen Americana, afroamericana? Incluso dos." In *Carmen global: El mito en las artes y los medios audiovisuales*. Edited by Rafael Utrera and Virginia Guarinos, 177–92. Seville: Universidad de Sevilla, 2010.

Krims, Adam. *Music and Urban Geography*. Abingdon, Routledge, 2007.

Manuel, Peter. "Introduction: Contradance and Quadrille Culture in the Caribbean." In *Creolizing Contradanze in the Caribbean*. Edited by Peter Manuel, 1–50. Philadelphia: Temple University Press, 2009.

McClary, Susan. "Carmen as Perennial Fusion: From Habanera to Hip-Hop." In *Carmen: From Silent Film to MTV*. Edited by Chris Perriam and Ann Davies, 205–16. New York: Rodopi, 2005.

Mérimée, Prosper. *Carmen*. Translated by Nicholas Jotcham. Oxford: Oxford University Press, 1989.

Mora, Kiko. "Carmencita en cinco fragmentos y una coda." *España Contemporánea* 25, no. 2 (2015): 223–42.

———. "Some Notes toward a Historiography of the Mid-nineteenth Century *Bailable Español*." In *Flamenco on the Global Stage: Historical, Critical and Theoretical Perspectives*. Edited by K. Meira Goldberg, Ninotchka Devorah Bennahum, and Michelle Heffner Hayes, 103–16. Jefferson, NC: McFarland, 2015.

Morales, Ed. *The Latin Beat: The Rhythms and Roots of Latin Music, from Bossa Nova to Salsa and Beyond*. Cambridge, MA: Da Capo, 2003.

Party, Daniel. "The Miamization of Latin-American Pop Music." In *Postnational Musical Identities: Cultural Production, Distribution and Consumption in a Globalized Scenario*. Edited by Ignacio Corona and Alejandro L. Madrid, 65–80. Lanham, MD: Lexington, 2008.

Pereira, Adriana. *Buscando el crossover: El mercado para la música latina alternativa en Estados Unidos*. Madrid: Fundación Autor, 2004.

Said, Edward. *Orientalism*. New York: Vintage, 1979.

Schroeder, David. *Cinema's Illusions, Opera's Allure: The Operatic Impulse on Film*. New York: Continuum, 2002.

3

Beyoncé Online, Re-presenting Beyoncé

EIGHT

Unlikely Resemblances

Beyoncé, "Single Ladies," and Comparative Judgment of Popular Dance

MARY FOGARTY WOEHREL

"SINGLE LADIES": THE CASE STUDY

By March 31, 2010, a YouTube clip called, "Baby Dancing to Beyoncé— ORIGINAL! @babycory on Twitter" has had 10,662,954 views.[1] The video is one shot, straight on, of a diapered baby leaning on a coffee table, with its back to the camera lens, in front of a large television set where Beyoncé's "Single Ladies (Put a Ring on It)" (2008) music video is playing. The baby bops along to the video, stretching out legs, and occasionally hands, almost in sync with the dancers. At moments the baby settles down on the floor, on knees and bottom, but quickly gets momentum back up to its feet to continue the dance.

This bouncing-baby vignette of the "Single Ladies" music video is part of a network of paratexts such as homages, parodies, mash-ups, and commentaries.[2] These raise questions about authorship in dance, as assigned by fans of popular music and dance. Many of the issues around popular dance "copies" of previous work reveal not only some inspirations or influences of the creators but also how often people in everyday capacities compare different performances to generate meanings.

When art critics are outraged at a popular reconstruction of a choreography they hold as sacred, what is revealed is not so much a consolidation of the sense of immorality surrounding artistic theft as the tumbling out of some deeper, problematic cultural biases. Often hidden in their critiques about cultural theft or misappropriation are derogatory, inflammatory comments about "trivial" entertainment settings and lowly performances not worthy even to be taken seriously as reference or reconstruction.[3]

In this chapter I focus both on popular artists' choreography and fan performances. The issue here is how copying dance moves is interpreted based on who is doing the interpretation, how well it is done, and to what (perceived) gain. Beyoncé's music video, "Single Ladies," together with the online commentary and the YouTube mash-ups inspired by it, provides a unique case study, offering insights into both artists and fans. This discussion concerns Beyoncé's "Single Ladies" music video, the question of Bob Fosse's influence, and, most important, the camp remix by Shane Mercado in his bedroom in a thong (a performance I champion as fabulous and necessary). Mercado's fan performance of Beyoncé's music video on YouTube, its million-plus views, and subsequent invited televised appearances by Mercado, will illustrate how fan judgments work in popular culture at the intersection of dance and music. Out of this discussion I will raise several issues around popular dance including popular reconstruction (or remixes), credit and authorship, and what audiences "do" with popular dance on the internet. Dance isn't a "thing" so much as it is a bodily experience and form of sociality. Part of that sociality involves audiences of dance who talk about dance practice, not only with moral judgments about authenticity and ownership, but also with pleasure found in incongruencies within the performances. In other words, audiences often value finding unlikely resemblances between different performances that are performed with pleasure, humor, and talent.

For audiences, meaning is often found at the intersection between music and dance, between artist and fan (with a curiously minor consideration of the choreographer). This exploration raises issues about casual, everyday assessments about dance in music videos, and, in particular, the way that these evaluations are performed.

Beyoncé's "Single Ladies" song premiered on October 8, 2008, on WWPR's Power 105.1 and was released on October 13, 2008. Music video aside, the music itself becomes a material object played in cafés, on YouTube, and in cars. As Sylvester argues, "in its own jump-rope sort of way . . . [it's] hustler music. Every aspect of the song comes secondhand or straight pilfered.

Producers The-Dream and Tricky Stewart swipe the heavy drops and double-time claps from Beyoncé's own 'Get me Bodied'; B's bubbly melody rarely changes mode, and to be sure, she walks down one note at a time from fifth to root for the chorus, third to root for the verse, cf. 'hot cross buns.'"[4] This reading is rather cynical. I would add that there's some tricky harmonic color as well in the chorus, where the dissonant bass-line move suggests a modulation that never arrives, adding a murky feel to the "bubbly melody" and giving an edge to the lyric's taunt that "you should have put a ring on it."

For fans of dance, the danceability of a song is an aesthetic criterion for musical judgments about the song itself, a point that highlights fans' abilities to make abstractions about movement meaningful. Thus, the intersection of dance and music is an important place to begin to measure the meaning of music in the lives of people who love dance.

The "Single Ladies" music video was directed by Jake Nava and choreographed by Jaquel Knight with Frank Gatson. It was made cheaply to allow the more expensive "If I Were a Boy" video to be made.[5] "If I Were a Boy" appeals to viewers as a self-contained minifilm narrative (the original, paradigmatic mininarrative being, of course, Michael Jackson's "Thriller"), whereas "Single Ladies" appeals to appreciators of dance.

The video begins in darkness as the sound track kicks in. The lights fade in to three women—Beyoncé the central of the trio—in black leotards and black heels. The video has a stark, *Vogue*-inspired set, featuring one celebrity pop singer and two back-up dancers, Ebony Williams and Ashley Everett. They dance throughout the entire music video as the lights fade in and out, the camera occasionally zooming in gradually, and out slightly more dramatically, panning from side to side, sometimes viewing the dancers from above (crucially at 2'05" and 2'27" at the beginning and end of the bridge) and generally playing with the distance between the lens and the dancers in a rather subtle way. The dancing itself could distract the viewer from the quality of engagement provided by the camera work. The obvious simplicity of the set and content (three women dancing, lights, camera movement, and fades) in many ways enhances an appreciation of just how stylized the dancing is, as if the dancers were video-game avatars. Beyoncé lip-syncs throughout, and most of the choreography is timed to match the structure and lyrical content of the song while allowing for some individual, kinetic interpretations by the dancers.

The gray-scale of colors with the black costuming allows the movement vocabulary to "pop," to be easily identifiable within the monochrome world. Movements of arms across the body or particular kicks are easily deciphered and, because most of the movement is frontal and doesn't use a lot of space, the performance invites a bedroom or living room response. Audiences can mirror the choreography back to the star, it's accessible enough that the viewer can pick up enough aspects of the movement to participate, whether sitting down, or after clearing out a bit of space. The video invites a participatory read as well as a voyeuristic one. One thing is clear, though, the video worked instantaneously with fans, and grew meaning with additional views.

The iconic music video "Single Ladies" has won music video awards and became a point of contention at award ceremonies when it didn't win.[6] The song topped US charts, and the music video has provided a theme song with some staying power, alluded to in such various contexts as *Alvin and the Chipmunks: The Squeakquel* (2009), the US television show *Glee*, and footage of Barack Obama waving his hand with the "should have put a ring on it" gestures from the music video.[7] Furthermore, wedding disc jockeys are requested to play it for bouquet tosses.[8] Beyoncé has also remade the video into numerous live performances on award shows and television programs.[9] Not every video that is centered on dance commands this sort of attention. From babies to professional dancers, there was a quality to the "Single Ladies" video that motivated responses (whether motor reactions or professional parodies).

Casual, everyday assessments about dance in music videos and, in particular, the way that such assessments are performed and mobilized by YouTube audiences demonstrate the authority of dance. In the music video shoot, if one dancer makes a mistake, they all have to start over. The video is about three women together doing choreography in synchronization, and in call-and-response, which may be one of the most crucial elements of the video's aesthetic. It is about their relationship and spacing. Pamela J. Tracy's study of the practices of young Black girls demonstrates this point in relation to issues of race and social groups in "Why Don't You Act Your Color?" In her study, she found that young Black girls (ages nine to eleven) didn't like when their white friends "acted Black" or listened to artists such as Destiny's Child and TLC. Part of their annoyance reflected their deep affinities with particular artists, and felt ownership of their musical content.[10]

Beyoncé wins in the global pop-culture wars because club dancers in, say, Korea all prefer to do the same dance routines at the same time, and so videos like "Single Ladies" provide a complete choreography for an entire song. The package is ideal for selling both the song and Beyoncé's branding. Dance crazes in the past have similarly been used to sell music.[11]

The "Single Ladies" song and music video were not universally praised. Some of the comments on the online forums discuss how "this song sucks" and how the video is boring. Likewise, one music critic reviewing the single calls Beyoncé "out of touch with her audience."[12] The takeaway point here is that aesthetics isn't so much about agreed-upon value judgments as about how appreciation is fought over and debated. To add to that, those musical pleasures are often about dance practice and performance, and the impact of dance on the reception of music, because the two have a relationship that plays out in curious ways.

One YouTube commentator states that he, she, or they doesn't like the song but sees how it would be good to dance to in a club. The music video lays out that possible context, and that possible criterion, explicitly by means of the bare set and focus on dance. The video sells the song as danceable, in a way that the soundtrack alone might not. The danceability of the song is then an aesthetic criterion not only for the musical experience but also for a musical judgment about the (functional) worth of the song.

THE SHORT STORY OF SHANE MERCADO

Almost immediately after Beyoncé's music video aired, Shane Mercado, a New York City resident, learned the entire dance in his bedroom and performed the dance for a camera in his room, posting the result on YouTube. The video got more than a million hits very quickly. Not only is what Shane Mercado did common practice—there were many other imitations of Beyoncé's video—but the speedy rise to YouTube celebrity has also become commonplace. By the time Justin Timberlake and Beyoncé parody the "Single Ladies" video on *Saturday Night Live*, it is too late to have the same humorous impact. Shane Mercado has beaten them to the punch line. Since then, there has been a wide array of spoofs, advertising, and performances inspired by the Beyoncé video that I do not want to address here.[13] I focus instead on the two figures most discussed initially online: Shane Mercado and Bob Fosse. And I do so using a linear, real-time recall of the events, trying to lay out online commentary in the order that it unfolded, both for historical accuracy and because of what it might say about the role of timing in musical pleasures and judgments. The YouTube event narrative has two plot lines, both starting at the same point: the airing of Beyoncé's "Single Ladies (Put a Ring on It)" music video.

Shane Mercado performed the "Single Ladies" choreography in his bedroom seemingly a matter of moments after the music video came out in October 2008. His performance dominated online attention, and shared space in online conversations about the influence of Bob Fosse on the choreography in the music video. Mercado's epic online bedroom version of the dance routine was so well received that inquiries by online communities grew to a frenzy, insisting that Mercado and Beyoncé needed to meet. The resulting awkward and unspectacular exchange can be viewed online.[14] Both are cordial and professional with one another. Mercado asks a simple question: What was the hardest part of the choreography for Beyoncé to acquire? She refers to the aspects that Mercado's bedroom performance did not include (running up the wall and dancing in heels) in her response. I interviewed Shane Mercado in 2009, and relate his responses here to add the perspective of a dancing participant.[15] Shane Mercado told me that "I chose to learn the choreography from 'Single Ladies' because I just immediately fell in love with it. And as a dancer, the opportunity to actually see choreography with no edits from top to bottom was a real treat. Just also loved the choreography as well. Yes . . . I know choreography from other videos . . . and most of all Beyoncé's other choreography."[16]

By this time, Mercado has been invited to appear on the *Bonnie Hunt Show* and is featured in television news slots, where he shows television journalists, for example, how to do the dance. The dance is difficult to learn for the amateur or untrained dancer, which reveals that Mercado is hardly average. It becomes apparent that he has more than twenty years of dance training, explaining why he could pick up all the choreography so quickly.

A new controversy now begins, and this one is a bit more playful: who is the better dancer? As soon as Mercado was juxtaposed on top of the original music video, this lively debate took off with polls on websites to decide.[17]

Mercado is invited back on the *Bonnie Hunt Show* to perform other dance routines from well-known movies. The invitation demonstrates the popularity of dance performances for television audiences alongside audiences online. This introduction is enough of a backdrop to begin to address some of the categories of knowledge that appear here, and what exactly is at stake for the participants and for dance culture research.

COMPARISON IN AESTHETIC JUDGMENT

The online commentaries involving Shane Mercado began to revolve around questions of comparison. For example, participants asked each other to decide online who is the better dancer, Shane Mercado or Beyoncé. As I mentioned previously, the place where the comparisons really begin is on the *Bonnie Hunt Show*. On it, Mercado dances for the live studio audience in front of the mediated image of the music video. As soon as Mercado is juxtaposed, he is no longer just a fan doing the routine; he is a contender for the best version of the choreography.

The dance technique itself provides a different set of criteria for the comparison. In the music video, the three women have to execute the choreography at the same time. Doing so is harder than Mercado's bedroom performance because he does not need to synchronize his movements with other dancers or take into account proximity and spacing while dancing. That said, it may very well be harder for Mercado to line himself up in front of the projected music video during the *Bonnie Hunt Show*.

People had already been making similar critiques about the official music video. There are three dancers doing the choreography, so comments began to develop around those performers and their abilities. Which one is the best dancer? Then, when all the mash-up videos appeared with Fosse's dancers, Beyoncé's dancers, and Mercado spliced to appear side by side, the comparisons continued.

When I asked Mercado what was different about the *Bonnie Hunt Show* performance from the one in his bedroom, he explained: "Well my bedroom performance was done on total impulse. When I want something I want it now. So when I said to myself ... I'm gonna do it ... so I did it ... LOL. It was pure FUN.... My Bonnie performance was FUN but added to it, not nervousness ... but total and utter excitement. I still can't believe this is happening to me.

It's incredible."[18] Thus, by his account, fun is the essence of his experience of music through dance, and achieving fun is the aim. Mercado is a classically trained dancer with more than twenty years of experience, so let's see how he lines up with Beyoncé for an aesthetic comparison.

Mercado's version is playful with elements of teasing and boasting. He adds a new layer of irony, too, by being a queer man dancing to a song called "Single Ladies." The song's lyric, rather than the actual dance movements, provides that humorous subtext. One of the reasons Mercado's *Bonnie Hunt Show* performance is better than the bedroom performance is the degree to which Mercado camps it up and increases his energy and range of motion for the predominantly female live studio audience. Rather than an aesthetics of fixed values, I argue that the interpretation of popular dance involves more fluid performances—of the dance and of argumentation and debate.

MUSIC VIDEOS AS CRIME SCENES: MASH-UPS AND AUDIENCES AS DANCE SLEUTHS

While Mercado was enjoying his rise to fame, another plot was developing simultaneously. A number of YouTube viewers began producing their own homemade mash-up videos. The dance sleuths began noticing a similarity between Beyoncé's moves and the choreography of Bob Fosse. It was an easy enough association to make, for Fosse's choreography would be familiar to dance fans, and also Beyoncé's choreographers had already created a music video homage to Fosse's work for a previous album promotion.[19] Then a YouTube clip titled "The Mexican Breakfast" surfaced,[20] featuring Fosse's dance moves from *Mexican Breakfast* (1969) set to the Unk track "Walk It Out" (2006), a video mash-up that is camp in its own right. The "Mexican Breakfast" clip had already developed a cult following of its own, but it quickly got tied into the Beyoncé mix. Here was a group of participants who acted the part of detectives,[21] uncovering the mysteries of Beyoncé's video and pulling the threads together as evidence accrued.

A controversy then started up on YouTube over what can be considered moral issues in popular dance. Commentators asked, Had Beyoncé and her choreographers stolen this choreography from Bob Fosse? Was Beyoncé an impostor, who hadn't created her own concept for the music video?

Was Beyoncé not *creative*? All these questions appeared in various commentaries following the Beyoncé-inspired music video posts and "Mexican Breakfast."

A different sort of debate soon interrupted these verbal controversies. It arose from new YouTube videos that split the video screen, splicing together pieces of Bob Fosse's choreography in "Mexican Breakfast" with Beyoncé's music video. The dance sleuths began to debate the extent to which Beyoncé had borrowed movements from Fosse, using the dance clips themselves. Some of the mash-up videos included Shane Mercado as well, to make a threesome.

One dance fan,[22] in defense of Beyoncé, posted a television talk-show excerpt in which Beyoncé admits not only to being influenced by Fosse but, more importantly, to being influenced by precisely the YouTube clip that laid Unk's "Walk It Out" over the Ed Sullivan show feature of Gwen Verdon's "Mexican Breakfast." The posting sleuth writes that the haters can stop complaining because there it was from Beyoncé's own mouth, Beyoncé having offered the credit Fosse's inspiration deserved. The post appeased the online discussions.

In other words, Beyoncé credited her influences, and by doing so assuaged the adverse discussions and dampened the moral judgments. The matter has to do with one of the crucial aesthetic criteria for judging a music video, and one that has previously gone unanalyzed: the demand by fans that the choreography be original, something new, or something new that is borrowed above-board from something old.

Dance choreographers are generally not among the credits at the bottom of music videos before they start and just as they end.[23] The YouTube fans want to know who came up with the moves, who the influences were, who should get credit. What is perhaps equally interesting is that the YouTube viewers' controversy was to do with the originality of Beyoncé's concept and choreography without a mention of, or even an interest in, whether she wrote the song (she didn't) or which music producers she worked with. YouTube audiences are most (or certainly significantly more) interested in the relationship of sound to image.

In this story, however, the fans generally hold Beyoncé, rather than her choreographers, responsible for the originality, or lack of it, in the moves. In other words, the pop artist is being given credit for the dance performance in a way that suggests a collapse of typical distinctions between choreographer and dancer (with no mention of the music video director either).

The conception of the dancer as their own choreographer is a prevalent characteristic for some dance practices such as breaking, but more general hip hop dance styles still tend to split choreographers and dancers. The reason is the dominance of routines in this dance culture, which is to say, crudely, people doing dances in synchronicity. So it is significant that Beyoncé, rather than her choreographer(s), is given credit for "creating" the dance, and is also the one held "liable" in public opinion for the creative choices of the choreographers. The attitude relates to the branding of Beyoncé as the artist, and the status of choreographers as hidden laborers. In other words, Beyoncé—the star—is held accountable for all the choices even though it is unclear how much of a role she had, or could have had, in the creative decisions of the music video: choreography, lighting, costuming, and so on.

The history of music videos provides some explanation for this attribution of authorship to female artists, at least. For example, Lisa Lewis argues that artists such as Cindy Lauper used music videos precisely as a way to claim ownership of their songs and images.[24] Lauper not only changed key lyrics in a song that she didn't own (but thus authored, through her reinterpretation of the meaning) but also contributed to almost every aspect of the music video. She also employed her mother to play the part of her mother in "Girls Just Wanna Have Fun," adding an autobiographical aspect to the song and thus, again, claiming ownership of more facets of her star-text. It would be impossible for a Beyoncé fan, familiar with the star's life (in particular with her real-life marriage to Jay-Z), to miss the zoom-in toward the end of "Single Ladies" onto the expensive wedding ring on Beyoncé's gloved hand, a marker, in this representation, of Beyoncé's "real-life success" of getting her man to "put a ring on it."

The story continues as a new claim arises about the meaning of the dance moves. An intermediary dance style that had developed after Fosse and before Beyoncé, called "J-Setting," appeared in the discussions about credit and ownership. J-Setting apparently started in the 1970s with the Jackson State University marionettes, who were known as the "prancing J-setters." It developed originally as a popular dance in Black gay clubs in the United States, especially in Atlanta. The style involves a leader and a group that mimics the movements of the leader. (One common practice is called the

Eight Count, which involves eight counts of choreography with a leader and a group copying the movements.) The style, J-Setting, is itself based on Bob Fosse's choreography for *All That Jazz* (1979) and *Chicago* (1975). At a few key moments in "Single Ladies," there appears to be a call-and-response moment (with Beyoncé doing a movement sequence first, copied by the other dancers). Thus, the J-Setting style is seen to be, at the very least, an influence on Beyoncé's choreographer, Jaquel Knight. The sleuthing continues apace.

MORALITY ISSUES

The first issue at stake for audiences is morality. As is clear from the preceding discussion, Beyoncé, as an artist, has a stake in creativity. When Beyoncé addresses why she made the decisions she did about the music video, such as admitting to seeing "Walk It Out" and being influenced or inspired by it, then the fans are subdued. They aren't only subdued over ownership debates, but many actually respond with glee. They say that she's not hiding anything, and that other posters are "haters" (people who just want to put everyone down). She has cited her influences and therefore is still creative, and finally they say, "She's just like us! She watches YouTube clips for inspiration." These responses seem to come from the Beyoncé fans, but there is still a particular breed of dance fan that has a different set of criteria.

For some audiences, if most of the movements are from Fosse, then Fosse is the creative one (the artist) and Beyoncé is just a copy (therefore derivative and, in short, no good). But what happens with judgments about Shane Mercado's performance result from an entirely different set of judgmental criteria. Here the issue isn't a moral one. In other words, the viewers don't mind that he is imitating Beyoncé and not creating his own choreography. He is copying her because he is a fan and is therefore not measured for his ability to create anew, but rather his ability to copy precisely. (Indeed, it is only when Beyoncé situates herself as a fan that she is released—by some— from the judgment of being derivative.) Regardless, the issue is always about the relationship between aesthetic and moral judgments as they relate to different positions. So, it seems that comparison and copying have their foothold in judgments in popular culture with unlikely resemblances: those performances that are accurate in a surprising way supply a particular kind of pleasure.

AESTHETIC EXPERIENCE OF MUSICAL MEDIATION

An *unlikely resemblance* is a comparison that seems improbable because of the contemporary discursive context of the experience, yet immediately registers as a comprehension of a similarity.[25] In the "Walk It Out" video, for example, meaning is generated through "resemblances" between music and movement that strike one as unlikely, and which are therefore intriguing. Three visibly white women, including Fosse's wife, dance around a barren stage in colorful costumes (more covered than Beyoncé's dancers, who wear leotards, although Beyoncé's costumes signal back to a *Cabaret* and *All That Jazz* aesthetic). The general movement of the dancers around the stage is comparable to that in Beyoncé's video, although not all the Fosse movement motifs seem to be borrowed from this particular sample. The unlikely resemblance for the viewer is that between music and dance: a contemporary hip hop track set to white women dancing from decades earlier. The resemblance was clearly engaging for spectators because the synchrony between sound and image not only worked but also changed the interpretation of the music.

In the YouTube mash-up, the YouTube audience recycles material for new creative reconfigurations. Musical YouTube mash-ups, where two or more musical tracks are layered together, serve up similar unlikely resemblances that engage fans. They also provoke consideration of the music, video, and dance artists who contribute to the making of the mash-ups, and of the reception that follows their production.

The Fosse choreography is an interesting and original choice because it works as a critique. What Beyoncé admitted to liking about the YouTube clip was that Fosse's choreography, set to "Walk It Out," worked with an unlikely musical sound track. It isn't ahistorical or postmodern borrowing; it doesn't even depend on the articulated intentions of the performer, Beyoncé, or her choreographers. What is striking about the borrowing is the layers of parody that begin not with Beyoncé's remake of Fosse's choreography but rather with the Unk soundtrack for "Walk It Out" being laid over the top of the Fosse choreography for the "Mexican Breakfast." The playful borrowing, an unlikely resemblance that synchronizes movement and sound to create new comparisons, is the layered, recycled, and imaginative creation at the core of the present discussion.

YouTube, as I have suggested, provides a venue for a social group (in this case fans) to establish its own aesthetic criteria, which need not map precisely—or at all—onto historically sedimented schemes of artistic value. The YouTube community says that this video is interesting and worth investigating on YouTube. Social or amateur dancers like the video because they can imitate the dance, and professional or aspiring dancers can use the forum of the video and YouTube to get exposure. Fosse is credited, and so his legacy continues with newer generations. The argument that I have developed here reflects new approaches to and interpretations of the pop aesthetic that are clearly centered on dance practice, rather than on the issues of authenticity built into the requirement for songwriters to perform their own materials.[26]

DANCE AND MUSICAL JUDGMENTS

What does it mean that the performances of fans are judged differently from those of artists? Artists have not only constantly to refresh their reputations but also update them, and this is always in conversation with the everyday responses to their work that shape their reputations. In the preceding discussion, Shane Mercado's performance is not judged in the same way as Beyoncé's because the criteria of and for judgment are different. In addition, the distinction between amateurs and professionals becomes blurred as the context of dancers' lives is revealed. In this case, when a professional dancer (Mercado) does a remake of a Beyoncé music video in his bedroom, it is read as amateur, and the measures of his talent are enhanced through that reading. Artists, on the other hand, are judged on their originality (and, in this situation, Mercado is necessarily not judged as an artist in this sense). The critical environment is complicated in several ways for dance artists. On the one hand, choreographers for music videos are required to be original but are not typically given onscreen credit. Similarly, dancers often audition using their own choreography, as in the case of street dance, but are not paid for choreography but rather for their performance: choreographic royalties are higher than performance ones.

In the first place, popular artists are performers themselves and often dance in their own shows. Although popular music scholarship and everyday press comments focus mainly on the artistry of whether singers play their own instruments, fans clearly appreciate dance performances by these artists. In this sense, popular artists when performing are given credit for and ownership of the choreography they choose. Thus, they also become responsible for the choreography to fans. So, if Beyoncé's choreography looks identical to Bob Fosse's, it is her issue to contend with, and her choreographers aren't called out in the fan conversations about it.

Second, popular music artists appreciate dance artists, and vice versa. The relationship between dancers and music involves artists who also perform to music by others, and thus, in popular dance terms, are fans themselves. On occasion, pop stars are fans of dancers, as in the case of Sia and Madison Nicole "Maddie" Ziegler, who have performed in music videos for "Chandelier" and "Elastic Heart," or when Beyoncé and Jay-Z tracked down Les Twins from France whom they had seen on YouTube. Les Twins then went on to tour with Beyoncé for years. In such cases, both television and the internet can be seen as vehicles for dance stardom.

Yet, for audiences, fans are judged by different standards. As I mentioned earlier, they are not expected to be original. To this, I would like to add a modification. Audiences often appreciate the "unlikely resemblance" created by fans, like the baby who bounces to Beyoncé. Shane Mercado's dance to "Single Ladies" in his bedroom is read as all the more interesting because it is unlikely. Here, the judgment is a comparative one, with different sets of criteria for each performer that depend on the performer's position (as fan or artist). The goal for the fan sometimes is to perform the choreography as accurately as possible while seeming to be the most unlikely candidate in performance.

One of the notable aspects of Shane Mercado's performance of "Single Ladies" was how quickly it went viral. The speed with which he released the video had an impact on its reception, for audiences were impressed by how quickly he had acquired the choreography perfectly. His skills are underpinned by the years required to acquire such dance competence. In other words, although he performed in a bedroom, representing fan culture, he was a skilled and proficient dancer.

Popular music artists performing dance and having a dance component in their live dance shows and music videos links the visual with the audible. The conjunction raises questions about the music industries, labor, and especially hierarchies within union rates. Dancers in music videos are often precariously employed. Often dancers on tour are overworked, given few days off with long working hours. This labor reflects unethical and problematic choices by artists, their management, and production companies. Both television and the YouTube bedroom have provided backstage access to the lives of dancers and created star vehicles. The exposure provides enough attention to advocate for more rights and pay for dancers but such has not been the result in recent years. In fact, popular music artists and their companies find ways to lowball choreographers and dancers.[27]

Dancers are also trendsetters, which informs music's popularity. For example, Tanisha Scott popularized dancehall in music videos and has worked with popular artists such as Sean Paul, Beyoncé, Rihanna, and Drake. Dance provides the authenticity and credibility ("street cred") for their songs. Authenticity and credibility are crucial qualities; Tracy has identified how essential affinities and identifications are for youth audiences.[28] They want fantasy and representation, and role models and songs to dance to. But social media has proven the veracity and volume of popular dance practices, and the forms of dance that become popular are those that work best with the aesthetic of a music video style.

COMPARING PERFORMANCES: WHAT ARE WE ACTUALLY LOOKING FOR?

Popular dance and music judgments have often been relegated to comparative category of pleasures, as opposed to aesthetic categories of absolute art. In the Scottish Enlightenment of the eighteenth century, scholars such as Francis Hutcheson argued that pleasure was often found in "relative or comparative beauty" spawned from the likeness of "a copy and an original."[29] Pleasure can also be found in comparisons between copies and originals, and that pleasure might even motivate a whole discourse around those two categories for discussions of popular culture.

Nelson Goodman distinguishes between "allographic" art (where every performance is a legitimate instantiation of the artwork and forgery is impossible) and "autographic" (where there is a single "original" that can indeed be forged). Theodore Gracyk uses this distinction in his discussion of songs performed versus songs recorded.[30]

The historical distinctions between the pleasures of the body and the seriousness of the mind meant that in concert-hall performances there is a (perceived) "denial of any bodily response while the music plays."[31] On the other hand, in popular music concerts, listeners engaging with music often enter the performing process, which involves an emphasis on a first response to the music. I like to compare this tradition of conceptualazing the "work" to Orhan Pamuk's novel *My Name Is Red*, in which artists aren't judged by their originality but by their ability to craft a rendition so accurate with respect to the original as to be indistinguishable. Suddenly an aesthetics of forgery doesn't have the same stigma because, at the end of the debate, what is at stake isn't the great work of art but the relationships between people.

The aesthetic experience that is given multiple and conflicting meanings by a diverse audience is simutaneously commodifiable and democratic. Musical gesture and dance gesture are in every aspect of the song itself from its production through its marketing and its promotion (as a music video) and including Beyoncé's live performances, where she does the dance every single time she performs the song, with various mutations. Mercado's *Bonnie Hunt Show* performance of the song actually gave the song new meaning.

Audiences are as likely to listen to this song on a laptop, through YouTube filters and tinny speakers, as on a stereo system at home. The aesthetic framework developed here emphasizes not only this first response but also involves, in all cases, the repetitive listening required to learn, or investigate, dance moves. The experience for the dancer of getting dance synced with the music is fragmentary and repetitive, for all the parts of the routine come together gradually. I suggest then that, for certain listeners, knowing the music well involves learning how to dance to it (to represent, express, or perform its sounds and rhythms) along with the acquisition of the skills necessary to present a recognizable version of the song. Moreover, the video works for those smaller screens because the action is centered. These conditions set the stage for aesthetic appreciation.

Shane Mercado dances to Beyoncé's song because he likes her music, but his dance practice also clearly informs his musical taste and preferences. In other words, people who love dance are worthy of study for the field of popular music studies not only because they tend to be such creative and invested participants, but because they also seem to be having the most fun with it. And those who fly into a rage that their important art has been forged ("Fosse has been plagiarized") are showing more about their condescending attitudes to raced, classed, and gendered spaces than to the nobility of their cause. It is their morality that I am calling into question in this chapter. In other words, just as "taste classifies the classifier," as Pierre Bourdieu famously put it, so does moral judgment.[32] But there is one more step to this number. In dance choreography in music videos, just as in the way someone walks down a street, we can see the limits of copyright: the human body and its movement choices.

MARY FOGARTY WOEHREL is Associate Professor in Dance at York University. She is coeditor of *Movies, Moves and Music: The Sonic World of Dance Films*.

NOTES

1. CGElliot09, "Baby Dancing to Beyoncé—ORIGINAL! @babycory on Twitter," January 26, 2009, https://www.youtube.com/watch?v=ikTxfIDYx6Q.
2. See Genette, *Paratexts*.
3. I discuss similar themes in "Gene Kelly," in relation to Gene Kelly's performance in *Singin' in the Rain* and a 2008 Volkswagen commercial featuring b-boys.
4. Nick Sylvester, "Hiphop Reviewed," *The Wire* 298 (December 2008): 74.
5. Dan Cairns, "YouTube Plays Part in Beyoncé Knowles' Life," *Sunday Times*, May 10, 2009, https://www.thetimes.co.uk/article/youtube-plays-part-in-beyonce-knowles-life-mcbl6j8djp8.
6. This includes, perhaps most famously, Kanye West's onstage protest, which interrupted Taylor Swift's acceptance speech for her "You Belong with Me" video, which beat "Single Ladies" to win Best Female Video at the 2009 MTV Video Music Awards. See Rosie Swash, "Kanye West Apologises for Interrupting Taylor Swift at VMAs," *Guardian*, September 14, 2009, https://www.theguardian.com/music/2009/sep/14/kanye-west-taylor-swift-vmas.
7. "Glee: Season One, Episode Four," *Guardian* (blog), January 25, 2010, https://www.theguardian.com/tv-and-radio/tvandradioblog/2010/jan/25/glee-season-one-episode-four; "Obama Tells Beyonce He Likes 'Single Ladies,' Does Hand Flip," *Huffpost*, February 28, 2009, http://www.huffingtonpost.com/2009/01/28/obama-tells-beyonce-he-li_n_161978.html.
8. See online lists of top requested disc jockey tracks for weddings, such as WeddingBee's "Top 100 Most Requested Songs at Weddings—2016," https://www.weddingbee.com/ceremony-and-reception/top-200-most-requested-songs-at-weddings/, where "Single Ladies" appears as number fourteen.

9. See, for instance, 100marilla, "Beyonce Single Ladies (Live Tyra Banks Show)," November 3, 2009, https://www.youtube.com/watch?v=KQRTswWnLsk.
10. Tracy, "Why Don't You Act Your Color?"
11. For a good example of this, see Dawson's *The Twist*.
12. Sylvester, "Hiphop Reviewed," 74.
13. For a more comprehensive overview, see Pullen, "If Ya Liked It."
14. Shane Mercado, "Single Man Dances to SINGLE LADIES," October 18, 2008, https://www.youtube.com/watch?v=SGemjUvafBw.
15. For a case study in the variety of ways that videos can be analyzed methodologically from perspectives of participants to audiences to cultural critics, see Fogarty, "Gene Kelly."
16. Mercado, personal correspondence, January 13, 2009.
17. Last time I checked, Mercado was winning easily.
18. Shane Mercado, personal correspondence with the author, January 13, 2009.
19. The music video "Get Me Bodied", dir. Beyoncé and Anthony Mandler (2007), was based on a Fosse number from *Sweet Charity* (1969).
20. Hobson, *Body as Evidence*, 44. The clip presents Gwen Verdon and two backup dancers as featured on the Ed Sullivan Show, but the original music is dubbed over with Unk's "Walk It Out."
21. Carlo Ginzburg (*Clues*, 88–89) notices the unlikely resemblance: "The art connoisseur resembles the detective who discovers the perpetrator of a crime (or the artist behind a painting) on the basis of evidence that is imperceptible to most people."
22. BeyonceStans4, "Beyonce Confirmed That Single Ladies Video Was Indeed Inspired by Broadway Choreographer Bob Fosse," November 18, 2008, https://www.youtube.com/watch?v=e-SlfHHd3qI.
23. Director X is an exception and is often credited in his music videos.
24. Lewis, "Female Address."
25. The term "unlikely resemblances" is my inversion of Ludwig Wittgenstein's notion of family resemblances, a term that has received quite a popular reception (Wittgenstein, *Philosophical Investigations*, 32, §67).
26. Frith, *Performing Rites*.
27. For more about commercial dance pay rates and issues, see Fogarty, "Struggle of Independent Artists."
28. Tracy, "Why Don't You Act Your Color?"
29. Francis Hutcheson, quoted in Wetmore, "Sympathy Machines," 50.
30. See, for instance, Gracyk, *Rhythm and Noise*, 38.
31. Frith, *Performing Rites*, 124.
32. Bourdieu, *Distinction*, 6.

BIBLIOGRAPHY

Bourdieu, Pierre. *Distinction: A Social Critique of the Judgement of Taste*. Translated by Richard Nice. Cambridge: Harvard University Press, 1984.
Dawson, Jim. *The Twist: The Story of the Song and Dance That Changed the World*. London: Faber, 1995.
Fogarty, Mary. "Gene Kelly: The Original, Updated." In *The Oxford Handbook of Dance and the Popular Screen*. Edited by Melissa Blanco Borelli, 83–97. Oxford: Oxford University Press, 2014.
———. "The Struggle of Independent Artists: A Toronto Snapshot." *Dance Equity Quarterly*, June 2017. http://danceequity.com/wp-content/uploads/2017/06/EQ-Spring-2017-Final-D-E-Only-LR.pdf.
Frith, Simon. *Performing Rites: On the Value of Popular Music*. Cambridge, MA: Harvard University Press, 1996.
Genette, Gérard. *Paratexts: Thresholds of Interpretation*. Translated by Jane E. Lewin. Cambridge: Cambridge University Press, 1997.
Ginzburg, Carlo. *Clues, Myths, and the Historical Method*. Baltimore: Johns Hopkins University Press, 1989.
Gracyk, Theodore. *Rhythm and Noise: An Aesthetics of Rock*. Durham: Duke University Press, 1996.
Hobson, Janelle. *Body as Evidence*. Albany: State University of New York Press, 2012.
Lewis, Lisa. "Female Address on Music Television: Being Discovered." *Jump Cut* 35 (1990): 2–15.
Pullen, Kirsten. "If Ya Liked It, Then You Shoulda Made a Video: Beyoncé Knowles, YouTube and the Public Sphere of Images." *Performance Research* 16, no. 2 (2011): 145–53.
Thomas, Philippa. "Single Ladies, Plural: Racism, Scandal, and 'Authenticity' within the Multiplication and Circulation of Online Dance Discourses." In *The Oxford Handbook of Dance and the Popular Screen*. Edited by Melissa Blanco Borelli, 289–303. Oxford: Oxford University Press, 2014.
Tracy, Pamela J. "'Why Don't You Act Your Color?': Preteen Girls, Identity, and Popular Music." In *Cultural Studies: An Anthology*. Edited by Michael Ryan, 610–16. Malden, MA: Blackwell, 2008.
Wetmore, Alex. "Sympathy Machines: Men of Feeling and the Automaton." *Eighteenth-Century Studies* 43, no. 1 (2009): 37–54.
Wittgenstein, Ludwig. *Philosophical Investigations*. 3rd ed. Translated by G. E. M. Anscombe. Oxford: Basil Blackwell, 1968.

NINE

"I See Music"

Beyoncé, YouTube, and the Question of Signed Songs

ÁINE MANGAOANG

Beyoncé embodies the very notion of a twenty-first century multidisciplinary artist. She is an award-winning artist known for releasing surprise visual albums and staging intricate photoshoots to reveal public announcements,[1] with widely perceived personal narratives of feminism, female empowerment, and gender equality. At the time of this writing, the thirty-seven-year-old's twenty-year artistic career is intertwined with capitalist brand Beyoncé, for she serves as the celebrity face for the L'Oréal group, Tommy Hilfiger, and her own fragrance and fashion lines House of Dereón and Ivy Park.[2] Beyoncé is also known for her virtuosic choreography, impressive intermedia award show performances and arena tours, and, more recently, her crossover to Hollywood cinematic endeavors. For an artist like Beyoncé, perhaps it is no surprise that music is a quintessentially audio-*visual* experience that goes beyond an imagined segregation of the senses. Beyoncé's public announcement of her visual approach to music then speaks to the common belief that music begins and ends as an auditory phenomenon. "I see music," she argued, promoting 2013's visual album, *Beyoncé*. "It's more than just what I hear."

In the field of music studies, literature on music that does not privilege the auditory experience remains somewhat limited. Within musicology, music performance, and music education, scholarship on hearing loss and deafness is noticeably scarce, and when it does appear, it is primarily published in music psychology and disability studies journals.[3] Only in recent years is the area starting to be recognized among wider musicology through the hard work of a small but growing number of individuals bridging the gap between music and disability studies.[4] In the past two decades especially, a number of studies from audiology and the health sciences have connected the risk of acquired hearing loss and the extended use of personal listening devices. Such studies have found that noise-induced hearing loss is steadily on the rise among youth populations and, despite being preventable, basic hearing conservation information remains largely absent from school and university curricula.[5] At best, discussions of music and deafness may result in a cursory nod to Beethoven's later years, or perhaps a mention of the performances of Scottish percussionist (and jewelry designer) Dame Evelyn Glennie. Indeed, among music educators as well as the general population, widely held assumptions persist that deaf culture is one without music, a community devoid of sonic experiences and of expressions of sound.[6]

My chapter aims to incorporate these various voices to contribute to the wider discourse on popular music and fandom and music and Deaf culture by offering an alternative way of thinking about Beyoncé's music through the vibrant subculture of Beyoncé videos created by hearing, hard of hearing, and d/Deaf fans.[7] This plethora of works, primarily published, shared, and interacted with through new media platforms like YouTube, operate outside traditional understandings of music and hearing, challenging the audist, phonocentric hegemony. Through a close reading of three case studies from the wealth of Beyoncé fan videos, I demonstrate how unique Web 2.0 practices combine important elements of Deaf and hearing cultures to create a "new model of cosmopolitan cultural citizenship" by providing "spaces for engagement and community formation."[8] I posit that the popularity of Beyoncé signed-song videos among hearing audiences—amateur homemade works that they are, incorporating a range of musical sensibilities and audiovisual experiences—is especially remarkable because it highlights the ways in which d/Deaf and hearing audiences seek new, meaningful ways for embodied expression and communication. I argue that such performances of Beyoncé's songs transform and recontextualize music and music video for both deaf and hearing audiences, ultimately revealing the limitations of an exclusively phonocentric approach to music, and ultimately demonstrate how Beyoncé's Deaf fan communities—and their reappropriation of her music—can help expand critical interpretations of Beyoncé's work.

MEDIATING MUSIC IN DEAF CULTURES

Sign languages are the indigenous languages for most, but not all, members of the Deaf community.[9] A completely separate language from English, sign languages (e.g., American, Australian, British, and Irish sign languages) are visual methods of communication and expression that utilize hand shapes, direction and motion of the hands, and body language all in conjunction with facial expressions. Each sign in a sign language is composed of three basic constituents: handshape, location, and movement. At least one handshape must be present in a sign. Signs may be located on the body or off it, to one side or the other, in the so-called neutral space in front of the body, or outside the neutral space. The other, less well-defined features of a sign are the orientation of the hand and nonmanual cues. Facial expressions are especially crucial for understanding signed languages; thus, in any sign language, the importance of facial expressions for comprehension should not be underestimated.

Contrary to the stereotype of deaf experience as one of absolute silence, the Deaf community is far from homogeneous, comprising diverse individual experiences across a spectrum of residual hearing. Many deaf individuals have various degrees of sound memory, and even those who do not are certainly not oblivious to the consequences of sonic frequencies. In addition to sound, a range of tactile, visual, and kinesthetic elements play important roles in deaf perceptions of music.[10] Studies of music as a multisensory phenomenon—in particular those who consider its tactile-kinesthetic, visual, or gestural character—have shown that these forms of perception have significance far beyond the Deaf and hard-of-hearing community, since musical experience in general involves sensory input from multiple sources.[11]

Media—and more recently social media—have opened a myriad of potential avenues for greater accessibility to a range of information as well as social and cultural experiences among Deaf communities. Media platforms have also been instrumental in shaping how hearing people perceive deaf individuals and Deaf culture. Few hearing people have regular interaction with people who are deaf and so film and television become portals through which Deaf culture is witnessed, as explained in Darrow and Loomis's 1999 study on media depictions of Deaf culture: "Most film and television viewers have never seen depictions of persons within the deaf community—communicating effortlessly and engaging freely in life's activities. As a result of our one-sided view of deaf persons, they are usually seen as less than fully functioning and dependent upon persons who hear."[12] As Darrow and Loomis argue, traditional Hollywood cinema tended to portray deaf characters negatively, widely distributing dangerous stereotypes of deaf people as bitter individuals, disappointments to their families, or characters worthy of pity.[13] Television and documentary formats make it possible to support a more progressive approach that could, in theory, draw attention to the realities and multiplicities of deaf experience in honest and more positive ways. At the time of this writing, however, there is no evidence that explicitly supports such advances in representation.[14] But progress in technological apparatuses have drastically improved and facilitate communication between deaf people and nonsigning individuals via technological third parties.[15] The visual nature of sign languages hypothetically allows for greater visibility of, and accessibility for, deaf audiences through sign language and interpreting or captioning on televisual media, although such accessible incidents remain on the margins, rarely implemented in any regular, sustained, or systematic fashion. The aforementioned televisual developments of web series and shorter audiovisual video-sharing content have thrived on new media platforms like YouTube, which has become increasingly ingrained as a form of everyday communication, serving as a mode of formal and informal education and a source of news and entertainment, and performs social-networking goals as well. For communities who continue to be marginalized by mainstream media, such as the Deaf community, YouTube's chaotic cultural archive offers untold opportunities for media representation, participation, and creation.

"SINGING WITH MY HANDS": SIGNING BEYONCÉ'S SONGS ON YOUTUBE[16]

During the past decade, tens of thousands of amateur, user-generated videos have emerged featuring an individual or group interpreting or translating popular songs into a variety of sign languages. Among them are fan-made videos of Beyoncé songs translated into recognized sign languages; a thriving signed-song subculture has grown out of various online video-sharing and social media platforms, including YouTube, Instagram, Vine, Vimeo,

Facebook video, Twitter, and DailyMotion, to name a few. Once the exclusive reserve of the deaf community, signed-song interpretations have, in the past few years, garnered popularity among hearing communities, who view popular signed songs on YouTube both by accident and by design. While it is impossible to ascertain the precise number of online videos of Beyoncé's songs performed by and through sign languages, on YouTube alone the body of works easily spills into the thousands.[17] The online repository of Beyoncé music videos use American Sign Language (ASL), Nicaraguan Sign Language (Idioma de Señas de Nicaragua), Swedish Sign Language (Svenskt teckenspråk), and many more besides. The result has been an impressive network of Beyoncé signed-song fan videos dating back to the early days of YouTube.[18]

Many of these Beyoncé signed-song videos can be categorized as "home-mode" videos, adapting anthropologist Richard Chalfen's expression "home mode," which refers to the amateur filmmaker's representation of the private world of the domicile. Home-mode footage is material that may not necessarily be made within the home but at least deals primarily with the home and domesticity.[19] The Beyoncé videos I discuss here are recorded performances that are uploaded online, primarily to the user-generated site YouTube, in which individuals usually play back pop songs in private, often in a domestic space and interpret or sign to them. These homemade videos construct a kind of ordinariness, wherein the home is displayed as a domestic yet theater-like space. The awkward shots in front of kitchen cupboards, in dimly lit bedrooms or framed by chintzy curtains, serve to construct a sense of copresence, inviting interaction from the viewer's home to the sign-singer, even though none of these videos is actually live, of course. Set against YouTube's self-conscious self-referentiality, such videos appear dark and grainy, habitually captured on camera phones or low-resolution webcams. Despite the remarkable quantity of signed-song videos that exist in YouTube's cultural archive, the low view count received by many such videos demonstrates that they are largely ignored or overlooked.[20]

New media practices often recall old media, and the Beyoncé videos are no exception. Such signed-song videos clearly build from a tradition of combining music and signs or gestures performed solo, in pairs or groups at organized Deaf public events or in private domestic settings: the earliest archival footage of deaf song signing comes from the early 1900s—of

Americans signing "Yankee Doodle." Deaf groups performing signed songs began to emerge in the 1980s, such as the California-based Musign Theatre Company and, later in the 1990s, Talking Hands, who performed songs signed in true ASL. The last decade's explosion in signed-song practices and public dissemination can be directly correlated with YouTube's growing popularity. These recorded signed-song performances are reminiscent of basic forms of broadcast presentation such as television or MTV-era music videos. They contrast, however, with traditional forms of broadcast media that operate across a one-way stream. YouTube's Web 2.0 make-up enabled viewers to be active participants by responding directly to uploaded videos, with their own videos, likes, and, more commonly, text comments left on the video page—what Burgess and Green describe as the "conversational character" of YouTube. Yet in most Beyoncé signed-song comments, users are not really commenting in a conversational sense. Rather, they are giving direct responses to the video's appearance, primarily commenting directly on the signer's presentation. Like YouTube's comment sections in general, the comments under Beyoncé signed songs use colloquial language, as well as emoticons and conventional abbreviations (OMG, LOL, WTF) associated with text messaging; the frequent spelling mistakes and nonstandard punctuation contribute to their general impression of immediacy and spontaneity.

In short, these Beyoncé videos neatly summarize YouTube's call to "broadcast yourself," as proclaimed in You Tube's early tagline, and so it is from this global environment that the recent renaissance in signed-song videos emerged.[21] Ben Bahan describes song signing as a traditional form of storytelling from Deaf culture, especially in ASL, which he divides into two distinctive types: "percussion" signing and "translated songs."[22] Building on Bahan's work, research on music and Deaf culture includes musicologist Anabel Maler's detailed discussions on song-signing.[23] Maler organized the practice of song-signing into four broad categories: live music interpretation services, live performances by song-signing artists, videos featuring the performance of an original song, and videos featuring the performance of a preexisting song.[24] Although not exhaustive, Maler's categories include the most common contemporary occurrences of signed songs, and Maler goes on to acknowledge the many challenges that exist in creating signed-song music videos fit for both deaf and hearing audiences. As a practice performed by both Deaf and hearing cultures, yet never fully claimed by either, song signing occurs in diverse contexts and among mixed audiences, who will each have different concerns, prerequisites, and priorities. Darrow pointed out the many limitations in direct sign-language translations of pop lyrics that feature a large number of nonsense words.[25] One generalization is that deaf audiences desire more translation and meaningful sign, while hearing audiences favor signs closely synchronized to the beat and a close ordering of individual signs with the song lyrics, regardless of how idiomatic the signing is in itself. For a mixed deaf and hearing audience then, at the very least a successful sign language music video is one that meets both criteria and serves both imagined audiences well. The Beyoncé videos I present hereafter fall under Maler's fourth category of signed songs, namely, videos featuring the performance of a preexisting song. The most popular Beyoncé signed songs on YouTube include interpretations of "Best Thing I Never Had," "Dangerously in Love," "Flawless," "Halo," "I Was Here," "If I Were a Boy," "Irreplaceable," "Listen," "Love on Top," "Pretty Hurts," "Run the World (Girls)," and "Single Ladies (Put a Ring on It)." In what follows, I focus on three examples that represent a range of approaches to Beyoncé signed songs available on YouTube: "If I Were a Boy," "Halo," and "Run the World (Girls)." I discuss each of these songs and their original music videos against the correlating signed-song videos and reception thereof in order to examine the aesthetic implications and sociocultural meanings of the fan-made versions of Beyoncé's songs.

CASE STUDIES

Trainee Sign Language Instructor's Performance of "If I Were a Boy"

"If I Were a Boy" is an emotive yet puzzling pop ballad taken from Beyoncé's third studio album, *I Am . . . Sasha Fierce* (2008). Released as a lead single alongside the contrastingly upbeat, up-tempo "Single Ladies (Put a Ring on It)," "If I Were a Boy" was the only song from the album not cowritten by Beyoncé.[26] Lyrically, the song provides a commentary on the socially prescribed nature of gender roles through an imaginative gender-swapping narrative, in which Beyoncé imagines what life would be like if she were male rather than female. Singing directly to an imagined partner, Beyoncé implores the listener to be attentive to perceived fundamental inequalities that persist between the genders through the stereotypical tropes of an inattentive lover who goes and drinks "beer with the guys and chase[s] after girls." The official "If I Were a Boy" music video, directed by Jake Nava, follows this lyrical theme of gender role reversal and identity play. Shot in stark black and white, the video displays Beyoncé as a female police officer and wife of a supportive on-screen husband. The music video turns the tables on traditional gender roles, culminating in a dramatic twist in the final section that reveals that Beyoncé is really the supportive spouse and her husband is the playboy police offer who takes his partner for granted. The overall effect of both song and music video makes attempts—however clichéd—to highlight the complex yet stereotyped dynamics of heteronormative relationships and queries the implicit assumptions built into societal gender roles.

Several signed-song versions of "If I Were a Boy" are available on YouTube. They include three ASL music video versions of "If I Were a Boy" produced by YouTuber and Deaf/hard-of-hearing advocate Jade Films (2009)—released as part of a visual music campaign "on a mission to educate those to create access to music videos or live events for deaf and hard of hearing consumers"—and sign-language interpreter soph1951's low-fi, direct, word-for-word translations of the lyrics from English to ASL (2011),[27] and Doua Saleh's 2013 sparse, beginner video made as part of her college ASL class. I will focus here on the remarkable, thoughtfully rendered "If I Were a Boy" ASL video uploaded by Dan McDougall (2010). With more than eighty thousand views to date, McDougall's music video is the product of fifteen weeks of translating, filming, and editing work undertaken by students from Madonna University's Sign Language Studies department to discover whether there is "such a thing as an 'ASL Music Video.'"[28] Their video was uploaded with a linked guide to help viewers understand the interpretive choices rendered in the video, including the features of ASL poetry, original lyrics in English, an ASL glossary, and further explanation on their creative choices. The five-minute-and-twenty-two-second video builds on the song's emotive themes of gender stereotypes and heteronormative relationships; in it, four female, trainee sign language interpreters act out the song's lyrics in an imagined group-therapy setting. The video traces the four actors' figurative transitions from female protagonists to male characters through the use of hats, suits, and other ostensibly masculine props as the song builds, with each transition further marked by symbolic cinematic shifts from their "real-life"

Table 9.1. Beyoncé's "If I Were a Boy" chorus from Madonna University's ASL Music Video, directed by Alyse Paquin (2010).

English lyrics	American Sign Language (ASL) glossary
If I were a boy	Imagine, trade-places
I think I would understand	Understand
How it feels to love a girl	You, feel-inside
I swear I'd be a better man	Instant understanding (head)
	Instant understanding (heart)
	Oh-I-see
	Honor you, respect you

world of color (female) to the imaginary "if" world in black and white (male). Rather than providing a direct and literal mapping of the English lyrics into ASL, the team chose to use the song's lyrics as the basis for creating a poetic interpretation that would be lyrical in ASL, which instantiates both the differences between English and sign language and the subjective nature of pop song lyrics. For example, the song's chorus changes in their version from the original, as depicted in table 9.1.

This example details two interrelated facts. First, it shows that the linguistic shape and contours of English are not easily or readily mapped onto ASL. As we can see in table 9.1, interpreting English song lyrics into ASL is complex, with some level of creativity and critical analysis to determine which signs would best fit. For example, the relatively short line "I swear I'd be a better man" is, in this instance, interpreted into four "phrases" if you will, using the signs for instant understanding of the head and heart, an "oh, I see" gesture, followed by the signs for "honor you" and "respect you." A creative approach to signed song requires considerable time (in this case, up to fifteen weeks), effort, and collaboration between Deaf and hearing communities to ensure a successful, meaningful, and imaginative outcome. Second, it demonstrates that significant modifications must be made to original texts in order to make the song adhere to the rhythm and rhyme techniques of ASL. The phrase "instant understanding" was repeated for rhythmic purposes and the location of the sign against the body was modified to deepen the concept that was to be conveyed: to demonstrate matters of the head and the heart. Following the precedent set in Beyoncé's original music video, the ASL signed-song video ends with its own narrative twist in the final scene. Each of the four protagonists returns to the group-therapy room carrying a portion of a ripped photograph, which they throw on the table, and it is revealed that the men at the root of their heartache are not four different men, but rather one and the same man. This playful, humorous take on the original dramatic, sober twist is further juxtaposed against the lamenting, melancholic mood in Beyoncé's original song and music video.

"Halo" Transgressions

Cowritten by Beyoncé, Ryan Tedder, and Evan Bogart, "Halo" was the fourth single released from *I Am... Sasha Fierce* in January 2009. A global chart-topper, the emotive, driving power ballad has been covered extensively by many artists, including English band Florence and the Machine, a hip hop-meets-dancehall "reggaeremix" by US electronic trio Major Lazer and Jamaican singer Elephant Man (Oneal Bryan), an upbeat mash-up with "Walking on Sunshine" by the cast of *Glee*, the stripped-down, ethereal cover by English singer-songwriter Jasmine Thompson, and an acoustic collaboration by Swedish cellist Linnea Olsson and Norwegian singer Ane Brun. This profoundly popular practice of recording a myriad of covers of Beyoncé's "Halo" extends no less to sign-language video covers. After the song's release in 2009, a flurry of ASL versions (see videos by Diego Anthony Sanchez, Tiffany T. Hill, and Juvenile Jacob to name just a few) were uploaded to YouTube, followed swiftly by Swedish Sign Language (such as that by Dennis Kihlgren from 2009) and British Sign Language (like Lucinda Murray's 2017 video) signed-song versions.

The most popular signed-song version of "Halo" was uploaded by Paul Sirimarco and Tina Cleveland, a Los Angeles couple who gained notoriety for their carpool karaoke-style signed-song performances, and their "Halo" achieved viral success in 2014.[29] A hearing team, Tina is a qualified ASL interpreter and Paul is "a supportive husband who learns signs for every signalong created."[30] Their impromptu performance of "Halo" is representative of their signed-song approach. The song is played on the car stereo while Paul drives and Tina takes the song's lyrics and directly translates them word for word into ASL, synching the ASL signs to match Beyoncé's rhythm and tempo. The results of this "caught off guard," improvised signalong were mixed. According to feedback from hundreds of self-identified hearing and non-ASL literate audiences, the video looks visually appealing for many hearing audiences, who (excessively) compliment Tina's physical appearance and comment on her rhythmic coordination to the music, without apparently understanding any of the signs she used. YouTuber Paula Thompson commented that in "Halo," "Tina's inner beauty radiates forth in this video and in her sign language expression. I have seen others attempt similar videos, but I just have not felt the same beauty of the soul and emotional expression that touches me although I do not know American Sign. Her love for what Paul and what she does is very obvious. Lucky guy."[31] Shared extensively on the internet, Beyoncé herself joined in the conversation by sharing a link to the video on her official Facebook and Twitter pages—an action read by many fans as a form of official endorsement of the couple's signalongs and of ASL and Deaf culture.

Yet many d/Deaf and hard-of-hearing viewers took to the comment section to complain that Tina's interpretations are completely unintelligible in ASL.[32] YouTuber Hartmut Teuber describes what a more thoughtful and rehearsed signed-song performance would have been, stating that "An ASL rendition of the song would be different and far better. Tina's is not poetic at all. It is just mongrelized ASL-English which are often seen done by ASL-English interpreters. With her hands under the dictatorship of music, her signing becomes incomprehensible. . . . Her signing for 'halo' exactly describes her. She signed 'BIG-SWOLLEN-HEADED.' . . . Don't corrupt the music by your lousy rendering into swollen-headed ASL."[33] Such critical comments have not deterred the couple from establishing a crowdfunding campaign to cover the production of higher-quality signalong videos that would include accessible features for all viewers (such as closed captions) and facilitate fan visits across the United States. In support of their mission, they received widespread mainstream media attention and appeared on television as advocates for ASL, which led to a formal award during the Los Angeles Deaf Awareness Month in recognition of their work in bridging the gap between d/Deaf and hearing audiences. These actions—and international attention—were problematically perceived by many as monetizing her (mis)use of the Deaf community's native language, and it was the focus of intensely polarizing debates on social media platforms.[34] The debate largely addressed questions of who has the right to use—or misuse—the Deaf community's native language. Opinions were divided among d/Deaf and hearing commenters, but the overwhelming consensus from the Deaf community was that there were more qualified and better representatives for ASL and Deaf culture than a skilled but not fluent ASL interpreter and her partner who had only basic ASL skills.

"Run the World (Girls)" ASL Music Video

The final example I will draw attention to is Beyoncé's rousing hit "Run the World (Girls)," taken from her fourth album 4 (2011). Cowritten by Beyoncé and songwriter-producer Terius "The-Dream" Nash, the song is built on extensive drum samples from Major Lazer's dancehall-meets-electro track "Pon de Floor" (2009). The up-tempo percussive riff from "Pon de Floor" forms the backbone of Beyoncé's assertive delivery in "Run the World," an emancipation anthem to "girls" that commands listeners' attention like a battle cry. The song begins with Beyoncé shout-singing the refrain's call "Who run the world?" with the responding answer "Girls!" sung by an alternating chorus of female shouts and primal harmonies in thirds, fifths, and octaves. The quasi-rapped, staccato verses and melodic bridge sections are lyrics of female empowerment:

> Help me raise a glass for the college grads ...
> I work my 9 to 5 and I cut my check
> This goes out to all the women getting it in
> ... we're smart enough to make these millions
> Strong enough to bear the children

Variations of the empowering chorus lyric—"Who run the world? Girls! / Who run this motha? Girls!"—are sung more than fifty times, repeatedly driving home the song's declaration of girl power. This extreme aesthetic is suitably matched in the accompanying music video directed by Francis Lawrence, during which the lyrics appear on our screens infused with defiant gestures (fist pumps to the sky, military salutes, flipping her middle finger to the camera) with hip hop references to her hometown: "This is how they made me / Houston, Texas, baby."

Set in a postapocalyptic desert against a desolate backdrop of burnt-out cars, flags, and battalions, the official music video is a lesson in audiovisual excess. The overtly stylized, sexualized presentation of Beyoncé and her group of female dancers calls into question the complex and contested role of sexuality in discussions of empowerment. Indeed, the combination of militarized, hypersexualized, and phallic opposition to traditional associations of feminine "girls" evokes a reworking of Aristophanes's *Lysistrata*, where Beyoncé thus assumes the role as a postfeminist protagonist leading her army of sexually powerful women. At various points in the video, a blond-haired Beyoncé is flanked by a golden lion, a pair of fierce hyenas on chains, and an army of women clad in high-fashion costumes using song and dance to fight an anonymous male militia clad in black riot gear. Devised by a team of international choreographers and derived from a combination of emphatic shoulder shrugs, crawling on all fours, and contemporaneous "African movement vocabularies,"[35] the "Run the World" dance sequence received acclaim from fans and critics alike. It won the 2011 MTV Video Music Award for Best Choreography, and the song and associated dance sequence was performed at several high-profile events that year, including its public premiere at Oprah Winfrey's televised farewell concert, a memorable live-action multimedia performance at the 2011 Billboard Music Awards, and an appearance as the penultimate song in Beyoncé's notable headline at the 2011 Glastonbury festival.[36] Beyoncé's cultural presence around this time further intertwined her "Run the World" message with a personal feminist manifesto. Media features and interviews, such as the 2011 *Harper's Bazaar* cover feature, were quick to cite Beyoncé's calls for equality between the sexes as evidence for her belief in feminism, even if at that time Beyoncé seemed to distance herself from the term itself.[37] In short, though not without issue or divisions, the song—along with its corresponding dance and music video—has largely come to stand for an extensively mediated, multimodal manifesto of female empowerment. It is perhaps unsurprising then that thousands of fans answered Beyoncé's sonic call to arms by creating the host of cover versions that now proliferates on YouTube.

Among them are several sign language interpretations made by d/Deaf and hearing individuals and groups that run the gamut of ages, ethnicities, genders, and sexualities. Lauren Hostovsky's low-budget ASL Music Video for "Run the World (Girls)" is particularly noteworthy for its imaginative approach, starring seven young d/Deaf women who fluently sign-rap and dance in a great variety of locations in Washington, DC. Uploaded on May 5, 2013, the music video was filmed and directed by Hostovsky and Marisa Mills. To date this has received more than 150,000 views. Categorically produced with a deaf and hard-of-hearing audience in mind, the video visibly portrays the song-signers in well-lit scenes that aptly show their facial cues, as well as their signs, gestures, and dance moves. Unlike the previous two case studies, their "Run the World (Girls)" video is made more accessible through accurate closed-caption subtitles throughout the video. Although the directors exercise artistic license in their ASL interpretation, it is clear that the directors have given much thought to constructing their music video so that it replicates the key tropes from Beyoncé's music video. Such sequences include adding Beyoncé's signature "Run the World" chest-popping, bust-thrust movement (1:00–1:04), skillfully incorporating Beyoncé's overhead fist pumps and salutes to follow the ASL signs for the "Who run the world? Girls!" chorus (1:05–1:28 and 3:50–3:59; see figs. 9.1 and 9.2), to a scene where a blond protagonist in a white dress walks a leashed dog, instantly recalling the original music video scene in which a blond, beehived Beyoncé in white leads her chained hyenas (see figs. 9.3 and 9.4).

Hostovsky, who self-identifies as hard of hearing and culturally Deaf—with ASL as her first language—describes her project as motivated by the desire to create music videos that would inspire and appeal to d/Deaf and hard-of-hearing audiences through thoughtfully rendered ASL translations. She explains that she wanted d/Deaf audiences to experience "more" than only "hearing/feeling the beat and vibrations of the music, but also by having access to the message of the music, the words and the ideas behind them, in choreographed ASL. It is often difficult to translate songs into ASL, but as with any good translation you have to challenge yourself to be creative while also sticking to the original message as much as possible."[38] Hostovsky details her approach of collaborating with Deaf friends Kojo Amissah and Marisa Mills to work out new, dynamic ASL interpretations of Beyoncé's song because she believes "music is for everyone. Just because we are deaf or hard of hearing doesn't mean we can't enjoy the music. We enjoy hearing or feeling it, dancing to the beat of it, expressing ourselves with the music and through the music."[39]

VISUALIZING BEYONCÉ THROUGH DEAF YOUTUBE FANDOM

The preceding brief case studies reveal several emerging themes. In what follows, I focus on three key themes that run throughout Beyoncé signed-song videos.

Beyoncé as Audiovisual Artist

The visual turn in popular music—and Beyoncé in particular—is well documented.[40] What is still undocumented, however, is the wealth of Beyoncé signed-song videos that continue to appear on YouTube almost daily. This speaks to her immense and persistent popularity that extends across hearing and Deaf cultures and communities and attests as well to Beyoncé as a truly audiovisual, multimodal performance artist. Deaf, but more commonly

Figs. 9.1 and 9.2. Hostovsky's choreographed fist pumps in "Run the World" ASL video alongside Beyoncé and her army of fist pumps in the official video.

Figs. 9.3 and 9.4. *Left*: Hostovsky's protagonist in a white dress walking a dog on a leash in her "Run the World (Girls)" ASL video. *Right*: Beyoncé in a white dress holding a pair of chained hyenas in Lawrence's official "Run the World (Girls)" video.

hearing, fans are drawn to creating exciting interpretations of the lyrics, the rhythm, the energy, and the spirit of her songs through sign language. Since her songs are rife with possible interpretations, possible meanings can be gleaned by being attentive to Beyoncé's visual markers: her facial movements and physical gestures, as well as her energy and spirit. In an interview with Nashville Public Radio (2016), ASL interpreter Scott Baker—who has interpreted live concerts of Beyoncé, Garth Brooks, and Dolly Parton, among others—describes his approach to interpreting Beyoncé's songs. Baker highlights the fact that Beyoncé "exists visually as well as aurally," and so, for him, the explicitly multimodal nature of Beyoncé's work thus calls for a very particular kind of interpretation during her live shows, one that requires as close a reading of her body language as of the lyrics, words, and sounds she makes. Baker states that "her music is very often conceived in visual form ... and her persona, her body, the way that she moves with it is as much a part of her music as just listening to the sounds of it is."[41] For these reasons, Baker declares that he must make interpretative choices in the moment when interpreting her concerts, keeping one eye on Beyoncé in order to see exactly what she does with her face and her body, and how she sonically and visually delivers each song. Since there can be no objective meaning to many of her lyrics, he says, any interpretation of her songs requires a particularly multimodal reading to deliver an accurate, ethically sound translation. Each of the case studies demonstrates not only the ways in which meaning subtly shifts from original to cover versions through the lyrical translations and interpretations by and of these YouTubers, but also how agents within these communities capitalize on the language of sign itself as an opportunity to communicate new musical meaning.

Online Performance and Agency as Community Building

The Beyoncé signed-song music videos described above operate within and as an online community on a visceral level, though not necessarily in ways that were initially intended. Music plays a fundamental role in social, cultural, and personal identity formation, especially among youth populations, who account for a majority of practitioners of these works. Scholars have noted that users participate in YouTube as a way of being heard and building community ties.[42] Through music, communities and their members reassert basic bonds, which emphasize primordial ties rather than the contingent relations of everyday life. There is an aura of liveness, combined with a fleeting sense of community, through filmed song-signing performances, and the embodied practices of singing along and signing along connect individuals to a worldwide web of like-minded individuals with whom to exchange ideas, rehearse with, and learn from. As formalized sign languages are still relatively new languages, these performative texts offer a way for *all* users of the language to improve, get feedback, and develop their proficiencies in translating, interpreting, and creativity. Recording, uploading, and watching Beyoncé signed-song videos on YouTube serve to reify the social bond between predominantly hearing communities of Beyoncé fans that may not otherwise have intersected with d/Deaf communities, and vice versa.

The fact that beginner song-signers and sign-language interpreters upload such videos onto online social media platforms like YouTube, Instagram, and Facebook—using them as a remediated rehearsal space—clarifies how they operate socioculturally as a mirror for some. For others, they serve as a figurative, communicative channel to demonstrate more fluent, more creative, and more musical approaches to signed song. Recording sign language to music and as music and sharing it as videos online triggers one of the greatest drivers of human progress: the mirror neurons. According to neuroscience research, the existence of mirror neurons provides structural evidence that we are wired for harmonic social unity, and unified rhythmic movement reinforces these social bonds. Mirror neurons are found in the cortex, the brain's central processing unit, and activate when a person is performing an action as well as *watching* someone else do it. Increasing evidence suggests that sensory experiences are also motor experiences, and music, movement, and gesture may just be particularly pleasurable activators of these sensory and motor circuits. Research on mirror systems shows that through mere *observation*, the *movement* areas of an individual's brain are activated.[43] Therefore, it is highly plausible that the most fluent as well as the most viewed Beyoncé signed-song videos serve as pleasure activators, through the pleasure gained from seeing someone execute sophisticated signs and movements with skill and expertise. But the signed-song videos that achieve viral status and widespread notoriety are almost exclusively those made by members of the hearing community, as exemplified by Paul and Tina's video, with signed-song videos made by the Deaf community receiving considerably fewer views. Because the majority of the population are hearing, it may be unavoidable that signed-song interpretations by the hearing will be the easiest for nonsigners to relate to. Encountering truly original, creative, and linguistically precise signed-song performances are challenging even for those with basic sign language skills, let alone those who have stumbled onto sign language in action for the first time through one of YouTube's many signed-song videos.

YouTube's Mixed Audiences and Charges of Cultural Appropriation

Last, although the majority of dimly lit, low-resolution signed-song videos posted on YouTube are met with little to no fanfare, the response to Paul and Tina's off-the-cuff "Halo" signalong demonstrates how YouTube's collective policing policy means slapdash work is quickly—and very publicly—called into question. The problem of mixed audiences, to use Bahan's phrase, and the subsequent mixed reactions are exemplified in one particularly vigorous discussion on the Reddit.com/deaf forum, where d/Deaf Redditors took particular offense to Paul and Tina's signalongs and accused them of culturally misappropriating ASL.[44] Summarizing the views of many individuals offended by their signalongs and subsequent fundraising actions, commentator DuncantheWonderDog says, "What Tina & Paul are doing is cultural appropriation. It is on the same level as blackface. There are already many talented Deaf, CODA [Child/ren of Deaf Adult], and Interpreters (who are active part of deaf community) who are much better than Tina and Paul AND actively support the deaf community."[45] Other Redditors agreed with Duncan's assessment; Redditor kyabupaks declares that Paul and Tina's signing style appears unnatural and continues that Tina's

> signs are clear, but there is no flow and beauty to it. Instructional videos should only be created by longtime signers—such as deaf people or CODA's [sic]. ASL . . . is a part of a culture that is sadly misunderstood by the majority of outsiders. That's where I think Tina and Paul crossed the line. They are obviously not deaf nor CODA's [sic]; because their signed songs are like the visual equivalent of hearing nails screech across a blackboard. That's cringe-worthy, trying to make money off that, just because they can exploit on the ignorance of the majority of people who have no grasp on our community and its culture. When it comes to teaching ASL in its truest form, they are *not* qualified at all.[46]

The underlying question, according to kyabupaks, is one of nondeaf, nonfluent ASL users exploiting the Deaf community's native language for their own vanity and gain. Other members of the Deaf community disagreed with such readings of the signalongs, arguing that Tina and Paul's videos raise awareness about ASL among the general population and that in itself, while not unproblematic, is a positive activity. Yet Paul and Tina faced additional criticism for not *listening* to deaf audience feedback and for responding with hostility to constructive and negative comments on their signing posted on their YouTube pages. Somewhere in the contemporary practice of YouTube signed songs, the original function of sign language interpretation has been misplaced, if not lost. The primary goal of mediating information and dialogue between the deaf and hearing worlds has been, in several cases, replaced by the desires of interpreters and beginning sign-language students to become performers. Rather than signed-song interpreters being a conduit for deaf to can impart meaning and understand a particular work of art,[47] an overwhelming number of hearing sign-language interpreters have colonized the very function of interpreting for their target audience, seduced by the theatrics of performance for performance's sake.

As the foregoing presentation of the debate shows, considerable disparity remains in how best to approach the contentious topic of signed songs in Deaf culture and its community. A translated English-to-sign-language performance of any song can be crudely executed and grammatically absurd, which can lead to accusations that the works created are primarily or exclusively made to serve the hearing community. Persistently posting erroneous or inappropriately translated signed songs, no matter how noble the intention, is ethically dubious in that poorly prepared videos can exclude and offend the rich cultural heritage of the Deaf community's indigenous language, a language that is still forced to fight for legal recognition in many parts of the world. Against this struggle for fundamental human rights, any spontaneous expressions of song through sign language may be reviewed, critiqued, and scoured for flaws. This is especially the case when such DIY, user-generated videos remain publicly (and freely) available for an indefinite period. Hosting the world's largest collection of signed-song videos, in effect YouTube serves as an accidental archival resource for untold future generations interested in the art and study of music and sign languages. It is critical to note that this private resource remains subject to the covert, commercial ends of Google—YouTube's parent company since 2006—and, for that reason, every video could be edited, made unavailable except upon paid subscription, or removed outright.

CONCLUSION

The subgroup of Beyoncé signed-song videos illustrates how Beyoncé's music is distinctively distributed and embedded in the everyday lives of deaf and hearing individuals and communities around the world. Beyoncé's embodied music outputs can affect people who were once previously excluded from enjoying, creating, and participating in music. Analyses of YouTube videos often posit a reified division between amateur and professional content and creation, leading to vast assumptions about a video's attentional merit.[48] In the videos presented here, we see individuals and groups producing videos that move between categories and challenge binary conceptions about a video's quality or power to establish communicative connections with other people. Indeed, this chapter suggests that we can learn much about how Beyoncé's music functions by examining how her songs are mediated and practiced by her fans online. Focusing on the creative labor of the breadth of Beyoncé fans enables a glimpse into the analytical, critical, diverse, innovative, and socially energized possibilities of fandom. Her fans identify certain limitations afforded by traditional, mainstream, industry-led music videos, and in addressing the gaps, create signed-song videos that go beyond the stereotypical confines of YouTube's bedroom music-making culture.

Through Web 2.0 affordances, a combination of important elements of Deaf and hearing cultures are merged to create new spaces for maintaining and extending social networks and engaged communities. As these examples presented here illustrate, however, enthusiasm about such seemingly democratizing developments are uneven and are often unfairly positioned to the advantage of the hearing hegemony. The true potential in Beyoncé signed-song videos lies not only in their new expressive potential but also in their ability to ignite global debates on cultural appropriation of (Beyoncé's) music, on deaf discrimination. Such videos provide a platform for the audist majority to learn about sign language and Deaf culture, however inaccurate and misguided many of them may be. Remarkably, they help educate and empower hearing audiences with an awareness of the importance of embodied expression and multimodality as a foundation for musical communication. Signed performances of Beyoncé's songs transform and recontextualize her music and music videos for both deaf *and* hearing audiences, where the perception of Beyoncé as a multifaceted figure of empowerment is taken up by fans. In the process of doing so, Beyoncé's songs are employed to expose the fact that deaf rights are human rights, and ultimately reveal the limitations of an exclusively phonocentric approach to music.

ÁINE MANGAOANG is Postdoctoral Research Fellow at the Department of Musicology, University of Oslo. She is author of *Dangerous Mediations: Pop Music in a Philippine Prison Video* and coeditor of *Made in Ireland: Studies in Popular Music*.

NOTES

Earlier versions of this essay were written for a keynote address at a 2016 Beyoncé conference at Cardiff University, and read at University College Dublin, University of Oslo, and University of York. At those lectures and elsewhere I received invaluable feedback. I thank Tejaswinee Kelkar, Sam Murray, Marthe Ødegård Olsen, John Richardson, and the editors of this volume, Martin Iddon and Melanie Marshall, for their insights and encouragement offered on earlier drafts of this chapter.

1. Beyoncé's February 2017 maternity photoshoot photographed by Awol Erizku, for example, publicly announced her pregnancy and set a new world record for the most liked Instagram post of all time, with more than ten million likes.

2. Scholars have written about how pop artists make the majority of their money today through brand partnerships, synchronized deals, and merchandizing collaborations. See, for example, Marshall, "Consuming Gaga," esp. 233–34, on Lady Gaga's brand of decadent consumption, commodity feminism, and neoliberal selfhood.

3. Among others, Fulford et al. have made significant contributions to the work on d/Deaf musicians, in particular their use of hearing-aid technologies. See, for instance, Fulford et al., "Hearing Aids."

4. Howe et al. has several chapters on music and d/Deaf culture, including chapters by Maler, "Musical Expressions," and Jones, "Imagined Hearing." Other important contributions to the topic are Jessica Holmes's work on phonocentricism ("Singing beyond Hearing") and Christine Sun Kim's *Face Opera II* (2013) and scholarly networks such as the American Musicological Society's Music and Disability Study Group. I also draw attention to the many practice-based initiatives, both in and outside academia, that support the building of long-lasting musical relationships between hearing and deaf communities, for example, the *Summer Sing and Sign!* program in Cork, Ireland, that brings together choral music and sign language.

5. Some recent articles are Jansen et al., "Noise Induced Hearing Loss"; Morata, "Young People"; and Śliwińska-Kowalska and Davis, "Noise-Induced Hearing Loss."

6. Darrow has written extensively on the misconceptions about music among d/Deaf communities. Darrow found that particularly in educational settings, most teachers have the misconception that a student who is deaf has no hearing at all and that music instructors are unsure what instructional methods and strategies to use with d/Deaf and hard-of-hearing students (Darrow, "Teaching Students with Hearing Losses," 27).

7. In this chapter, I reject the label "hearing-impaired," which is still used by some to describe d/Deafness, because it implies a pathological illness to be cured rather than d/Deafness as a linguistic and cultural minority and difference in human experience. As consistent with the culturally accepted standard, I adhere to James Woodward's ("Implications," 1972) definition of "deaf" and "Deaf," in which *deaf* refers to the physical condition of deafness and capital-D *Deaf* refers to an understanding of the Deaf community and culture. Not all deaf people identify as belonging to Deaf culture. When referring to both groups, I adopt the widely used term "d/Deaf" and I use "hard of hearing" to describe people like myself with less severe hearing loss from birth or acquired deafness later in life.

8. Burgess and Green, *YouTube*, 79.

9. Besides deaf and hard-of-hearing individuals, the Deaf community may include family members of deaf people and sign-language interpreters. Most children with hearing loss are born to hearing parents, and therefore Deaf communities are unusual among cultural groups in that most members do not acquire their cultural identities from their parents. Instead, cultural identity is often acquired through attendance at deaf schools or through deaf advocacy and social groups.

10. See Straus, *Extraordinary Measures*, 169; Maler, "Musical Expressions"; and Jones, "Imagined Hearing."

11. Examples of such studies are Godøy and Lehman, *Musical Gestures*; Stuart, "Enkinaesthesia"; and the work of Alexander Refsum Jensenius and colleagues in the Music, Mind, Motion, Machines research group at the Department of Musicology, University of Oslo.

12. Darrow and Loomis, "Music and Deaf Culture," 93.

13. Ibid., 89–90.

14. Anecdotal evidence points to a slight trend toward more positive televisual representation, particularly through new forms of web-streaming television series, such as a silent vignette in Aziz Ansari's Netflix series *Master of None* (season two, episode six, 2017), which follows a deaf woman's everyday life in New York city, where the characters flirt and converse exclusively in American Sign Language.

15. Examples of such communicative technologies are closed captions and subtitles on television and video streaming services, mobile telephone text and picture

messaging, and audio via induction loops and transmitters for hearing aids and cochlear implants.

16. soph1951, "About," January 19, 2009, https://www.youtube.com/user/soph1951/about.

17. A cursory search on YouTube using keywords "Beyoncé" + "Sign Language" yields just over 84,000 hits, as of August 20, 2016. Taking into account duplicate postings and irrelevant results, a conservative estimate would posit that at least a quarter (21,000) of these videos are original sign-language performances of Beyoncé songs.

18. It is important to note that although YouTube hosts an extensive back catalog of signed-song videos as a private, commercial business owned by Google, it is not and cannot be considered an archive in the sense of being a complete or open public record. The earliest Beyoncé signed-song video that remains publicly available on YouTube is YouTuber dominique07's signed performance to "Listen," March 21, 2007, https://www.youtube.com/watch?v=vZWH7B53Vqk.

19. Chalfen, *Snapshot*.

20. A significant number of the more recent low-fidelity, amateur, signed-song videos have received fewer than one thousand views, and many received fewer than one hundred views.

21. For further details on early YouTube DIY aesthetics as they relate to music video, see Mangaoang, *Dangerous Mediations*.

22. Bahan, "Face-to-Face."

23. Maler, "Songs for Hands," and Maler, "Musical Expressions."

24. Maler, "Musical Expressions."

25. Quoting the comedian Dave Barry, Darrow ("Sounds," 12) details a number of songs with the lyrics "uh huh, uh huh," "la la la," and "na na na na na."

26. "If I Were a Boy" was written by Brittany Jean Carlson (known as BC Jean) and Toby Gad.

27. The quotation from the Jade Films YouTube page continues, "We promote equal access through partnership. Enjoy the video in American Sign Language! It's music for everybody. VMP campaign project is not making money. We produced these videos to show the growing needs and the demands for accessibility to music videos and online playback contents." Several deaf-made signed-song videos include a disclaimer stating that the videos are intended for educational purposes only and not for financial gain (Jade Films, "Ver. 2 as a Boy 'If I Were a Boy' by Beyonce—ASL Music Video [en-gender marlene dietrich]," February 3, 2009, https://www.youtube.com/watch?v=ZRHKBkt9h9E). soph1951 is a sexagenarian US female sign-language interpreter with an extensive YouTube catalog of more than eight hundred signed-song videos spanning eight years.

28. Dan McDougall, "ASL Music Video Project," circa February–March 2010, http://madonnasls.com/sls4650/index.html.

29. Paul and Tina's Signalong, "Paul Films Tina Signing Sign Language, Beyoncé 'Halo' with No Practice," August 5, 2014, https://www.youtube.com/watch?v=dt_nQ3Vnoxw.

30. Paul and Tina's Signalong, "About," July 30, 2014, https://www.youtube.com/channel/UCzLrixb9uh7plQYgZSFmaYQ/about.

31. Paula Thompson, 2015, comment on Paul and Tina's Signalong, "Paul Films Tina."

32. Maler provides examples of some hearing song signers who privilege translating the beat and rhythm of the preexisting song—via constant head-nods or body pulses—rather than adhering to the prosody of ASL ("Musical Expressions," 83–86).

33. Hartmut Teuber, 2015, comment on Paul and Tina's Signalong, "Paul films Tina."

34. A very brief overview of the Paul and Tina social media platforms and coverage include Paul and Tina's Signalong Official YouTube account and Facebook page, multiple posts on the Deaf YouVideo blog and vlog, several Reddit posts via the subreddit r/deaf community (with their tagline "we cannot hear! yay!"), and various personal blogs and Deaf discussion boards (such as Amy Cohen Efron's deafeyeseeit.com, danielgreene.com, and joshiesworld.com).

35. Amin, "Girl Power."

36. It should be noted that Beyoncé's 2011 Glastonbury performance signaled the first solo female headline act there in twenty-one years, the last previous being Sinead O'Connor's 1990 performance.

37. When asked about her thoughts on feminism in the 2011 *Harper's Bazaar* interview, Beyoncé states that "It's just something that's kind of natural for me, and I feel like . . . you know . . . it's like, what I live for. I need to find a catchy new word for feminism, right? Like Bootylicious" (quoted in Davidson, *Black Women*, 91). Beyoncé went on to fully embrace, use, and, to some, sell out the terms *feminist* and *feminism* in the years that followed. For further discussions on Beyoncé's complex narratives of feminism, see Hansen, "Empowered or Objectified?"

38. Lauren Hostovsky, "ASL Music Video—Run the World (Girls)," May 5, 2013, https://www.youtube.com/watch?v=yCBk4C1_90A.

39. Ibid.

40. For references to the visual turn in popular music see Holt, "Is Music Becoming More Visual?" For further reading on Beyoncé's assertion of "pop's visuality as a parameter of added value and heightened meaning" in her visual album see Harper, "BEYONCÉ," 70.

41. Scott Baker, in Emily Siner, "When Interpreters Can't Translate Everything," *Nashville Public Radio*, October 12, 2016, http://nashvillepublicradio.org/post/8-when-interpreters-cant-translate-everything#stream/0.

42. Lange, "Videos of Affinity."

43. Much has been published on mirror neurons or mirror systems since their discovery in the early 1990s. Of particular relevance to music research are works by Kohler et al., "Hearing Sounds," and Molnar-Szakacs and Overy, "Music."

44. Bahan, "Face-to-Face," 45.

45. DuncantheWonderDog, 2015, comment, accessed August 24, 2017, https://www.reddit.com/r/deaf/comments/2hhujj/deaf_reaction_to_tina_paul_sirimarco/ckt7v1j/.

46. kyabupaks, 2014, comment, accessed August 24, 2017, https://www.reddit.com/r/deaf/comments/2hhujj/deaf_reaction_to_tina_paul_sirimarco/cksx4yo/.

47. Caroline Zola, "Let's Talk (or Sign!) about the Deaf, Not Hearing Interpreters," *Slate*, June 10, 2015, http://www.slate.com/blogs/lexicon_valley/2015/06/10/sign_language_let_s_talk_or_sign_about_the_deaf_not_hearing_interpreters.html.

48. Lange, "Videos of Affinity," 83.

BIBLIOGRAPHY

Amin, Takiyah Nur. "Girl Power, Real Politics: Dis/Respectability, Post-raciality, and the Politics of Inclusion." In *Oxford Handbook of Dance and the Popular Screen*. Edited by Melissa Blanco Borelli, 255–67. Oxford: Oxford University Press, 2014.

Bahan, Ben. "Face-to-Face Tradition in the American Deaf Community: Dynamics of the Teller, the Tale, and the Audience." In *Signing the Body Poetic: Essays on American Sign Language Literature*. Edited by H-Dirksen L. Bauman, Jennifer L. Nelson, and Heidi M. Rose, 21–50. Berkeley: University of California Press, 2006.

Burgess, Jean, and Joshua Green. *YouTube: Online Video and Participatory Culture*. Cambridge: Polity, 2009.

Chalfen, Richard. *Snapshot Versions of Life*. Bowling Green, OH: Bowling Green State University Popular Press, 1987.

Darrow, Alice-Ann. "Sounds in the Silence: Research on Music and Deafness." *Update: Applications of Research in Music Education* 25, no. 1 (2006): 5–14.

———. "Teaching Students with Hearing Losses." *General Music Today* 20 (2007): 27–30.

Darrow, Alice-Ann, and Diane Merchant Loomis. "Music and Deaf Culture: Images from the Media and Their Interpretation by Deaf and Hearing Students." *Journal of Music Therapy* 36, no. 2 (1999): 88–109.

Davidson, Maria del Guadalupe. *Black Women, Agency, and the New Black Feminism*. New York: Routledge, 2017.

Fulford, Robert, Jane Ginsborg, and Alinka Greasley. "Hearing Aids and Music: The Experiences of D/deaf Musicians." In *Proceedings of the Ninth Triennial Conference of the European Society for the Cognitive Sciences of Music*. Edited by Jane Ginsborg, Alexandra Lamont, Michelle Phillips, and Stephanie Bramley. Manchester: Royal Northern College of Music, 2015. http://www.escom.org/proceedings/ESCOM9_Manchester_2015_Abstracts_Proceedings.pdf.

Godøy, Rolf Inge, and Marc Lehman, eds. *Musical Gestures: Sound, Movement, and Meaning*. New York: Routledge, 2010.

Hansen, Kai Arne. "Empowered or Objectified? Personal Narrative and Audiovisual Aesthetics in Beyoncé's *Partition*." *Popular Music and Society* 40, no. 2 (2017): 164–80.

Harper, Paula. "*BEYONCÉ*: Viral Techniques and the Visual Album." *Popular Music and Society* 40, no. 1 (2019): 61–81.

Hawkins, Stan. *Queerness in Pop Music: Aesthetics, Gender Norms, and Temporality*. New York: Routledge, 2016.

Holmes, Jessica. "Singing beyond Hearing." *Journal of the American Musicological Society* 69, no. 2 (2016): 542–48.

Holt, Fabian. "Is Music Becoming More Visual? Online Video Content in the Music Industry." *Visual Studies* 26, no. 1 (2011): 50–61.

Howe, Blake, Stephanie Jensen-Moulton, Neil Lerner, and Joseph Straus, eds. *Oxford Handbook of Music and Disability Studies*. Oxford: Oxford University Press, 2016.

Jansen, E. J., H. W. Helleman, W. A. Drechsler, and J. A. de Laat. "Noise Induced Hearing Loss and Other Hearing Complaints among Musicians of Symphony Orchestras." *International Archives of Occupational and Environmental Health* 82, no. 2 (2009): 153–64.

Jones, Jeannette DiBernardo. "Imagined Hearing: Music-Making in Deaf Culture." In *Oxford Handbook of Music and Disability Studies*. Edited by Blake Howe, Stephanie Jensen-Moulton, Neil Lerner, and Joseph Straus, 54–72. Oxford: Oxford University Press, 2016.

Kohler, Evelyne, Christian Keysers, M. Alessandra Umiltà, Leonardo Fogassi, Vittorio Gallese, and Giacomo Rizzolatti. "Hearing Sounds, Understanding Actions: Action Representation in Mirror Neurons." *Science* 297, no. 5582 (2002): 846–48.

Lange, Patricia G. "Videos of Affinity." In *The YouTube Reader*. Edited by Pelle Snickars and Patrick Vonderau, 70–88. Stockholm: National Library of Sweden, 2009.

Maler, Anabel. "Musical Expressions among Deaf and Hearing Song Signers." In *Oxford Handbook of Music and Disability Studies*. Edited by Blake Howe, Stephanie Jensen-Moulton, Neil Lerner, and Joseph Straus, 73–91. Oxford: Oxford University Press, 2016.

———. "Songs for Hands: Analyzing Interactions of Sign Language and Music." *Music Theory Online* 19, no. 1 (2013), http://mtosmt.org/issues/mto.13.19.1/mto.13.19.1.maler.html.

Mangaoang, Áine. *Dangerous Mediations: Pop Music in a Philippine Prison Video*. New York: Bloomsbury, 2019.

Marshall, Melanie L. "Consuming Gaga." In *Lady Gaga and Popular Music: Performing Gender, Fashion, and Culture*. Edited by Martin Iddon and Melanie L. Marshall, 231–44. New York: Routledge, 2014.

Molnar-Szakacs, Istvan, and Katie Overy. "Music and Mirror Neurons: From Motion to 'E'motion." *Social Cognitive and Affective Neuroscience* 1, no. 3 (2006): 235–41.

Morata, Thais C. "Young People: Their Noise and Music Exposures and the Risk of Hearing Loss." *International Journal of Audiology* 46, no. 2 (2007): 111–12.

Śliwińska-Kowalska, Mariola, and Adrian Davis. "Noise-Induced Hearing Loss." *Noise and Health* 14, no. 61 (2012): 274–80.

Straus, Joseph N. *Extraordinary Measures: Disability in Music*. New York: Oxford University Press, 2011.

Stuart, Susan A. J. "Enkinaesthesia: The Essential Sensuous Background for Co-Agency." In *The Background: Knowing without Thinking: Mind, Action, Cognition and the Phenomenon of the Background*. Edited by Zdravko Radman, 167–86. New York: Palgrave Macmillan, 2012.

Woodward, James. "Implications for Sociolinguistic Research among the Deaf." *Sign Language Studies* 1 (1972): 1–7.

TEN

"Girl I'm Tryna Kick It with Ya"

Tracing the Reception of the Embodiment of Girl/Bedroom Culture in "7/11"

MELISSA AVDEEFF

The initial release of Beyoncé's "7/11" single and music video caused a minor flurry of activity online among audiences trying to "figure out" how to interpret the track—one that's admittedly quite different from the artists' previous aesthetics at the time. On November 22, 2014, SupDaily06 (Chris Thompson) posted the YouTube video "Beyoncé—'7/11'—EXPLANATION." While reflecting on Beyoncé, he admits he has "not really enjoyed her voice that much since 'Dangerously in Love,' but . . . [does] dig the new album." Then he offers his interpretation of what the new "7/11" video "is really about":

> OK, so what I think that this whole thing . . . it's about being fit and healthy and having a proper diet. So she starts off and she is KALE. She's got a KALE shirt on and she's letting you know that kale is a great vegetable. Here she shreds some Parmesan cheese onto it; here she gives it a little bit of a bite with some vinaigrette like an alligator. Here she's focusing on dairy products: whole milk, 1%, skim. And here she enjoys a milkshake; you have to treat yourself to treats every once in a while. Milkshake. This next section is about juicing, about super-charging your food. Take your kale, mix in some fruit, add water—healthy! You gotta mix it all up. Boom! Superfood! The next is just stay hydrated. Stay hydrated with your friends. If water is boring, put it in a party cup; party cups make everything fun. And this represents the food pyramid. You gotta make sure you get a little bit from each section of the food pyramid to have an all-around

balanced diet. Here represents that when you get to the holidays you'll have a gift of a new body for yourself. You are the gift. She gets out, she's the gift, the gift of a sexy body from eating properly. That is just Beyoncé talking to her foot; she really might have lost her mind.

The video ends with Thompson remarking that "To be honest, I don't understand what this video was. It's super low quality, which is not usual for her. But I will say this: she looks like she's having a great time. So tell me in the comments below: is there a purpose behind what this video is, because it's so different from what she normally does? Or is she just losing it a little bit?"[1]

This reaction to Beyoncé's "7/11" video is not exemplary; it does not have a tremendous number of views and generally reads like an ironic response with an underlying serious desire to decode the "7/11" text. But it's the key moment at the end, in proclaiming his confusion and inability to adequately *explain* Beyoncé's music video, where Thompson's video reveals wider issues in both the reception of the girl culture embodied in Beyoncé's "7/11" music video and the subsequent trivialization of girl culture that is perpetuated in Thompson's response. In his video, Thompson, a self-identified heterosexual male, signifies the historical "unknowingness" of the girl culture media practices that have historically been conducted in the private sphere by young girls.

This chapter is an examination of the reception of Beyoncé's "7/11" video by music critics and YouTubers, focusing specifically on the music video's cultural embeddedness and relationship to recent evolutions in girl culture, particularly in the digital shift that expanded domestic and private activities online and brought them into the public sphere. Through such analysis, I argue that "7/11" is illustrative of a shift in media practices wherein girl culture has gone public on social media, and listening is increasingly both a participatory and a productive practice. After situating Beyoncé's music video within the evolution of girl culture and the historical distinctions between public and private spheres, this chapter explores how music critics respond to the "7/11" video and explicates their attempts at decoding the thematic elements. This chapter then outlines how YouTubers decode the embodiment of girl and bedroom culture in "7/11" through their reaction videos. This form of textual poaching is influenced by the visual aesthetics of "7/11" and affords online spaces for consumption practices that had previously been privately mediated.

Beyoncé's "7/11" music video is an important moment in the transition from bedroom girl culture to an online and public incarnation. Her video divulges these practices, which have a history of being trivialized or misunderstood in the mainstream media. Viewers may identify with Beyoncé's practices and are thereby assured by their normalcy or commonality. Just as mainstream discussion of girl bedroom culture is lacking, so are analyses of how viewers respond to public displays of these practices. This chapter provides new forms of analysis by comparing this open format of cultural criticism with the more traditional form of gatekeeping through mainstream music criticism.

THE VISUALITY OF THE DIGITAL BEDROOM IN "7/11": MUSIC CRITICS RESPOND

"7/11" was slated for release on the *Platinum Edition* (2014) reissue of *Beyoncé* (2013) on November 25, 2014. On November 19, 2014, a thirty-second sample of the song was released as a teaser, the whole song was leaked on November 20, and the music video was officially released on November 21, presumably as a way to counteract the impact of the song leak. The track "broke the internet," so to speak, sparking numerous YouTube reaction videos and critical reviews from the mainstream press. Undoubtedly, the scale of the reaction was not unique to "7/11," but for the purpose of analysis, the reactions provide an intriguing look into the fan and critic response, as well as the video's relationship to wider shifts in digitality.

"7/11" as a song was, at the time of its release, the closest that Beyoncé has thus far ventured into more overtly hip hop-influenced vocal delivery accompanied by sparse trap-influenced beats. Written by Beyoncé and Alonzo Holt, with producers Bobby Johnson, Detail, and Sidney Swift, the song's style is frenetic, and the lyrics are intricate and difficult to discern even after repeated listenings. First reactions to the song by the mainstream press were mixed: some appreciating the song for its uniqueness, others calling it a throwaway track meant as album filler. The release of the video helped to explain the song for some, but it also added to the general confusion. Allison Piwowarski of *Bustle*, for example, writes, "But what the fresh hell is '7/11' about? Even members of the Beyhive are scratching their heads over this one" before deducing that she "can confidently say—as confident as one can be while deciphering Bey lyrics—that '7/11' is about the drinking game 7/11 Doubles."[2]

Mainstream press reviews, largely positive, focus on four themes: the supposed low-budget video aesthetics; the idea that Beyoncé is queen and therefore above criticism; the idea that, instead, Beyoncé is "just like us," curating an illusion of intimacy; and the importance of fun, which will be discussed further in this chapter. Mike Wass of *Idolator* notes "this looks like it was filmed on Queen Bey's iPhone but it's still hands down the best thing you will see today ... or, quite possibly ever,"[3] which is mirrored by Patrick McDermott of *The Fader* when he asks, "Did Beyoncé make the best video ever with an iPhone?"[4] The video "looks like it was a blast to film" and demonstrates that "at the end of the day, we very much do care about having fun."[5] "7/11" features "quirky dance moves and wardrobe changes" by Beyoncé,[6] who is "wearing no make-up, panties and baggy sweaters,"[7] with her dancers, making "a human pyramid and straight up playing around with friends in what looks like a hotel,"[8] and is described as "one long selfie."[9] It is important to note that, in its embodiment of girl culture, the video features "sexiness swapped for silliness"[10] as a "fantastic ode to slumber parties and dancing in your underwear."[11] Even if Beyoncé is described as being "just like us,"[12] hers is a highly crafted and manufactured version of intimacy. It may be a "surprisingly personal video,"[13] but it is still, nevertheless, a *product* and, as such, meticulously controlled.

A number of critics have attempted to establish a relationship between "7/11" and the digital turn, but they seem unsure of what form that relationship may take. Leandra Medine writes, "this semi-crude selfie video, when held up against the highly produced and incredibly styled videos that are typically indicative of a Beyoncé production, could theoretically make a much larger statement about the way in which we consume digital entertainment."[14] Further, Phillip Maciak notes that "7/11" is "crafted to take full advantage of the interactive possibilities of Twitter, Vine, and Tumblr." It "feels a bit like a revolution" in which Beyoncé has "made a joyful, living, shareable piece of digital art that's fully of this moment."[15] Maciak further argues that the interactivity represented in the video encourages a sense of viewer ownership: the selfie medium represents ownership of self-representation, and Beyoncé upholds the control she possesses over her persona within this video.

The video's arrangement of neatly parceled dance moves, location changes, loops, and repetitions invites audiences to deconstruct the video into shareable GIFs; to participate, remix, and circulate, broadening the dissemination and discourse surrounding Beyoncé as idol and brand. In creating a video that is essentially composed of a sequence of potential GIFs, Beyoncé is harnessing participatory culture, supplying materials clearly intended to be poached and remixed in ways that are implicit within the medium. To examine "7/11" as a medium is to recognize the interactivity and convergence of digital culture; taken together with the visual narrative of the video, however, the presentation of Beyoncé and her dancers enjoying the *best slumber party ever* marks Beyoncé's involvement and legitimization of girl culture and its online transference. Beyoncé, perhaps recognizing that a generation of girls grew up dancing along to her videos in their bedrooms with friends, gives their voices and experiences representation and visibility in "7/11," thereby drawing attention to fan activities that have historically been trivialized in the mainstream press.

"7/11" is the clearest example of Beyoncé's acknowledgment of a girl culture that has often depended on her own music: her prior solo albums, and many Destiny's Child albums, have also integrated themes of girl power, postfeminism, Black feminist thought, and sex-positivity. For example, *Writing's on the Wall* (1999) can be understood as a call to action for women to assert their independence and agency in relationships. Tracks such as "Independent Women" (2001) by Destiny's Child further this narrative by comparing Destiny's Child to the rebooted *Charlie's Angels* in 2000, both implied as postfeminist idols, noting in the chorus that "The shoes on my feet / I've bought it / The clothes I'm wearing / I've bought it / The rock I'm rockin' / I've bought it / 'Cause I depend on me / If I wanted the watch you're wearin' / I'll buy it / The house I live in / I've bought it / The car I'm driving / I've bought it / I depend on me." In addition, "Girls" (2004), based on the sex-positive female characters of *Sex and the City*, is an ode to female relationships and the strength that women can draw from each other, as opposed to struggling to compete with one another. These examples are not exhaustive, and it is clear that not all Destiny's Child and Beyoncé songs can be decoded as postfeminist, especially when considering that a small selection of their songs and music videos can be interpreted as destructive in their portrayals of women and female-centered relationships: see "Nasty Girl" (2001), with lyrics that shame an unnamed woman for her clothing choices.

Angela McRobbie and Jenny Garber coin the term "bedroom culture" in their 1975 essay "Girls and Subcultures," and the concept is critically explored at length elsewhere.[16] McRobbie and Garber originally used the term to describe how teenage girls use domestic spaces, such as the bedroom, as alternative means of organizing cultural life, in opposition to the more public subcultures that young males involve themselves in. McRobbie and Garber argue that the absence of females in the male-driven subcultures discussed in the literature is startling, and "when they *do* appear, it is either in ways which uncritically reinforce the stereotypical image of women with which we are now so familiar . . . or they are fleetingly and marginally presented."[17] The academic examination of bedroom and girl culture has greatly expanded since the 1970s, but the personal and journalistic documentations of girl culture's socialization process still often diminish its importance as a phenomenon or trivialize it as a trifling and liminal moment in adolescent growth.[18]

Sian Lincoln's ongoing research into bedroom and girl culture emphasizes the importance of music in the contemporary teenage bedroom, functioning as a catalyst in the negotiation of identity and sociability. As with Tia DeNora's examination of female music practices,[19] Lincoln notes the essential nature of music as the sound track of everyday life, serving as a site of meaning creation and a backdrop to collective social experiences. Consuming music, as a medium, "is both an individualized and a unifying practice,"[20] characterizing biography as well as a symbol for the exertion of control over personal space, distinct from parental control (to a certain extent). Noting that much of the literature about bedroom culture examines media engagement as a secondary activity within one's personal space, instead focusing on the *artifacts* in a bedroom and their importance in biography and identity formation, Lincoln examines music as a primary site of engagement and recognizes the significance of media in youth socialization, regardless of gender identification. I have been using "bedroom culture" and "girl culture" somewhat interchangeably, but it should be noted that although consuming music in one's bedroom is not inherently a "girl" activity, it is often gendered as such in mainstream discourse, based on historical associations of femininity and domestic spaces. Nevertheless, as later discussions here will explore, digitality increases the visibility of participation in domestic media practices, regardless of historical binary gender assumptions.

Beyoncé's "7/11" video may also be interpreted as a documentation of pre-going-out rituals wherein groups of friends prepare for a night out (to a club or to a party, for example) by gathering in a domestic space beforehand. Usually accompanied by music, these rituals signify a more adult version of young girl collective media practices in domestic spaces. The young girl mimicking her favorite idol by singing into her hairbrush may still occur (as exhibited by Beyoncé in "7/11"), as well as the exchanging of clothing, makeup, and gossip, but the addition of alcohol alters the meaning of the gathering. In addition, the bedroom here acts as a liminal (but highly important) space, leading up to the main event of the club or another party. Much like the collective meaning-making activities of young girls, these rituals are important bonding experiences. Nick Agafonoff describes his participant observation of a pre-going-out ritual by a group of girls as follows:

> During the three hour pre-going out ritual I documented an extraordinary array of behaviours. Jane and Celeste changed their clothes three or four times. They made and received dozens of phone and text messages to and from their friends constantly, getting and making reports on what everyone in their female social group was wearing, who was already at the club and what reactions they were getting. They did their make-up and hair using a profusion of hair and make-up products, which Jane had to tip from the make-up drawer onto the bed in order to sort through all the products. They graduated from cheap UDL's [sic; canned cocktails] to the more upmarket Bacardi Breezers towards the end of the night. By the end of the session the room was a huge mess with clothes and make-up and empty bottles of UDL and Bacardi Breezers strewn throughout. Celeste was unhappy with the outcome of her first hairstyle and so she started making it up all over again. At one point there was a fight between Celeste and her mother as to how she was presenting herself. It just made Celeste go away and create an even more controversial look. Throughout this entire time, the stereo pumped electronic dance music as Jane and Celeste sipped UDLs and then Bacardi Breezers.[21]

Alcohol, as highlighted in the "7/11" video, often plays a central role in these rituals and enhances the group's participation in their chosen music or media. Through an alcohol-induced lessening of inhibitions and an increased focus on sex and sexuality, the performance and creation of a sexualized ideal may be explored prior to leaving the domestic space. For many, these rituals are more important than the actual event and are a signficant point of contact for friendship and bonding from college age to one's midtwenties. It is a time for validation; during a period of relative uncertainty and instability in a woman's life, these rituals validate one's position within a community, creating an in-group of support and a safe space for explorations of identity, sex, and sexuality.[22]

In the "7/11" music video, it is unclear whether Beyoncé and her backup dancers will be going out, but their actions portray the typical elements of pre-going-out rituals: clothing changes, alcohol consumption, makeup and clothing strewn about, dancing, and group bonding. The video correspondingly highlights the performativity of these rituals. The *performance* of femininity is on display, made to appear more authentic as its construction is viewed through the lens of Beyoncé's smartphone or Go-Pro, in opposition to the way in which these rituals are often constructed on film and television.[23]

Beyoncé's "7/11" video is deeply embedded and representative of mid-2010s digital media practices, and it reflects the shift of bedroom girl culture, and the rituals and performances that define them, to the online and public sphere. As noted earlier, there are countless portrayals of these practices on other media, such as film and television, but the agency of representation exhibited by Beyoncé, connected to the self-publishing format of selfies and other user-generated media, is distinct in its form of participation. The movement of bedroom activities online has a contested history, from a theoretical perspective. Practices change as technologies create space for new modes of sociality, seen in the way many social media platforms underwent a visual turn, leading up to "7/11"s 2014 release, with video increasingly becoming the primary sharing format. After the rise of YouTube as the primary site of music engagement for youth, many platforms have either adapted, or new ones have been created, to accommodate the emphasis on visuality, such as Musical.ly (now TikTok) and SnapChat.

LEGITIMIZATION THROUGH PARTICIPATION: YOUTUBE REACTION VIDEOS

Social media have brought greater democratization to media production. The technical power of ubiquitous technologies, such as Smartphones, has increased the potential for shared attention during media events and provides "individuals with the technical capability to compete with mass media in disseminating information, setting agendas, and framing conversations."[24] One of these competing practices is the publishing of critical responses to media texts, historically produced by journalists, critics, and the like, and restricted by gatekeepers and shareholders. Platforms such as YouTube facilitate collective sensemaking by diversifying the voices and systems of participation. YouTube reaction videos have become an alternative response to media texts as a form of vernacular criticism. Although they are a common YouTube genre and trope with a comparatively long history (considering the ephemeral nature of digital user-generated content), the practice is particularly undertheorized. The next section examines "7/11" reaction videos, situating them within the nexus of practice of online bedroom and girl culture.

Though the content and mood of reaction videos vary, a reaction video can largely be understood as a "meta-video that documents in real-time individuals watching another video usually for the first time."[25] The most common configuration involves a face-focused, seemingly self-produced video that documents the viewer's reaction to a media text. Reaction videos tend either to show the viewer's face and upper body alone or insert the media being reacted to on the reactor's image. The history of reaction videos has been traced to a home video recorded in 1998 and uploaded to YouTube in 2006 in which two children react to unwrapping their Christmas gift of a Nintendo 64 console. These children are not reacting to an audiovisual text, but their reaction (uninhibited screaming) has come to epitomize the fundamental moment of authentically spontaneous vocalizations that reaction videos strive for. The reaction video in its current form is more directly traced to YouTube in 2007 with the proliferation of reactions to the "gross-out fetish porn clip" "2 Girls 1 Cup." Writing in 2011, when the reaction video went mainstream, Sam Anderson notes that the spread of "2 Girls 1 Cup" reaction videos was "like a social periscope" that allowed people to "watch this taboo thing by proxy, to experience its dangerous thrill without having to encounter it directly—like Perseus looking at Medusa in the reflection of his shield."[26] Like the genuine screams of the children on the Christmas Day video, reaction videos strive for the documentation of surprise, with authenticity of emotion being valued above all else. They also emphasize fascination with everyday life: screens of people watching other screens, a cognate of reality television and other visually driven social media such as SnapChat and Instagram.

Elaine Chun, in an examination of K-Pop reaction videos, notes that reaction videos produce a "layered participant structure" consisting of three nested texts: the original video, the reaction video, and the comment spaces across both texts.[27] Interactions therefore occur between the creators of the original text and the reactive fan and also between fan communities who participate. In combination, they extend the transmedia storytelling potential of the primary text. In some ways, they connote an older genre of web broadcasting: the vlog. As a video version of the *LiveJournal* diaries, early video blogs from 2005 and 2006 contain many of the same key features of reaction videos: an authentic conversational approach; face-forward recording; low-budget aesthetics; and an invitation to viewers to enter a personal space, usually the bedroom. Rainer Hillrichs mirrors much of the literature on bedroom culture more broadly when he argues that early vlogs, by using the bedroom (or other domestic spaces) as their setting, not only show these private spaces "as they are" but offer "their own materiality and meanings for adoption or manipulation." The performativity of bedroom culture is recorded for broadcast through the presentation of *self* and domestic artifacts. These vlogs, like the reaction videos, are a "window into the home" and, as such, cannot be conceived as a neutral performance.[28]

There is a distinct lack of research available on YouTube reaction videos, but as Jean Burgess notes about vlogs, which I find applicable to reaction videos, such videos are not merely messages or products but they are "mediating mechanisms via which cultural *practices* are originated, adopted and (sometimes) retained *within* social networks."[29] To return to Beyoncé's "7/11" video, its reaction videos may also *represent* cultural practices, in this case pre-going-out rituals and girl culture, thereby generating value through spreadability of cultural practices. Chris Thompson's reaction, shot in conversational style, is very much a part of the vlog lineage but, at the same time, demonstrates a thorough misunderstanding of the cultural practices portrayed in "7/11," which are informed by the development of the vlog format.

Heather Warren-Crow furthers this discussion by gendering the reaction video genre as feminine, regardless of the sex of the YouTuber, because of the "foregrounding of voice over speech and body over words."[30] As she notes, the original wave of reaction videos demonstrated a fascination with "screaming like a girl, as girls are discursively understood."[31] Aestheticization of the *voice* comes about through the perceived authenticity of the reaction, favoring an embodied, natural response that makes the labor involved immaterial. Warren-Crow fosters an interesting connection between the feminine vocalizations on reaction videos and the "pink labor" that is prevalent throughout social media platforms. The work of reaction videos, as a form of participatory medium, defines users as producers (akin to Chun's concept of layered participation) and draws attention to the rising importance of "feminine skills" in the digital economy. Participatory media are operational because of unpaid labor, as part of "a larger trend of the feminization of labor."[32] In Warren-Crow's analysis, this feminization occurs regardless of the identified gender or perceived sex of the participant; male voices are common in reaction videos, but they often display an element of feminine performativity, through a focus on embodied reactions and a privileging of a natural over an intellectualized response. I also note that these binary distinctions are highly problematic and draw attention to much larger issues of labeling that are outside the scope of this chapter.

As will be explored in a later section, numerous reaction videos for "7/11" differ from the typical reaction-video format; many still do, however, combine the simultaneity of viewing and responding with the conversational approach of early vlogs and are usually filmed in private domestic spaces. Using YouTube's search function, forty "7/11" reaction videos were identified using the queries "7/11 reaction" and "7/11 review." It is possible that more videos could be found with other search terms. My analysis is primarily concerned with how people are reacting to the *content* of "7/11," particularly how bedroom girl culture takes on meaning through the broadcast reactions. In this analysis, the reaction videos are examined as a site of engagement for mediated actions by YouTubers; the agency of their reactions to "7/11" defines a vernacular response to bedroom culture and demonstrate both an understanding of, and contribution to, such cultural practices.

From what can be identified, the majority of the "7/11" reaction videos are filmed in domestic spaces. For many, in what room of the house the video is shot is unclear, but all appear to be domestic private spaces. Some are clearly filmed in a bedroom. Connecting this observation to the literature on vlogging, the subjects of these videos appear to invite viewers into their homes and private lives. The conversational tone of the participants is also quite familiar, further enhancing the connection between reaction YouTuber and audience. Hillrichs notes that, in the early era of vlogs, the visible bedroom artifacts on the video can be identified for their meaning-making potential because of the agency of the vlogger, but for the "7/11" videos, the domestic space seems to serve a secondary function or no function at all. None of the YouTubers appears to put thought or effort into where the video is created, and only one person calls attention to the artifacts in the bedroom by declaring that she had not cleaned up for the video (owing to the surprise nature of the "7/11" music video's release).[33]

Overall, the response to Beyoncé's "7/11" music video markedly differs from the reception of the song. Because the song was leaked a day before the video, most of the reaction YouTubers had already heard the song and formed their opinions. The song "7/11" is outside the norm of Beyoncé's typical outputs, and a small number of YouTubers display difficulty negotiating their love for Beyoncé in opposition to their dislike for the song, and some assert that they enjoy the song despite the negative reviews they had heard elsewhere. Ching Ching Speaks, for example, is unsure how to react to the song or the video and goes back and forth in her real-time reaction between calling the video and Beyoncé "cute," "silly" (and that she "liked seeing her really goofy") and proclaiming her aversion: "the song was OK. I'm impartial, and I know people are gonna hate that I said that. Still a huge fan of Beyoncé.... I didn't hate it, it's not my favorite video."[34] Ron Vuggotta shares his confusion about the negative reviews: "basically a lot of people are, like, really dissing the song, and I don't really understand why."[35]

Those who clearly indicate that they were not Beyoncé fans before this video do not hesitate to announce their distaste for the song and appear less likely to enjoy the song than Beyoncé fans. For example, YouTube user Official Zgibode calls "7/11" the "worst song I've ever heard," further explaining "I don't know what this is.... Now it's over. Thank the heavens. I hated it."[36] Zedakiah Koterba asks his mom to react to the song, and she spells out her feelings, noting "Beyoncé I love you, but no. Just no. I really did not care for this one."[37] Most of the song-response YouTubers do not provide reasons beyond visceral reaction; trever pitts is the only YouTuber who qualifies his distaste of the track, using it as a way to proclaim his dissatisfaction with most contemporary music:

> This is a horrible song. Where is the passion? I remember in music it used to always be about passion and writing meaningful songs. And yes, Beyoncé is a decently good singer, not hating on her.... People like this type of stuff? For me, music is about passion, expression, it gives you chills up and down your spine.... Music nowadays seems to lack

the passion and drive that it used to. Music used to all be about passion and drive and creativeness. This song doesn't have passion or drive or creativeness.[38]

It is interesting to hear trever pitts discuss the lack of creativity he perceives in "7/11," because the general consensus with YouTubers is that the song and video are Beyoncé's most creative outputs thus far: thisISmartinJR calls the music video "completely original. This video was everything,"[39] Dylan Will Not Participate says it's "the greatest video of all time,"[40] and AdrianXpression notes that "it's so quirky; it's completely different than what I expected."[41]

In Tom Sherman's examination of vlogs as vernacular video, he identifies video as the primary medium of contemporary communication. Vernacular video, therefore, serves to establish the video producer's presence as fixed within the video; video "exhibits its own consistencies of form,"[42] influenced by what appeals to advertisers (if involved in the market economy) or draws on video techniques to appeal to "shorter attentions spans," such as "a fascination with crude animation and crude behaviour, quick-and-dirty voice-overs and bold graphics that highlight a declining appreciation of written language."[43] It is intriguing that the reaction-and-review video genre's aesthetics did not significantly evolve between 2006 and 2014, and they remain one of the lowest-budget YouTube video formats, requiring only a camera, a location, and an internet connection. These videos do not often rely on interesting camera techniques, allowing the focus to be the reaction of the viewer to the media being reacted to (or reviewed). What is noteworthy about the "7/11" reaction videos is that their vernacularism resides in their use of language. The expression and mood of these videos is varied, but there are also established ways of speaking that are exhibited throughout. The videos that do not conform to these ways of speaking tend to be created by those who do not establish themselves as Beyoncé fans. In addition to referring to Beyoncé as a "bitch"—used here as a term of endearment—commonly used reaction terms include "killed it"; "winning and/or owning the world"; Beyoncé, or the video, "is everything"; "a goddess"; "giving me life." The use of strategic, commonly used terms fixes the YouTuber's presence in relation to the "7/11" music video and as a Beyoncé fan, or member of the Beyhive. Fandoms often create in-groups through communication methods, and the vernacular becomes a central tactic of orienting groups in this way.

Many reaction YouTubers found that their opinion of the song changed with the release of the music video; it helped them to make sense of the song, as it did for the mainstream press critics reviewed in a previous section. Still, the song and video elicit a lot of confusion, whether one identifies as a Beyoncé fan or not. The central opinion is that the song is not meant to be taken seriously: its authenticity is located in its representation of fun and championing of fun as a serious undertaking. The difficulty for many reviewers in how to approach Beyoncé's music video is summarized quite well by ReddArrow: "This is kinda like my emotional state every time I see anything Beyoncé related. You can't say a word. You can't verbalise. You've been hit by a brick. You don't know how to react, how to feel, and every thought that comes into your head might be inadequate and you don't want to say anything."[44] His reaction contrasts with 4everBrandonTV: "If some of you don't get the aspects of this song—y'all are blind.... Basically, this song was not made to have meaning to it. Get it? Everything an artist tells us does not have to have meaning to it."[45] YouTubers address the camera to note that "it's not a song that I take seriously, and it's not a song that you're supposed to take seriously,"[46] "it ain't trying to win no Grammy. ... Don't read into it too much because there's nothing to read into, she's just goofing off."[47] The video "makes you want to get up and dance—I think that was the whole point of it,"[48] or "it good in that 'Bitch, let's go to the club, let's get turned up.' But it's not good in the sense that you want a Grammy."[49] REAl REAction makes the point that "the song meant nothing to me, but I'm sure it meant the world to her."[50]

The focus on fun is common throughout the reaction videos. Viewers feel that the humor and silliness of the video humanizes Beyoncé: her goddess (or Queen B) persona is supplemented by a facet of her performativity that positions her as "just like us." The music video "shows Beyoncé's humorous side, opposed to the typical goddess glamour type aura that she usually has. It shows a down to earth side of Beyoncé that we rarely see."[51] Ching Ching Speaks can "see why it's popular. It's Beyoncé totally not being herself. We all know Beyoncé to be super classy and, you know, at events and tight-lipped. And she's silly but not, like, crazy. And it was kinda like seeing Beyoncé with the door closed.... I like seeing her really goofy."[52] These reactions to seeing what viewers perceive as Beyoncé's authentic self mimic the phenomenon in bedroom culture when young people use domestic spaces to explore their identity, in a way that they may not feel comfortable doing in public.[53]

YouTubers' reactions to Beyoncé's humor and play embody bedroom girl culture; not in precisely those terms, but by considering this backstage performance of self to be what she, and other girls, do in their personal spaces. Male and female YouTubers associate "7/11" with a girls' slumber party and, in doing so, further the discussion by noting that the song makes them want to get involved in the same way, perpetuating the active media consumption of girl culture through dance and collectivity. Beyoncé seemed to have "called her friends over for a slumber party it looks like,"[54] while the resulting video "was fun. I liked the fact that it was done in, like, a hotel or a motel. And she's just having fun with her girls—they're using blow-dryers, she's doing crazy silly dances, her room is messy, her house is a mess.... I like to see this girl get loose like this."[55] Other responses:

> ReddArrow: this is what Beyoncé's slumber party looks like.... This is what she looks like preparing for a night out.[56]

> MessyMyles: She made this song so I can turn the fuck up.... The video "7/11" makes me want to grab all my friends, bitch, and rent out a hotel room—we ain't gotta get nothing expensive like the Hilton. We can go on down to the Super 8 ... and turn the fuck up.[57]

> STORY OF CHINA: When Beyoncé comes on it makes you want to put some sunglasses on, shake your weave, dance for your man, drink your drink. With "7/11" she's giving you all of that because she do shit that you do at home when you think nobody's watching—you do the little Tae Bo moves, that little leg thing she was doing, you practice twerking your butt in the mirror ... she gives you it all, like.... It looked like they were friends for like seven girls and they was hanging out, drinking in the hotel room, acting stupid.... It was like one of them songs for girls' night out—you just don't give a damn, you just want to turn up and drink. You trying to get away from your kids, you man, got your friends with you, you're just trying to have some fun.[58]

> Samore Love Real TV: I wanna learn how to do those moves, shaking my butt like that.[59]

> thaghettoview: Me and my girls have fun, have a night—you know, girls night. It just looked fun.... They were just having fun and it made me want to go have a girls night and have fun and let loose and not have a care in the world.[60]

Only one response video contains a negative reaction to Beyoncé's fun persona and embodiment of pre-going-out rituals; DjZos Grotto, comments,

> It was a basic ass video. Basically a girl's slumber party.... Who cares! It was like she was having fun, which is fine... ratchet broads, and other broads treat this chick like a fucking goddess—she's a regular broad just like you, she's just got money. She's ain't do shit but record her and her fucking girls. I don't even know what they was doing... girls' night, slumber party, watching motherfucking Lifetime and *Exhale* and shit... go out on the balcony and dance and shit... and to be honest, who the hell cares?[61]

DjZos Grotto's video is one of the few truly negative reactions to Beyoncé's "7/11" music video. In addition to his misinterpretation of girl culture, he goes on to criticize Beyoncé's choice to wear white after Labor Day and he and his friend comment that she might be wearing butt implants, imply that Beyoncé is good at fellatio, and generally police Beyoncé's body and actions according to outdated constructions of femininity. A policing of Beyoncé's body and actions is also undertaken by one other YouTuber, a self-declared "Country Boy" with the handle The REALity Show in which he alternates between referring to Beyoncé as a "beautiful girl, there's no doubt about that.... Beautiful.... Body's in shape" and policing her choice to wear her underwear without pants. Problematically, his choice of language is reminiscent of body-politics discourse in its patriarchal policing of women's bodies, implying a degree of ownership over her body as a prop for male pleasure. For example, The REALity show remarks that "she needs to put some pants on, though.... I know her mommy and daddy ain't happy with her not wearing some pants. I know, I've got a daughter—I'll be danged if she's gonna dance on camera with no pants on."[62] The YouTuber infantilizes Beyoncé by comparing her agency to the parental constraints applied to his young daughter, simultaneously moralizing her clothing choices and taking pleasure in her revealed body.

While the focus on this chapter is primarily concerned with gendered performance and the production and reception of online bedroom girl culture, The REALity Show's comments point to longer histories of the policing of Black women's bodies, and Beyoncé's in particular. Throughout her career, Beyoncé has demonstrated a high degree of control over how her image is presented in the public eye, as well as agency over her body. Noël Siqi Duan, and others, note that Beyoncé's performances tap into a history of fetishization and sexualization of Black female bodies, which is linked to a number of systems, including slavery, colonialism, capitalism, and patriarchy. In criticizing Beyoncé's agency in this way, The REALity show runs the risk of eradicating difference through his policing. He situates his critique as an issue of morality but perpetuates the ideology that women, and Black women, are passive, or sexualized, props. Duan reports that bell hooks takes a similar approach, notoriously calling Beyoncé a "terrorist" because of her overtly sexualized performances, and the way in which she is infantilized on the cover of the May 2014 issue of *Time*. Beyoncé, in her choice to portray herself as silly or sexual (or both, as these are not necessarily mutually exclusive categories), reclaims ownership over her body and sexuality, something that has been historically denied for many Black women in US history. Duan's exploration of Beyoncé's 2013 Superbowl performance relates quite well to the "7/11" video when she notes that "she was not only claiming ownership of her body, but also demonstrating that black women, who are haunted by a long history of being perceived to have either animalistic sexual desires or be desexualized 'mammy' figures, can be admired for the very characteristics that have been considered negative race and sex traits."[63]

When Beyoncé fragments and draws attention to various body parts, especially her buttocks, it could be argued that through this mode of filming, she disrupts overt objectification and her own self-objectification becomes a form of empowerment.[64] As interpreted by the press, her sexiness is replaced by silliness; she focuses on play and humor, thereby defying the gaze-objectification cycle. In "7/11," Beyoncé is cute and natural as opposed to sexy: substituting one gendered performance for another. This dramaturgical presentation exhibits typically backstage, face-to-face, female bonding activities and moves them to a highly public arena.[65] The carefully curated illusion of intimacy achieved through the medium of the selfie video marks it as a more authentic performance of self and woman(girl)hood.

Although it is outside the scope of this chapter, it should be noted that the way in which Beyoncé is both subject to and also exhibiting her own controlling gaze is not only informed by historical gender conventions but also racialized. In some moments, she aligns with Aisha Durham's notion of the backward gaze, in which she invites viewers to gaze on her Black body, as an empowering move to counteract racialized objectification.[66] In addition, the way in which Beyoncé's gaze is often locked onto the camera can be read as both an invitation to intimacy and a Black feminist form of control. Nicole Fleetwood speaks of this Black gaze in visual culture wherein an agent's gaze serves to scrutinize the way in which race is imposed through a visual interpretation of one's body.[67]

Generally, Beyoncé's portrayal of girl culture and pre-going-out rituals is well received by YouTubers. Although very few YouTubers clearly identify the "7/11" video as representative of these cultural practices, they do identify key signifiers of the culture, such as the importance of fun and play, social gatherings with female friends, and physically reacting to media, in this case the "7/11" song. It is noteworthy to see that the identification of these signifiers, and desire to participate in these practices, does not correlate with gender. Rather, it seems that pre-going-out rituals, or slumber-party scenes, although associated with getting together with "the girls," are not necessarily coded as a girls-only activity by YouTubers.

Finally, the tacit connection between historically defined bedroom culture and contemporary digital bedroom culture that extends the domestic space to a collapsed private-public sphere is acknowledged by a number of YouTubers. Specifically, attention is paid to the technology that was (presumably) used to create the "7/11" video. Beyond merely noting that the video was most likely shot on a Go-Pro or iPhone, as most YouTubers did, some extend the idea by making connections with their own participation in video creation. The GIF-style filming is identified as analogous to the now-defunct Vine app by STORY OF CHINA when she says, "I think people will be like 'what the hell' because it looks like a Vine video. I think that's what they were trying to do, kinda like Vine, you know, plays for like seven seconds and it repeats itself."[68] Similarly, Ash Vee Catch'em All says: "As soon as I clicked play, I said, bitch is you giving me a vlog right now? Is you giving me a Vine, happy tease right now? Is you giving me an Instagram twerk video right now? Because when I honestly watched it, it was like seeing her have fun.... I am a fan of the video. I love seeing her vlog and do videos like that."[69] She goes on to comment that Beyoncé has "always been a vlogger," supporting the connections between Beyoncé's career development and social media platforms. "7/11" demonstrates elements of Vine filming aesthetics, like short sequences, repetition, humor, and dance and also aligns with the youth-oriented music app Musical.ly, which is indicative of the visual and prosumer shift in music consumption. Dylan Will Not Participate, whose reaction video was released much later than "7/11" in 2017, is "into it. It kinda reminds me of a really dope Musical.ly—like that app you can get."[70]

CONCLUSION

Video captures the ephemeral and, in the case of reaction videos, captures the simultaneity and immediacy of an authentic response to media. In "7/11," Beyoncé invites viewers into a carefully constructed backstage performance of self, embodying a cultural practice that has often depended on her own mediated outputs. Taken together, video, in the format of both YouTube reaction video and music video, becomes the way in which people situate themselves at events and describe what happened. "7/11" reaction YouTubers place themselves as witnesses to the "7/11" music video and as decoders of the cultural practices displayed by Beyoncé. Beyoncé, in turn, portrays a mode of media engagement that has historically been gendered female and associated with young females in particular. Beyoncé situates herself as a participant in bedroom and girl culture, displaying both the young girl practices of play and silliness and the older female's inclusion of alcohol and self-objectification. By drawing attention to these practices, she can be seen as legitimizing a practice that has often been trivialized by mainstream media and music critics in particular. By examining the ways in which YouTubers react and review "7/11" through video, the interconnectedness of these practices, and the position of both along a lineage of girl/bedroom culture and its transference to online participation and digitality, can be observed.

The performers in "7/11" are all presumably female, but the reaction of YouTubers appears to encompass a diverse representation of gender, sexuality, and race. Although it is problematic to assume someone's gender or sexuality, the fact that these videos are representative of their own cultural practices, points to the potential for a renegotiation of the genderization of bedroom culture. The participatory engagement with music in domestic spaces, as it moved online, increased the visibility of male and non-binary participants. Beyoncé's "7/11" occurs at a crucial moment in this shift, when the use of music-centered apps such as Vine and Musical.ly rose to prominence. These platforms combine humor, music, and self-representation, with a focus on authenticity, and are emblematic of the progressively active form of music engagement afforded by digital media.

The increasingly independent nature of cultural criticism, made possible through platforms such as YouTube, has allowed audience members to interpret and react to cultural texts in ways that were not previously available. The response to "7/11" demonstrates the distinctions between traditional gatekeepers and cultural critics in the form of music critics, and YouTube reaction videos, as observed in 2014. The visceral, and immediate, responses from the YouTubers demonstrates an immediacy of engagement, an immediacy that is reflective of the "7/11" video and participatory culture more broadly. The video is by no means the first time that girl culture has been seen in pop culture, but the music criticism and YouTube reactions to it suggest that although many social media platforms rely on the public presentation of intimacy and heavily curated performances of authenticity, the widespread understanding and knowledge of these practices was still restricted by cultural gatekeepers in the mainstream. It is remarkable that so widespread an activity as singing and dancing to music with friends in the private domain could provoke confusion when witnessed through music video. It raises the question of whether the confusion is centered on a misunderstanding of girl culture in general or Beyoncé's performance of spontaneous youthfulness in particular.

Throughout the 1990s and early 2000s, countless youths sang along to Destiny's Child songs in their bedrooms with friends, constructing dances, dressing up, and using hairbrushes as microphones. In 2014, Beyoncé let them all know that she's no different.

MELISSA AVDEEFF is Senior Lecturer in the School of Media and Performing Arts at Coventry University.

NOTES

1. SupDaily06, "Beyoncé—7/11—EXPLANATION," November 22, 2014, https://www.youtube.com/watch?v=AJd7Y8iWWzY.

2. Allison Piwowarski, "What Is the Meaning behind Beyoncé's '7/11'? Look to This College Drinking Game," *Bustle*, November 25, 2014, https://www.bustle

.com/articles/51135-what-is-the-meaning-behind-beyoncs-711-look-to-this-college-drinking-game.

3. Mike Wass, "Beyonce's '7/11' Video Is a Homemade Masterpiece Complete with Killer Choreography and Bathroom Twerking: Watch," *Idolator*, November 21, 2014, http://www.idolator.com/7571522/beyonce-7-11-video-twerking.

4. Patrick D. McDermott, "Beyoncé's '7/11' Video is One Long Perfect Selfie," *The Fader*, November 21, 2014, https://www.thefader.com/2014/11/21/beyonce-711-video.

5. Isha Aran, "Watch Beyoncé's Magnificent Bathroom Dance Party Music Video for '7/11,'" *Jezebel*, November 22, 2014, http://jezebel.com/watch-beyonces-magnificent-bathroom-dance-party-music-v-1662043078; Bridget R. Irvine, "Hear Me Out: Beyoncé, '7/11,'" *Harvard Crimson*, November 28, 2014, http://www.thecrimson.com/article/2014/11/28/hear-me-out-beyonce-7-11/.

6. Daniel Kreps, "Watch Beyoncé's Mesmerizing, Personal '7/11' Video," *Rolling Stone*, November 22, 2014, http://www.rollingstone.com/music/videos/watch-beyonces-mesmerizing-personal-7-11-video-20141122.

7. Wass, "Beyoncé's '7/11' Video."

8. Jessica Goodman, "Beyoncé's '7/11' Music Video Is Her Best Surprise Yet," *Huffpost*, November 21, 2014, updated November 23, 2014, http://www.huffingtonpost.com/2014/11/21/beyonce-711-music-video_n_6202824.html.

9. McDermott, "Beyoncé's '7/11' Video."

10. Kirsten Maree, "Single Review: Beyoncé—'7/11,'" *Renowned for Sound*, November 27, 2014, http://renownedforsound.com/index.php/single-review-beyonce-711/.

11. Aran, "Watch Beyoncé's Magnificent Bathroom Dance."

12. Rebecca Nicholson, "Beyoncé's 7/11 Video: Carefully Cultivated Candour," *Guardian*, November 24, 2014, https://www.theguardian.com/music/musicblog/2014/nov/24/beyonces-711-video-carefully-cultivated-candour.

13. Alice Vincent, "Beyoncé's 7/11 'Selfie' Music Video: Her Most Personal Yet," *Telegraph*, November 23, 2014, http://www.telegraph.co.uk/culture/music/11248820/Beyonces-711-selfie-music-video-her-most-personal-yet.html.

14. Leandra Medine, "Beyoncé's 7/11 Actually Succeeds in 'Breaking the Internet,' It's Just: Why?" *Man Repeller*, November 24, 2014, quoted by Micah Speaks, https://micahspeaksblog.wordpress.com/2014/12/03/beyonces-711/.

15. Phillip Maciak, "Is Beyoncé the Future of Digital Cinema?," *Slate*, November 24, 2014, http://www.slate.com/blogs/browbeat/2014/11/24/beyonc_s_7_11_video_vs_interstellar_is_this_gif_able_amateur_music_video.html.

16. Livingstone, "From Family Television"; boyd, "Why Youth ♥"; Driscoll, "Girls Today"; Kearney, "Productive Spaces."

17. McRobbie and Garner, "Girls and Subcultures."

18. Avdeeff, "Music of Twilight."
19. DeNora, *Music*.
20. Lincoln, "Feeling the Noise," 399.
21. Agafonoff, "Adapting Ethnographic Research," 122.
22. Connie Wang, "A Goodbye of Sorts to Pre-partying," *Refinery29*, December 18, 2015, http://www.refinery29.com/pre-gaming-female-friendship-bonding-rituals.
23. Butler, *Gender Trouble*.
24. Lin, "Rising Tides?"
25. Chun, "How to Drop a Name," 4.
26. Sam Anderson, "Watching People Watching People Watching," *New York Times Magazine*, November 25, 2011, http://www.nytimes.com/2011/11/27/magazine/reaction-videos.html.
27. Chun, "How to Drop a Name," 5.
28. Hillrichs, "From the Bedroom".
29 Burgess, "All Your Chocolate?," 102.
30. Warren-Crow, "Screaming," 1113.
31. Ibid.
32. Ibid., 1115.
33. Jardon Jayro, "BEYONCÉ—7/11 REACTION," November 21, 2014, https://www.youtube.com/watch?v=26Zn1KYARE0 [video has since been made private].
34. Ching Ching Speaks, "My FIRST VLOG! Beyoncé 7/11 First Time Watch and Reaction!!!," December 9, 2014, https://www.youtube.com/watch?v=MUl9OHZoL9I.
35. Ron Vuggotta, "Beyoncé—7/11—Review," November 25, 2014, https://www.youtube.com/watch?v=S7NLaO7faIk.
36. Official Zgibode, "7/11 BY BEYONCÉ—SONG REVIEW," September 13, 2016, https://www.youtube.com/watch?v=0Hd2eHX_Hac.
37. Zedakiah Koterba, "Mom Interprets Beyoncé 7/11," February 26, 2015, https://www.youtube.com/watch?v=2gmUAl3TGFg.
38. trever pitts, "Beyoncé—7/11 'Music New,'" November 22, 2014, https://www.youtube.com/watch?v=nL_M1HwrgWI.
39. thisISmartinJR, "BEYONCÉ—7/11 REACTION," November 21, 2014, https://www.youtube.com/watch?v=fvW_u14yHCo.
40. Dylan Will Not Participate, "Beyoncé—7/11 Reaction," April 5, 2017, https://www.youtube.com/watch?v=KvVGuDymqNk.
41. AdrianXpression, "Ring Off and 7/11 by Beyoncé REACTION," November 20, 2014, https://www.youtube.com/watch?v=PihZ0ksd2Ew.
42. Sherman, "Vernacular Video," 163.
43. Ibid.

44. Redd Arrow, "BEYONCÉ '7/11' MUSIC VIDEO #ReddReacts," November 27, 2014, https://www.youtube.com/watch?v=isV2B-WUT18 [video has since been made private].

45. 4everBrandon TV, "BEYONCÉ 7/11 VIDEO REACTION," November 21, 2014, https://www.youtube.com/watch?v=thQsbucDvso.

46. Vuggotta, "Beyoncé—7/11—Review."

47. Ashley Miller, "Beyoncé—7/11 (VIDEO & SONG REVIEW)," November 22, 2014, https://www.youtube.com/watch?v=Nxg2QFR00xs.

48. NJPrince, "Beyoncé—7/11 (Official Music Video Review)," November 22, 2014, https://www.youtube.com/watch?v=LYyXn-BsCUI.

49. OfficialKingcofield, "Beyoncé 7/11 Official Audio/Music Video {{Review}}," November 21, 2014, https://www.youtube.com/watch?v=jy73RLCU5hw.

50. REAl REAction, "Beyoncé—7/11 (REAction)," February 15, 2017, https://www.youtube.com/watch?v=bkgdIZQcAgQ.

51. Munk Man Will Not Lose, "BEYONCÉ—7/11 (Beyoncé New Music Video Released) Reaction!," November 22, 2014, https://www.youtube.com/watch?v=Bm3IDgSCnkw.

52. Ching Ching Speaks, "My FIRST VLOG!"

53. Larson, "Secrets."

54. REAl REACtion, "Beyoncé."

55. 4everBrandon TV, "BEYONCÉ."

56. Redd Arrow, "BEYONCÉ."

57. MessyMyles, "Beyoncé 7/11 Video Review," November 23, 2014, https://www.youtube.com/watch?v=Y6_KyVQ_JdsM.

58. STORY OF CHINA, "BEYONCE 7/11 REVIEW," December 5, 2014, https://www.youtube.com/watch?v=8JNBblfonMc [video has since been made private].

59. Samore Love Real TV, "Beyonce 7/11 Official New Music Video Released & So Damn BOOTYLICIOUS!! (Review)," November 22, 2014, https://www.youtube.com/watch?v=1IAEauFbtOM.

60. thaghettoview, "My Thoughts: Beyonce 7/11 Video Review," November 21, 2014, https://www.youtube.com/watch?v=o3poLkOXOQU.

61. DjZos Grotto, "Beyoncé 7/11 Video and Song Review by DjZo's," November 24, 2014, https://www.youtube.com/watch?v=88xXl8PCJBs.

62. The REALity Show, "Beyoncé 7/11 Reaction Video from a Country Boy," October 13, 2016, https://www.youtube.com/watch?v=rO-yHIO81RI.

63. Duan, "Policing," 60.

64. Hansen, "Empowered or Objectified?"

65. Goffman, *Presentation*; Grazian, "Girl Hunt."

66. Durham, "Check On It."

67. Fleetwood, *Troubling Vision*.

68. STORY OF CHINA, "BEYONCE 7/11 REVIEW."
69. Ash Vee Catch'em All, "Beyoncé's 7/11 Review!," November 23, 2014, https://www.youtube.com/watch?v=PWuNNLGbG-0 [video has since been taken down].
70. Dylan Will Not Participate, "Beyoncé—7/11."

BIBLIOGRAPHY

Agafonoff, Nick. "Adapting Ethnographic Research Methods to Ad Hoc Commercial Market Research." *Qualitative Market Research* 9, no. 2 (2006): 115–25.

Avdeeff, Melissa. "The Music of Twilight." In *Fan Phenomena: The Twilight Saga*. Edited by Laurena Aker, 64–74. Bristol: Intellect, 2016.

boyd, danah. "Why Youth ♥ Social Network Sites: The Role of Networked Publics in Teenage Social Life." In *Youth, Identity, and Digital Media*. Edited by David Buckingham, 119–42. Cambridge, MA: MIT Press.

Burgess, Jean. "All Your Chocolate Rain Are Belong to Us?: Viral Video, YouTube and the Dynamics of Participatory Culture." In *Video Vortex Reader: Responses to YouTube*. Edited by Geert Lovink and Sabine Niederer, 101–10. Amsterdam: Institute of Network Cultures, 2008.

Butler, Judith. *Gender Trouble: Feminism and the Subversion of Identity*. New York: Routledge, 1990.

Chun, Elaine. "How to Drop a Name: Hybridity, Purity, and the K-Pop Fan." *Language in Society* 46, no. 1 (2017): 1–20.

DeNora, Tia. *Music in Everyday Life*. Cambridge: Cambridge University Press, 2000.

Driscoll, Catherine. "Girls Today: Girls, Girl Culture and Girl Studies." *Girlhood Studies* 1, no. 1 (2008): 13–32.

Duan, Noël Siqi. "Policing Beyoncé's Body: 'Whose Body Is This Anyways?'" In *The Beyoncé Effect: Essays on Sexuality, Race and Feminism*. Edited by Adrienne Trier-Bieniek, 55–74. Jefferson, NC: McFarland, 2016.

Durham, Aisha. "'Check On It': Beyonce, Southern booty, and Black Femininities in Music Video." *Feminist Media Studies* 12, no. 3 (2012): 35–49.

Fleetwood, Nicole. *Troubling Vision: Performance, Visuality, Blackness*. Chicago: University of Chicago Press, 2015.

Goffman, Erving. *Presentation of Self in Everyday Life*. Garden City, NY: Doubleday, 1959.

Grazian, David. "The Girl Hunt: Urban Nightlife and the Performance of Masculinity as Collective Activity." *Symbolic Interaction* 30, no. 2 (2007): 221–43.

Hansen, Kai Arne. "Empowered or Objectified? Personal Narrative and Audiovisual Aesthetics in Beyoncé's *Partition*." *Popular Music and Society* 40, no. 2 (2017): 164–80.

Hillrichs, Rainer. "From the Bedroom to LA: Revisiting the Settings of Early Video Blogs on YouTube." *NECSUS*, Autumn 2016. http://www.necsus-ejms.org/from-the-bedroom-to-la-revisiting-the-settings-of-early-video-blogs-on-youtube/.

Hodkinson, Paul, and Sian Lincoln. "Online Journals as Virtual Bedrooms?" *Young* 16, no. 1 (2008): 27–46.

Kearney, Mary. "Productive Spaces: Girls' Bedrooms as Sites of Cultural Production." *Journal of Children and Media* 1, no. 2 (2007): 126–41.

Larson, Reed. "Secrets in the Bedroom: Adolescents' Private Use of Media." *Journal of Youth and Adolescence* 24, no. 5 (1995): 535–50.

Lin, Yu-Ru. "Rising Tides of Rising Stars?: Dynamics of Shared Attention of Twitter during Media Events." *PLoS ONE* 9, no. 5 (2014). http://journals.plos.org/plosone/article?id=10.1371/journal.pone.0094093.

Lincoln, Sian. "Feeling the Noise: Teenagers, Bedrooms and Music." *Leisure Studies* 24, no. 4 (2005): 399–414.

Livingstone, Sonia. "From Family Television to Bedroom Culture: Young People's Media at Home." In *Media Studies: Key Issues and Debates*. Edited by Eoin Devereux, 302–21. London: Sage, 2007.

McRobbie, Angela, and Jenny Garner. "Girls and Subcultures." In *Resistance through Rituals: Youth Subcultures in Post-war Britain*. Edited by Stuart Hall and Tony Jefferson, 209–21. London: Routledge, 1977.

Robards, Brady. "Randoms in My Bedroom: Negotiating Privacy and Unsolicited Contact on Social Network Sites." *PRism* 7, no. 3 (2010), https://www.prismjournal.org/uploads/1/2/5/6/125661607/v7-n03-a2.pdf.

Sherman, Tom. "Vernacular Video." In *Video Vortex Reader: Responses to YouTube*. Geert Lovink and Sabine Niederer, 161–68. Amsterdam: Institute of Network Cultures, 2008.

Warren-Crow, Heather. "Screaming like a Girl: Viral Video and the Work of Reaction." *Feminist Media Studies* 16, no. 6 (2016): 1113–17.

INDEX

Adele, 50
Adichie, Chimamanda Ngozi, 11, 93, 94–95, 101–4, 105–6, 109, 111n35
Agafonoff, Nick, 232
aggressive femme persona, 143–47
"Aggressives, The" (2005), 144
Ahmed, Sara, 6, 7
albums: iconography of, 45; number of songs considered for, 53, 64n44
Alexander, Elizabeth, 35
Alexandra, Rae, 94
"All I Could Do Is Cry" (2008), 122
allographic vs. autographic art, 193
Amanfu, Ruby, 56–57
Amissah, Kojo, 211
"Amor Gitano" ("Gypsy Love") (*Carmen: A Hip Hopera*, 2001), 157, 170–71, 172
Anderson, Sam, 234
André, Naomi, 162–64
antipolice sentiments, 5
appropriation, creative, 43–44, 179–80. *See also* borrowing
Archive Effect, The (Baron), 102
"Are You My Woman (Tell Me So)" (Chi-Lites), 3, 9
artistic theft, 179–80. *See also* borrowing
artists, core discourses of, 160–61
Arzumanova, Inna, 116
"At Last" (2008), 115, 122, 123–25, 126–28
attention to detail, Beyoncé's, 23–24

audiovisual performance artist, Beyoncé as, 198, 211, 214
Austerlitz, Saul, 50
"authentically" black music, 47–48
authorship: Beyoncé as coauthor, 59–60, 61; Beyoncé's process of, 50–60; of choreography, 13, 186–89, 192; collaboration in, 40–41, 54, 57, 61, 72; and copyright, 43, 44–45, 52, 57–59, 60, 61, 64n39; and critical reception of black music, 47–50; and "Don't Hurt Yourself," 56–59; and gender differences in critical reception, 43; and "Hold Up," 42, 52–56; and Led Zeppelin's "Dazed and Confused," 45–47; and mixing music in recording studios, 56; problem of, in popular music, 43–45; and royalties for radio play, 64n39; and sampling, 41, 45, 57–59, 107–8; and singer-songwriters, 43, 49–50; and songwriting credits, 51; and "write a word, get a third" practice, 51, 52, 61. *See also* borrowing; collagist creative practice
Avdeeff, Melissa, 12, 13, 226–50
"Ave Maria" (2008), 79–82, 82, 84, 96

Bach, Johann Sabastian, 60, 80
"Back to Business" (2012), 29
backward gaze, 242–43
Bahan, Ben, 203, 216
Baker, Josephine, 1, 117, 138

251

Baker, Scott, 214
Baldwin, James, 120, 132n26, 164
Bambara, Toni Cade, 33
Baraka, Amiri, 33–34
Baron, Jaimie, 97, 102
"B'Day" (2006), 26
B'Day (2006), 12, 25, 26–27, 171
Beach Boys, 42
Beatles, 42
Beck, 40–41, 45
Becoming Beyoncé (Taraborrelli), 118–19
"bedroom culture" (term), 231. *See also* girl/bedroom culture
Belles of Chateau Vidal, The (Le'Doux), 145
"Bello Embustero" ("Beautiful Liar") (*Carmen: A Hip Hopera*, 2001), 157, 171
"Best Thing I Never Had" (2011), 204
Beyince, Angela, 51
Beyoncé (2013): and collagist creative practice, 52, 61; critical/commercial success of, 32; disruption of pop-song structure on, 98–99; imperfection embraced in, 25, 30, 31, 32; and marriage of Beyoncé, 111n27; and narrative about meaning of, 30; recording and compositional style of, 53; and rejection of labor/hustle, 10, 25, 29–32, 37n20; selecting songs for, 64n44; sexuality referenced in, 111n27; and Simone's influence, 108; versatility demonstrated in, 31. *See also specific songs, including* "***Flawless"
Beyoncé (documentary), 30–31, 32
Beyoncé Effect, The (Trier-Bieniek, ed.), 115
Beyoncé: Life Is but a Dream (2013 documentary), 28, 108, 129–31
Beyoncé: Platinum Edition (2014), 228
"Beyoncé Takes Credit for 'Writing' Songs" (Friedman), 49
Billboard Awards of 2011, 28
"Bills Bills Bills" (1999), 25, 79
bitch term: "bow down bitches" catchphrase, 93, 94, 99–100, 105, 109, 110n6; male rappers' use of, 100; women rappers' reclaiming of, 110n6
Black Arts Movement, 33–34
"Black Bitch" archetype, 75
Black Book, The (Middleton et al., eds.), 33

Black Entertainment Television Awards show (2007), 119
Black History Month, US, 2, 3, 5
Black Lives Matter movement: Beyoncé's support of, 3, 5, 8, 15n6; and "Formation," 8, 35; and *Lemonade*, 33; and Super Bowl (2016) half-time show, 1, 3, 5
Black Panthers, 1, 2, 4, 33, 93, 110n2, 128
"black political relief," 127
Black Power movement, 130
Black Woman, The (Bambara), 33
Bland, Sandra, 136
Blender, Jr, 53
blues tradition, 47
Bogle, Donald, 120
Bonham, John, 57
"Bootylicious" (2001), 86n7
bootylicious term, 86n7, 222n37
borrowing: and allographic vs. autographic art, 193; Beyoncé's self-awareness of, 52; debates on Beyoncé's use of, 186–89; and J-setting, 188–89; outrage in response to, 13, 179–80, 194–95; in "Single Ladies" video, 13, 186–89, 190–91; tradition of, 42, 43–44, 45. *See also* authorship
Bourdieu, Pierre, 195
"bow down bitches" catchphrase, 93, 94, 105, 109, 110n6
Boyd, Rekia, 34
Bradley, Regina, 99
Brion, Jon, 57
Brody, Adrien, 122
Brody, Jennifer, 148–49
"Broken-Hearted Girl" (2008), 72, 80
Brooks, Daphne, 26–27, 34
Brown, James, 23, 24
Brown, Susana, 161
Brown Sugar (Bogle), 121
Burgess, Jean, 203, 235
Burke, Alexandra, 81
bus boycotts, 140, 141–42
butch lesbians, 148

Cadillac Records (2008), 12, 107, 115, 120–25, 127, 130
Cadrez, Tahnee, 41
call-and-response, 76, 182, 189
Calloway, Rheema Emy, 3

"Can't Get Used to Losing You" (1963; Williams), 53
Carey, Mariah, 48, 64n39, 74
Carmen (Bizet, 1875), 158, 160, 163, 164, 172
Carmen (Mérimée, 1845), 159, 160, 164, 172
Carmen: A Hip Hopera (Townsend, 2001): criticisms of, 164; and Latin crossover of Beyoncé, 169; and Pepsi spot, 165–66; role of race in message of, 165; and solo career of Beyoncé, 12, 157, 158, 159, 165; and star image of Beyoncé, 163, 172
Carmen Jones (1954), 159, 161–63, 165
Cashmore, Ellis, 126
Caten, Dean and Dan, 14n2
Cecire, Natalia, 30
celebrity of Beyoncé, 114
Chalfen, Richard, 202
Chandler, Kimberly, 145
"Change Is Gonna Come, A" (Cooke), 128
Chappell, Marisa, 142
chastity, 77, 85
"Check On It" (2005), 73, 73, 79
Chess, Leonard, 122, 123, 130
Chess Records, 122
Chi-Lites, 2–3, 9
choreography: artists given credit for, 187–88, 192; authorship of, 13, 186–89, 192; and dancers, 191, 192–93; expectations of choreographers, 191fans' performances of, 191, 194 (*see also* Mercado, Shane); forgery/plagiarization of, 194–95; and "J-Setting" dance style, 188–89; judgments of performances of, 191–92; and treatment of choreographers, 193; uncredited status of choreographers, 187, 188; unlikely resemblances in, 190, 192
Christianity, 69, 79–82
Chun, Elaine, 235, 236
civil rights, 1, 5, 127–28, 129, 140, 141–42
classical music, allusions to, 79–82
class identity, 76–82
Cleopatra Jones films, 148
Cleveland, Tina, 207–8, 215, 216–17, 222n34
Clinton, Hillary, 128–29
Clúa, Isabel, 160
Coachella performance of Beyoncé, 8–9, 14n3
Coldplay, 2, 7

collaborative production: benefits of model, 61; and Beyoncé's process, 54, 57, 61; and modes of vocal delivery, 72; perceived as inferior, 40–41. *See also* authorship; collagist creative practice
collagist creative practice: in *Beyoncé*, 52, 61; and Beyoncé's process, 42, 51, 52, 59–60, 61; and borrowing tradition, 42; as exercised in literature, poetry, and music, 43–44; in "Formation," 56, 65n45; in "Hold Up," 52, 54, 56; in *Lemonade*, 52, 61; of Simone, 108. *See also* authorship; collaborative production
Collins, Kip, 163
Collins, Patricia Hill, 75
Colmeiro, José, 167
colonial gaze, 68
Color Purple, The (Walker), 136
Colton, Lisa, 9, 10, 68–90
Colvin, Claudette, 142
composers and musical copyright, 43
concerts, labor performed by Beyoncé in, 24
contributors to Beyoncé's music, 60, 61. *See also* collaborative production; collagist creative practice
control exercised by Beyoncé: and *B'Day*, 26; and *Beyoncé*, 30; and *I Am . . . Sasha Fierce*, 78; and *Lemonade*, 149; over artistic expression, 149; over identity and image, 69, 241–42; over musical works, 61; over sexualized image, 69, 78; and "7/11," 229
Cooke, Sam, 128
cool, aesthetic of, 141
Cooper, Brittney, 95, 100, 140–41, 142
copyright, 43, 44–45, 52, 57–59, 60, 61, 64n39
"Countdown" (2011), 27
Cox, Julia, 5, 11, 93–113
"Crazy in Love" (2003), 3, 9, 15n4, 75
Creole culture, 168, 170
critical reception of black music, 47–50, 60
cultural appropriation, 9, 38n39, 216–18

"Daddy Lessons" (2016), 111n26
dancing and dancers: authenticity/credibility associated with, 193; authorship of, 179; and danceability of songs, 181, 183; judgments of performances, 191–93; treatment of dancers, 192–93

Dandridge, Dorothy, 12, 161, 162
"Dangerously in Love" (2003), 204
Dangerously in Love (2003), 25
Daptone, 64n39
Darrow, Alice-Ann, 200–201, 204, 220n6
Dash, Julie, 33, 109
Daughters of the Dust (Dash), 33, 109
Day Beyoncé Turned Black, The (Saturday Night Live), 5
"Dazed and Confused" (Led Zeppelin), 45–47
d/Deaf community and culture, 198–225; and challenges of song-signing, 203–4, 206; and closed-caption subtitles, 210; and community building, 214–16; and criticisms of song-signing efforts, 208; and cultural appropriation, 216–18; *deaf/Deaf* terms, 220n7, 220n9; media depictions of, 200–201, 220n14; misperception of music accessibility for, 199, 220n6; popularity of Beyoncé in, 211; and reception of signed-song videos, 215–16; and rising rates of hearing loss, 199; scholarship on, 198; and signed-songs from hearing community, 215, 216–17; song-signing tradition in, 202–3; and varying degrees of sound memory, 200; and visual aspects of Beyoncé's performances, 198, 214. *See also* sign language
Def, Mos, 165
"Déjà Vu" (2006), 26, 33, 143
DeNora, Tia, 231
Destiny's Child: and education of Beyoncé, 79; empowerment themes of, 230; father as producer/manager of, 36n1; girl power message of, 94; and influence of Beyoncé, 1; and labor/hustle of Beyoncé, 23, 25; and Latin music market, 166; and modes of vocal delivery, 74; and solo career of Beyoncé, 12, 23, 118, 157, 158; songwriting in, 51; and the Supremes, 118
Destiny's Child (1998), 26
Diplo, 42, 51, 53, 55
"Disappear," 72
disco, 48–49, 60
"Diva" (2008): lack of melody on, 86n21; and modes of vocal delivery, 72, 74, 75; and rejection of labor/hustle, 37n20; video for, 84, 85; wealth references in, 78

divas: cultural narratives about, 27; and persona cultivated by Beyoncé, 26; and political/social activism, 130; predecessors of Beyoncé, 116, 130–31; and stardom of Beyoncé, 131; and vocal display of Beyoncé, 74
Dixie, Derek, 57
dog-whistle politics, 5
"Don't Hurt Yourself" (2016), 10, 15n4, 42, 56–59
Downs, Kenya, 142
Drake, 31, 32
Dreamgirls (2006), 107, 115–19, 122, 123, 129, 130
DRUMLine Live, 9
"Drunk in Love" (2013), 30, 31, 37n26
Dsquared2, 14n2
Duan, Noël Siqi, 242
DuBois, W. E. B., 77
Dudamel, Gustavo, 2
Durham, Aisha S., 70, 76, 79, 84, 95, 100, 242–43
Dyer, Richard, 115
Dylan, Bob, 48
"Dy-na-mi-tee" (2002), 74

eccentricity, 160
Eckstein, Lars, 43
education of Beyoncé, 79
Edwards, Erica, 35
Eidsheim, Nina Sun, 5, 71, 76
Eliot, T. S., 60
Elliot, Missy, 51, 110n6
Ellison, Ralph, 35
empowerment: Beyoncé as figure of, 1, 61, 198, 219; Beyoncé's lean-in style of, 28; and *Carmen* character, 158, 163, 165, 172; and Destiny's Child, 230; disruption of objectification as exercise in, 242–43; and "***Flawless," 107; and predecessors of Beyoncé, 116; and "Run the World (Girls)," 209, 210; and Sasha Fierce alter ego, 70, 85
ethnic identity of Beyoncé, 79, 83
exoticism, 160

fatality, 160
Faupel, Alison, 43

Feast of All Saints, The (2001), 144
"female quest" defined by Kubitschek, 95–96
feminism, 93–113; and Adichie's TEDx talk, 93, 94–95, 101–4; in Africa, 103; and Beyoncé's performance of "At Last," 128; Beyoncé's self-identification with, 1, 94, 110n4, 146, 152n13, 210, 222n37; and civil-rights movement, 128, 129; and "***Flawless," 11, 94–95, 101–4; hip hop feminism, 95; and labeling feminists as the problem, 16n22; and *Lemonade*, 109; and materialism, 105–6; ratchet feminism, 140–41, 142, 146; and sexualized image of Beyoncé, 95; and twerking, 146. *See also* empowerment
femmes: aggressive femme persona, 143–47; and Black femme-inist criticism, 137–38, 151; black femme power in "Sorry," 139–42, 144–50; and butch lesbians, 148; definition of, 137; high femme, 140, 141, 146; in *Lemonade*, 137; and ratchet femme, 140–41, 142, 146; representation of, 137, 138; and stone femme, 147–50
Fernández, Alejandro, 170
fetishization of black, female bodies, 68, 242
film career of Beyoncé: *Cadillac Records* (2008), 12, 107, 115, 120–25, 127, 130; *Dreamgirls* film, 107, 115–19, 122, 123, 129, 130; and superstar status of Beyoncé, 115–16. See also *Carmen: A Hip Hopera*
filmmaking, "home mode," 202
flashbacks, 97
"***Flawless" (2013), 93–113; Adichie's TEDx talk sampled in, 93, 94–95, 101–4, 105–6; aesthetic of, 107; "bow down bitches" catchphrase, 93, 94, 99–100, 105, 109, 110n6; and feminism of Beyoncé, 11, 94–95, 101–4; and "flawless" label of affirmation, 104–6; and iconic black women, 107–8; interiority/performance tension in, 97, 103–4; "I woke up like this" catchphrase, 31, 93, 95, 105, 112n42; lack of chorus in, 98–99; mixed media of, 94, 95–96, 97, 108–9, 110n10; and political engagement of Beyoncé, 93–94, 109; quest stages represented in, 95–96; sign language interpretation of, 204; *Star Search* narrative in, 96–98, 100, 101, 103; structure of, 98

Fleetwood, Nicole, 116–17, 243
folk traditions, 44, 48
football, American, 7. *See also* Super Bowl halftime show, 2016
forgeries, 193–94. *See also* borrowing
"Formation" (2016), 32–35; and Black Lives Matter movement, 8, 35; as call for collective stillness, 35; and Clinton rally, 128–29; at Coachella, 9; and collagist creative practice, 56, 65n45; compensation valorized in, 34; Illuminati reference in, 33; labor articulated in, 23, 25; and Simone's influence on Beyoncé, 130; and Super Bowl (2016) half-time show, 2–3, 110n2, 128; video, 33; white responses to, 6
"Forward" (2016), 110n2
Fosse, Bob, 13, 180, 184, 186–89, 190–91, 192
4 (2011), 25, 26, 27
Fox News, 49
Franklin, Aretha, 127, 128
Friedman, Roger, 49
Frith, Simon, 47, 48
Fulton, Will, 9, 10, 40–67
Fulwood, Ramon "Tiki," 58
funk, 2
Funkadelic, 58

Garber, Jenny, 231
Garrett, Sean, 51
Garza, Alicia, 3, 15n7
Gatson, Frank, 52, 59
Gaunt, Kyra, 146
gender inequality/differences: in critical reception of music, 43, 48, 49; and hustle of neoliberalism, 28; and "If I Were a Boy," 204–5; in music production, 50–51; and reactions to authorship questions, 47
"Get Me Bodied" (2006), 26, 171
Ghost, Amanda, 80
Ginzburg, Carlo, 196n21
girl/bedroom culture: academic examination of, 231; Beyoncé's legitimizing of, 230, 244; embodied in "7/11," 227, 229, 230, 239–40, 243, 244, 245; lack of understanding of, 227; terms, 231; transition from bedroom to online/public incarnation, 228, 230, 233, 243; and vlogs, 235, 236–37

"Girls" (2004), 230
"Girls and Subcultures" (McRobbie and Garber), 231
"Girls Just Wanna Have Fun" (Lauper), 188
Girl's Tyme: Beyoncé's departure from, 23; father as producer/manager of, 36n1; and labor performed by Beyoncé, 23; and *Star Search* competition, 11, 96–98, 100, 101, 103
glamour of Beyoncé, 3
"God Bless America" (Berlin), 5
Goldberg, Meira, 161
Goodman, Nelson, 193
"Good Old Music" (Funkadelic), 58
Goodwin, Andrew, 115
Gopinath, Gayatri, 137
Gordon, Diana "Wynter," 42, 57, 65n47
Gore, Sydney, 136
Gorfain, Eric, 57
Gounod, Charles, 80
Gracyk, Theodore, 193
Gradney, Mia, 149
Grammy Awards, 2015, 40
Grant, Peter, 58
Green, Joshua, 203
Griffin, Farah Jasmine, 111n34, 126
Guarinos, Virginia, 164
Gucci, 128
gypsy identity, 157–76; authenticity associated with, 159; of Carmen, 160–61, 172; displayed in various musical genres, 168; evoked by Beyoncé, 165–66, 172; and female artists, 160–61; and "Habanera," 167–68; history of, 159–60; and mainstream artists, 169; as mutable, 161; orientalization of, 158, 161, 167; as Other, 158–59, 160–61; and panhispanic music, 167–68; and Spanishness, 160–61, 167–68; stereotypes of, 157–58, 160, 164

"Habanera" (Bizet), 157, 165, 167–68
Hall, Terryn, 136
"Hallelujah" (Cohen), 81
"Halo" (2008): and Beyoncé's growth as vocalist, 27; and modes of vocal delivery, 72, 74–75; and religious identity of Beyoncé, 83; sign language interpretation of, 204, 207–8, 216; video for, 84; vocal achievement in, 31
happiness, demand for oppressed person's, 7
hard-of-hearing audiences, 211. *See also* d/Deaf community and culture
Harper, Philip Brian, 33–34, 150
Harris, Aisha, 94
Harris, Tamara Winfrey, 3
Harris-Perry, Melissa, 140
"Haunted" (2013), 32
Haynie, Emile, 54
Headlam, Dave, 43
hearing loss, rising rates of, 199. *See also* d/Deaf community and culture
"He Don't Love You (Like I Love You)," 53
Hendrix, Jimi, 47
high femme, 140, 141, 146
Hill, Hadassah, 150
Hill, Napoleon, 24
Hillrichs, Rainer, 235, 236–37
hip hop, 45, 77
hip hop feminism, 95
historically black colleges and universities (HBCUs), 9, 14n3
Hobson, Janell, 102, 146–47
"Hold Up" (2016), 10, 42, 52–56
Holiday, Billie: and black femme imagery, 138; legendary status of, 120–21; Ross's portrayal of, 115, 120, 122, 132n26; Ross's tribute to, 117; struggles of, 120, 130
Holliday, Jennifer, 119
Hollywood, 116, 130
Holmes, Jake, 45–47
Homecoming: A Film by Beyoncé (2019), 8–9, 14n3
Hood, Ace, 24
hooks, bell, 4, 9, 242
Hostovsky, Lauren, 210–11, 212–13
Houston, Whitney, 1, 48, 74, 107, 116, 117–18
Hudson, Jennifer, 118, 119
human rights, 1
Hunter, Margaret, 146
Hurricane Katrina, 5, 26, 33
Hurston, Zora Neale, 95–96, 101, 138
Hutcheson, Francis, 193
Hutchinson, Jenny, 142

I Am... Sasha Fierce (2008): class identity represented on, 77–79; and DeGeneres interview, 125; and "good girl" persona of Beyoncé, 85; and labor/hustle of Beyoncé, 25, 27; and personality of Beyoncé, 84; religious identity represented on, 78, 79–82; and Sasha Fierce alter ego, 70, 85, 96; voice as signifier of identity on, 71–76; wealth references in, 78, 78. *See also specific songs, including* "Single Ladies (Put a Ring on It)"
I Am... World Tour (2009–10), 127
"I Care" (2011), 27, 31
identity, cultural, 68–90; Beyoncé's control over, 69; and class, 76–82; and feminism of Beyoncé, 94, 104; and "good girl" persona of Beyoncé, 85; influence of foremothers on, 108–9; and middle-class background of Beyoncé, 79; religious identity, 69, 79–82; and Sasha Fierce alter ego, 70, 85, 96; self-identification of Beyoncé, 68–69; as signaled through her voice, 71–76, 79; and Simone's influence, 108
"I'd Rather Go Blind" (2008), 122
"If I Were a Boy" (2008), 78–79, 78, 181, 204–7, 206
"I Have a Dream" speech (King), 123, 126, 127, 128
independence, 110n3
"Independent Woman" (2001), 33, 79, 94, 110n3, 230
infantilization of women, 241–42
infidelity theme of *Lemonade*, 149
intellectual property, 60–61. *See also* authorship
invisibility/hypervisibility, 35
"Irreemplazable" (2006), 171, 204
Irreemplazable (2007), 157, 166–71
"I Was Here" (2011), 204
"I woke up like this" catchphrase, 31, 93, 105, 112n42

Jackson, Janet, 107, 116, 117
Jackson, Michael: and Beyoncé's costuming in 2016 Super Bowl, 2; "Black or White" video of, 33; and critical reception of black music, 48; debut of moonwalk, 93; stardom of, 1; and Tidal, 34; and work ethic of Beyoncé, 23
Jade Films, 205, 221n27
James, Etta: and Beyoncé's performance of "At Last," 127, 128; Beyoncé's portrayal of, 117, 120–25, 130, 131; Osha's comparison of Beyoncé to, 115; and political culture, 130; reading Beyoncé in relation to, 12; soulful authenticity of, 116, 120, 122–23, 124, 130; as source of inspiration for Beyoncé, 107; stardom of, 1
James, Robin, 29, 37n20
Jay-Z: and Black Lives Matter movement, 15n6; and creative labor performed by Beyoncé, 23; and "Déjà Vu," 143; and marriage to Beyoncé, 81; media empire of, 105; and neoliberal ideology, 24, 36n8; and personal life with Beyoncé, 31; professional influence of, 36n1
Johnson, Ronnisha, 3
Jones, Sharon, 64n39
Joseph, Khalil, 143
Joshua Fit the Battle of Jericho, 83
"J-Setting" dance style, 188–89
Just My Soul Responding (Ward), 121
Juzwiak, Rich, 27

Kaepernick, Colin, 8, 17n36
Kaplan-Levenson, Laine, 144
Kebaili, Rachelle, 50
Keeler, Patrick, 56
Kehrer, Lauron, 5
Kelly, Chris, 140
Keyes, Cheryl, 44
Keys, Alicia, 74
Kimble, Kim, 147
King, Martin Luther, Jr., 123, 126, 127, 128
Knight, Jaquel, 189
Knowles, Mathew, 23, 36n1, 129
Knowles, Tina, 23, 36n1
Koenig, Ezra, 52–53
Kohlman, Marla, 42
Kooijman, Jaap, 10, 11, 12, 114–35
Kroft, Steve, 68
Kubitschek, Missy, 95

labor, resilience as gendered form of, 29.
　See also work, Beyoncé's performance of
Lady Gaga, 5–6, 13, 16n21
Lady Sings the Blues (1972), 115, 120, 132n26
"La Isla Bonita" (Madonna), 168–69
Lane, Ahmad "Javon," 46
Larsen, Nella, 138
Latin music/crossover, 158, 166–71, 172, 174n29. *See also* gypsy identity; Spanish and Spanishness
Lauper, Cindy, 188
Laurie, Timothy, 133n34
Lawlars, "Memphis" Minnie, 57–59
Le'Doux, Leonard, 145
Led Zeppelin, 42, 57–59
Lee, Spike, 165–66
Lemonade (2016): aesthetics of, 109; black female constituency of, 33; and Black Lives Matter movement, 3; and collagist creative practice, 52, 61; and contributors, 60; and "Crazy in Love" thematic link, 15n4; critical/commercial success of, 34; disruption of pop-song structure on, 99; and feminism of Beyoncé, 11, 109; hooks' reaction to, 4; infidelity theme of, 149; and "Lemonade syllabus," 34; and love between black Southern women, 11; Malcolm X's voice sampled on, 2; and political realignment of Beyoncé, 1, 3, 93, 109; recording and compositional style of, 53; and Simone's influence on Beyoncé, 108, 130; Southern imagery in, 109, 136; and work/labor, 10, 32–34. *See also specific songs, including* "Formation"
Lemonade (2019 rerelease), 60
Lennox, Annie, 146
Leonard, Marion, 43
lesbianism, 146–47, 148. *See also* femmes
Lewis, Heidi, 140
Lewis, Lisa, 188
Lewis, Sydney Fonteyn, 137–38, 139
"Lift Every Voice and Sing," 9
Light, Alan, 120
Lil' Flip, 99
Lil' Kim, 110n6
Lincoln, Rixford, 145

Lincoln, Sian, 231
"Listen" (2006), 127, 204
London, Dianca, 4
Loomis, Diane Merchant, 200–201
Lopez, Jennifer, 169, 172
Lorde, Audre, 11
Lordi, Emily, 4, 8, 9–10, 12, 23–39, 95, 99, 101, 124, 127
Love, Heather, 138
"Love on Top" (2011), 27, 31, 204
Lowery, Wesley, 15n6
lyrics, meanings of, 54, 65n47
lyric troping, 45, 53

Maciak, Phillip, 229
Madonna, 1, 82, 168–69, 172
Madonna University's Sign Language Studies department, 205–6, 206
male gaze, 68, 69, 98, 109, 242
Maler, Anabel, 203–4, 222n32
Mangaoang, Áine, 12, 13
Manuel, Peter, 168
"Maps" (Yeah Yeah Yeahs), 52–53
marching band tradition of HBCUs, 9, 14n3
marginalized populations, 38n39, 77
marriage of Beyoncé, 99, 111n27, 149. *See also* Jay-Z
Mars, Bruno, 2, 7, 8, 14n3
Martin, Chris, 2
materialism, 105–6, 110n3
Maultsby, Portia, 47–48
McClary, Susan, 43, 164, 165
McDermott, Patrick, 229
McDougall, Dan, 205
McKesson, DeRay, 15n6
McRobbie, Angela, 231
media fetishization of black, female bodies, 68
Medine, Leandra, 229
MeLo-X, 54–55, 65n49
memes, popular, 40–41, *41*
Mercado, Shane, 13, 180, 183–86, 191, 192, 194
Mérimée, Prosper, 159, 160
"Mexican Breakfast" (Fosse), 13, 186–87, 190, 196n20
middle-class identity of Beyoncé, 79, 82

Middleton, Robert, 43
Mike Will Made It, 42, 51, 53, 56, 65n45, 65n47
Mills, Marisa, 210, 211
"Mine" (2013), 31
mirror neurons, 215
misogynist reactions to Beyoncé, 49
Misty, Father John, 54, 55, 65n48
Mitchell, Anne, 5, 143
mixed media of "***Flawless," 94, 95–96, 97, 108–9, 110n10
MNEK, 42, 51, 54, 55, 65n47
Mora, Kiko, 161
Morales, Ed, 168
Morris, Susana, 95, 100
Morrison, Toni, 33, 138
Motown Records, 47, 122
MTV, 84
MTV Vanguard Lifetime Achievement Award, 93, 109n1
Muhammad Ali Legacy Award, 8, 17n37
Musical.ly, 233, 244
music industry, 27, 61
music theory, 87n18
music videos: and audience participation (*see* reaction-and-review videos); effect of, on song meanings, 83–84; and film homages, 45; and star image of Beyoncé, 115; visual linked with audible in, 192. See also *specific songs*
Musign Theatre Company, 203
Mya, Messy, 35
My Name Is Red (Pamuk), 194

"Nasty Girl" (2001), 230
National Football League (NFL), 2, 7, 8, 16n20
Native Americans, 17n35
Nefertiti imagery, 147–50
Negus, Keith, 43
neoliberalism, 3, 24–25, 29–32, 35, 36n8
New Musical Express, 47
New Orleans, Louisiana: Creole music tradition of, 168; and Hurricane Katrina, 5, 26, 33; queer musicians from, 5; and Super Bowl (2016) half-time show, 1, 3; and twerking, 146

Ngai, Sianne, 26
Ngugi, Evelyn, 138
"99 Problems" (Jay-Z), 100
Notorious B.I.G., 79

Obama, Barack, 3, 36n5, 115, 126, 127–28
Obama, Michelle, 26, 102, 105, 111n34
objectification, racialized, 242–43
O'Brien, Lucy, 121
Ocean, Frank, 31, 32
Olutola, Sarah, 4
Oprah Winfrey Show, The, 129
orientalism, 158, 161, 167, 172
originality, ideal of, 43, 45
Ortved, John, 140–41
Osha, Olusanya, 115
Otherness, 158–59, 160–61, 167, 172
"Oye" ("Listen") (2007), 171

Page, Jimmy, 46
Pamuk, Orhan, 194
panhispanic music, 167
Paquin, Alyse, 206
paranoid academic readings, 138–39
"Paranoid Reading and Reparative Reading" (Sedgwick), 138–39
parenthood of Beyoncé, 31, 32, 37n26
Parks, Rosa, 128, 142
Parkwood Entertainment, 61
participatory media, 236. See also reaction-and-review videos
"Partition" (2014), 31, 103
Party, Daniel, 168
Peddle, Daniel, 144
Pérez, Rudy, 170
perfectionism of Beyoncé, 25, 30, 31, 32
performance, core discourses for succeeding in, 160–61
Petridis, Alex, 87n21
Piwowarski, Allison, 228
plagiarism, 45–47. See also authorship; borrowing
Plastic Operator, 68
police brutality, 109, 136, 138
policing black bodies, 6, 241–42

political engagement of Beyoncé: in "***Flawless" (2013), 93–94, 109; in *Lemonade*, 1, 3, 93, 109; and Simone's political activism, 130; and stardom of Beyoncé, 3, 128–31. *See also* Black Lives Matter movement; feminism
"poptimism," 42, 50, 60
postracial era, belief in, 6–7
poverty, 77
power asserted by Beyoncé, 61
Presley, Elvis, 51, 64n40
"Pretty Hurts" (2014), 30, 31, 204
Prince, 1, 23, 48, 49, 87n18
producers, 51, 53

"Quadroon Ballroom, The" (Lincoln), 145
quadroon balls, 144–45
queer musicians from New Orleans, 5
queer regionalism, 137, 150
quotation practices, 45

R&B music, 48, 73, 74, 77
racism and racial inequality: and Beyoncé's performance of "At Last," 126; in critical reception of music, 47–49; football as vehicle for, 7; and "Formation," 128; and labor/hustle of Beyoncé, 28; and white supremacy, 5, 6
Radano, Ronald, 63n23
"Radio" (2008), 78
radio play, royalties for, 64n39
Radstone, Susannah, 97
ratchet femmes and feminism, 140–41, 142, 146
reaction-and-review videos, 233–44; aesthetics of, 238; authenticity conveyed in, 235–36; gendered as feminine, 235–36; layered participant structure of, 235; to "7/11," 226–27, 233–44, 245; vernacular of, 238; vlogs compared to, 235, 236–37, 238
Reagan, Ronald, 24
recording studios, 50–51, 59–60
religious identity of Beyoncé, 69, 79–82
remixes of Beyoncé's music, 65n49
reparative reading practice, 138–39
resilience as gendered form of labor, 29
respectability: aesthetics of, 141–42; politics of black, 94, 99, 100, 103, 109, 110n8; and ratchet feminism, 142

revenue streams available to artists, 61
Richardson, Riché, 150
Rihanna, 32
"Ring the Alarm" (2006), 37n17
Robb, Graham, 144–45
Roberts, Kamaria, 142
Robinson, Sylvia, 51
Robinson, Zandria, 35
Rock, Kid, 49
"Rocket" (2013), 103
"rockism," 42, 48–50, 60
Rolling Stone, 47
Ronson, Mark, 2–3
Rose, Tricia, 51
Rosen, Jody, 37n17, 130
Ross, Alex, 60
Ross, Diana: Beyoncé's portrayal of, 116–19, 130, 131; and black femme imagery, 138; glamour of, 107, 116; portrayal of Holiday, 115, 120, 122, 123, 132n26; reading Beyoncé in relation to, 12; star status of, 1, 116
royalties for radio play, 64n39
Royster, Francesca, 148
Run-DMC, 2
"Run the World (Girls)" (2011): awards for, 210; backing voices on, 29; and Beyoncé's empowerment philosophy, 28; and "Formation," 33; and neoliberal hustle, 28–29; sign language interpretation of, 204, 209–11, 212–13
Rushen, Patrice, 51

Said, Edward, 158, 164
Saleh, Doua, 205
same-sex marriage, 1
sampling: criticized as inauthentic, 41, 45; and Led Zeppelin's "When the Levee Breaks," 57–59; as means of engaging other black women, 107–8
Santana, Carlos, 169
Sanz, Alejandro, 166, 170
Sasha Fierce alter ego, 70, 75, 85, 96, 171
"sassy" speech style, 74
Saturday Night Live, 5, 183
"Say My Name" (1999), 37n17
Schmutz, Vaughn, 43
Schroeder, David, 162
Schubert, Franz, 80–82, 82, 84

Scott, Tanisha, 193
Sedgwick, Eve, 11, 138–39, 150
Sehgal, Parul, 105
self-articulation, struggle for, 97
selfie medium, 229, 233, 242
self-reliance, 110n3
Senbanjo, Laolu, 139
Servin, Dante, 34
"7/11" (2014), 226–50; aesthetics of, 243–44; arrangement of, 242–43; authenticity conveyed in, 233, 239, 242; fun/humor in, 239–41; and girl/bedroom culture, 227–28, 229, 230, 239–40, 243, 244, 245; interpreted as pre-going-out rituals, 232–33, 235, 240, 241, 243; interpreted as slumber party, 229, 230, 240–41, 243; mainstream presses' reactions to, 228–29; misinterpretations of, 226–27; and modes of vocal delivery, 72; and policing black bodies, 241–42; production of, 228, 243; reactions to song, 228, 237–38; and reaction videos, 226–27, 233–44, 245; release of, 226, 228, 236–37; video's effect on perception of song, 239
sexuality: and backward gaze, 242–43; in *Beyoncé*, 111n27; Beyoncé's control over, 69, 78; of black women's bodies, 242; and chastity, 77, 85; and feminism of Beyoncé, 95; role of, in discussions of empowerment, 209; in "7/11" video, 232, 242
Shackelford, Ashleigh, 137
Shakespeare, William, 60
Shakira, 169, 171, 172
Shakur, Tupac, 79
She Bop (O'Brien), 121
Sherman, Tom, 238
Shire, Warsan, 109, 139
sign language: challenges of song-signing, 203–4, 206; cultural misappropriation of, 216–18; earliest signed songs, 202–3; features of, 200; and interpretation of Beyoncé's lyrics, 214, 217; and mirror neurons, 215; and signed-songs from hearing community, 215, 216–17; and signing Beyoncé's songs on YouTube, 201–11, 206, 221n17; and technology facilitating communication, 201. *See also* d/Deaf community and culture

Simone, Nina: Beyoncé's identification with, 114–15, 131; collagist practice of, 108; and *Life Is but a Dream* documentary, 130; politics of, 116, 130, 131, 131n1; reading Beyoncé in relation to, 12
singer-songwriters, critical lauding of, 43, 49–50
"Single Ladies (Put a Ring on It)" (2008), 179–97; aesthetics of, 84–85; autobiographical aspects of, 188; awards for, 182; borrowings in, 180–81, 187; call-and-response of, 182, 189; commercial success of, 182; criticisms of, 183; danceability of, 181, 183; and "Formation," 33; Fosse's choreography referenced in, 13, 180, 184, 186–89, 190–91, 192; Mercado's performance of, 180, 183–86, 191, 192, 194; and modes of vocal delivery, 72, 75–76; paratexts of, 179; participation invited by, 182; premier of, 180; production of, 181–82; and Sasha Fierce alter ego, 96; sign language interpretation of, 204; *SNL* parody of, 183; VMA performance of, 84–85; wealth references in, 78, 79
Sirimarco, Paul, 207–8, 215, 216–17, 222n34
Smith, Barbara, 138
Smith, Erin Sweeney, 58
Smith, Valerie, 69
SnapChat, 233
solo career of Beyoncé: and *Carmen: A Hip Hopera* role, 157, 158, 159, 165; and Latin music crossover, 166–71; and turbulent era of music industry, 166
songwriting, 40–41, 51. *See also* authorship
"Sorry" (2016), 136–56; and aesthetics of respectability, 141–42; African aesthetics of, 139, 141; and aggressive femme persona, 143–47; original demo, 60; paranoid vs. reparative reading of, 138–39; and quadroon ball scene, 144–45; and ratchet feminism, 140–41, 142; and stone femme, 147–50; and twerking, 145–47; Williams featured in, 137, 143, 145–46, 147
"SOS" (Baraka), 33–34
Soulja Boy Tell'em, 56, 59
soul music: critical reception of, 47; and racialized forms of struggle and labor, 10, 24, 35; and soul singer/superstar dichotomy, 115

South and southern culture: Beyoncé's engagement of, 140; and "Daddy Lessons," 111n26; and *Lemonade*, 136; and quadroon balls, 144–45; Southern hip-hop persona of Beyoncé, 79, 99; and twerking, 146

Spanish and Spanishness: and *Carmen* character, 160–61, 167–68; and gypsies, 160–61, 167–68; and *Irreemplazable* (2007), 157, 160–61, 166–71, 172; and Latin music/crossover, 158, 160–61, 168–69, 172

Spears, Britney, 110n8

Spence, Lester, 24, 28, 36n8

spirituals, 76

Springer, Kimberly, 119

stardom of Beyoncé, 114–35; and authentic blackness/superstar dichotomy, 115, 130–31; and Beyoncé's appropriation of "At Last," 115, 116, 122, 123–25, 126–28, 129; and Beyoncé's portrayal of Diana Ross, 115, 116–19, 130; and Beyoncé's portrayal of Etta James, 115, 120–23, 130; and *Carmen: A Hip Hopera* role, 157, 163; and Latin crossover, 171, 172; and *Life Is but a Dream* documentary, 129–31; and music videos, 115; and Obama presidency, 127–28; and political/social justice causes, 3, 128–31; and predecessors of Beyoncé, 130, 131; "unapologetic Black" turn in, 128, 130

Star Search, 11, 96–98, 100, 101, 103

Stone, Sly, 47

stone femme, 147–50

Strummurd, Rae, 65n47

studio musicians, 41

Sublimefemme, 140

Sula (Morrison), 138

Summer, Donna, 138

Super Bowl halftime show, 2013, 15n4, 242

Super Bowl halftime show, 2016: and Black Lives Matter movement, 1, 3; Black Panther visual references, 2, 33, 110n2, 128; conservative/white commentators' reactions to, 4–5, 6–7; and "crashed" word choice, 7–8; and "Formation," 2–3, 110n2, 128; Malcolm X visual references, 2, 128; music performances of, 2–3

Super Bowl halftime show, 2017, 5–6

"Superpower" (2013), 31

superstar status. *See* stardom of Beyoncé

"Survivor" (2001), 23, 74, 94

"Sweet Dreams" (2009), 96

Sylvester, Nick, 180–81

Taraborrelli, J. Randy, 118–19

Tarpischev, Shamil, 145

technology in music production, 41, 52

"Telephone" (Lady Gaga), 73

Texas bama femme, 141

Their Eyes Were Watching God (Hurston), 95–96, 101, 106

"This Land Is Your Land" (Guthrie), 5–6

Thompson, Chris, 226–27, 235

Thompson, Robert Farris, 141

Tidal, 34, 61

Tillet, Salamishah, 149

Tinsley, Omise'eke Natasha, 4, 11–12, 15n4, 136–56

Tornoe, Rob, 16n20

Townsend, Robert, 163, 165

Tracy, Pamela J., 182

trademark performance elements of musicians, 44

troping, lyrical, 45, 53

Trump, Donald, 6, 16n21, 129

Turner, Tina, 107, 117

"Turn My Swag On" (Soulja Boy), 59

twerking, 145–46

"2 Girls 1 Cup," 234

universities, 7

unlikely resemblances, 180, 189, 190, 192, 196n21, 196n25

"Upgrade U" (2006), 34, 51

"Uptown Funk" (Ronson), 2–3, 14n4

Van Dessel, Pieter, 68

Versace, Donatella, 2

Video Music Awards, MTV, 2009, 84–85

"Video Phone" (2009), 78

Vine app, 243–44

Viñuela, Eduardo, 9, 10, 11, 12, 157–76

vlogs, 235, 236–37, 238

voice of Beyoncé: audiences' perceptions of, 76–77; cultural identity signaled through, 71–76, 79; and four modes of vocal delivery, 71–74, 72
Voltio, Julio, 171

Wald, Gayle, 8
Walker, Alice, 136
"Walk It Out" (Unk), 186, 187, 189, 190, 196n20
Wallace, Alicia, 4
Ward, Brian, 121, 142
Warren-Crow, Heather, 235–36
Was (Not Was), 14n4
Wass, Mike, 229
"Waterfall," 30
Watrous, Mark, 56
Waxman, Simon, 44
wealth, 3, 76–77, 78, 105
West, Kanye, 31, 40, 41, 53, 100
"When the Levee Breaks" (Led Zeppelin), 42, 57–59
White, Barry, 81
White, Jack, 42, 51, 56, 57
White, Stuart, 56
Whiteley, Sheila, 43, 86n2
white listeners: framed as victims of Super Bowl performance, 4–5, 6, 7; racially inflected listening by, 76
white privilege, 5, 6, 8
white supremacy, 5, 6
"Why Don't You Act Your Color" (Tracy), 182
"Why the Artistry Argument between Beck & Beyoncé Is a Stupid One" (Cadrez), 41

Williams, Andy, 53
Williams, Serena, 137, 143, 145–46, 147
Williams, Venus, 145
Winfrey, Oprah, 128
Woehrel, Mary Fogarty, 12, 13, 179–97
Wonder, Stevie, 47
Woods, Mario, 3
work, Beyoncé's performance of, 23–39; and attention to detail, 23–24; in *B'Day*, 26–27; *Beyoncé*'s rejection of labor/hustle, 25, 29–32, 37n20; Beyoncé's valorization of work, 25; and "Formation," 32–35; and hustle of neoliberalism, 24–25, 28; in *I Am . . . Sasha Fierce*, 27; and labor of black women, 26, 27; and perfectionism of Beyoncé, 25; in racist conditions, 28; work ethic of Beyoncé, 4, 23
"write a word, get a third" practice, 51, 52, 61
Writing's on the Wall (1999), 230

X, Malcolm, 2, 128
"XO" (2013), 46–47

Yeah Yeah Yeahs, 52–53
Young, Faron, 64n40
YouTube: community building/engagement on, 214–16, 218; control of content on, 217–18; conversational character of, 203; impact on industry, 233; mixed audiences of, 216; private back catalog of signed songs on, 221n18; signing Beyoncé's songs on, 201–11

Zimmerman, Amy, 149
Zorro archetype, 170–71, 172

www.ingramcontent.com/pod-product-compliance
Lightning Source LLC
Chambersburg PA
CBHW031310150426
43191CB00005B/160